Children of Methamphetamine-Involved Families

Children of Methamphetamine-Involved Families

The Case of Rural Illinois

Wendy Haight
Teresa Ostler
James Black
Linda Kingery

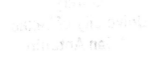

OXFORD
UNIVERSITY PRESS
2009

OXFORD
UNIVERSITY PRESS

Oxford University Press, Inc., publishes works that further
Oxford University's objective of excellence
in research, scholarship, and education.

Oxford   New York
Auckland   Cape Town   Dar es Salaam   Hong Kong   Karachi
Kuala Lumpur   Madrid   Melbourne   Mexico City   Nairobi
New Delhi   Shanghai   Taipei   Toronto

With offices in
Argentina   Austria   Brazil   Chile   Czech Republic   France   Greece
Guatemala   Hungary   Italy   Japan   Poland   Portugal   Singapore
South Korea   Switzerland   Thailand   Turkey   Ukraine   Vietnam

Published by Oxford University Press, Inc.
198 Madison Avenue, New York, New York 10016
www.oup.com

Oxford is a registered trademark of Oxford University Press

Library of Congress Cataloging-in-Publication Data

Children of methamphetamine-involved families : the case of rural
Illinois / Wendy Haight . . . [et al.].
p. cm.
Includes bibliographical references and index.
ISBN 978-0-19-532605-5
1. Methamphetamine abuse—Illinois. 2. Drug addicts—Family
relationships—Illinois. 3. Rural children—Illinois—Social conditions.
4. Rural children—Services for—Illinois. 5. Children of drug
addicts—Illinois—Social conditions. 6. Methamphetamine—Illinois.
I. Haight, Wendy L., 1958-
HV5831.I4C48 2009
362.29'9—dc22
2008017981

9 8 7 6 5 4 3 2 1

Printed in the United States of America
on acid-free paper

This book is dedicated to:

my sister, Laura, and brother-in-law, Bob, in appreciation of
their work and care for children from
substance-involved families.
WH

my husband, Sid, with thanks.
TO

my children, Matthew and Camilla.
JB

my husband, Carl, who is truly the wind beneath
my wings!
LK

Preface

The rural Midwest can be idyllic. Many residents and visitors alike enjoy its slow-paced small towns, four seasons, mature hardwood forests, peaceful lakes, and prairie meadows. The rural Midwest is not, however, immune to the social problems faced by larger communities throughout the United States, including poverty, violence, and substance misuse. Beginning in the 1990s, methamphetamine misuse became a significant problem, affecting not just individuals but whole families and communities in rural Illinois. Although substance misuse was not new to the rural Midwest, unlike alcohol and marijuana, addiction to methamphetamine was rapid and intense, bringing illness, violence, and crime to rural communities with limited law enforcement, medical, and social service resources.

In 2003, two experienced child welfare professionals practicing in rural Illinois approached us regarding a serious methamphetamine problem emerging less than 50 miles south of the University of Illinois at Urbana-Champaign. These child welfare professionals described an influx of children onto their case loads because of parental methamphetamine misuse. They observed that these children had multiple, complex needs for intervention. Our colleagues sought systematic research on the psychological functioning of children whose parents misuse methamphetamine, in order to design effective interventions to help these children to interpret their family experiences in a way that would allow them to recover from any trauma and develop in a positive direction within their foster families. Although some research had addressed the prenatal effects, as well as postnatal health and safety issues, research had not addressed the psychological consequences of growing up with parents who misuse methamphetamine. As we discussed their needs with our child welfare colleagues, four primary research questions emerged: What are the conditions in which rural children whose parents misuse methamphetamine are reared? How are these children functioning, psychologically? What are the implications for designing for them an effective mental health intervention, sensitive to the cultural context of the rural Midwest? How effective is this mental health intervention?

In addition to addressing these research questions, *Children of Methamphetamine-Involved Families* provides an example of a successful practitioner–researcher collaboration. Our transdisciplinary research team included Linda Kingery, LCSW, a social worker practicing in rural child welfare with over 20 years of experience with substance-involved families. Wendy Haight, PhD is a developmental psychologist and professor of social work at the University of Illinois at Urbana-Champaign with expertise in child welfare and applied qualitative research. Teresa Ostler, PhD is a professor of social work at the University of Illinois at Urbana-Champaign and licensed child clinical psychologist with experience working with traumatized children in foster care. James Black, MD, PhD is a professor of psychiatry at Southern Illinois University in Springfield whose medical practice includes rural children who have experienced trauma, children in foster care, and substance-involved families.

This book also illustrates how a sociocultural perspective and mixed-method approach emphasizing qualitative methods can be used to address social problems. Methamphetamine misuse in families is not an isolated phenomenon, but is embedded within a complex social and historical context. Understanding the impact of parental methamphetamine misuse on children's development requires analysis of this ecology. For many of the children introduced in this book, parental methamphetamine misuse is only part of an intergenerational family pattern of substance misuse, poverty, domestic violence, and rural isolation which, as a whole, impact their development and well-being. To provide a thick description of parental methamphetamine misuse in sociocultural context, we focus on rural Illinois from approximately 2003 to 2006, a time and place of intense drug activity. We use a case-based, mixed-methods research strategy combining approaches from cultural developmental and child clinical psychology and psychiatry. In the long run, this case-based study of rural Illinois will allow meaningful comparisons with other children, families, and communities affected by methamphetamine misuse. In the short run, thick, contextualized descriptions were used to design, implement, and evaluate a culturally sensitive mental health intervention for children in foster care whose parents misuse methamphetamine.

This book also is intended to encourage social workers to assume leadership roles in addressing the needs of children whose parents misuse methamphetamine. Social workers often have direct practice experience with children whose families are involved with methamphetamine within health, mental health, educational, and child welfare contexts. Furthermore, their ecological perspective is vital for addressing this issue, which impacts biological, psychological, social, and cultural systems. In addition, social workers are skilled in working within transdisciplinary teams. Addressing the complex

risks to children posed by parental methamphetamine misuse clearly will require sustained, transdisciplinary efforts from researchers, policy makers,
and practitioners.

Acknowledgments

This project was supported by the University of Illinois Research Board,
from which it received the Arnold O. Beckman Award for significant and
original research, and by the Children and Family Research Center, School
of Social Work, University of Illinois at Urbana-Champaign, which is
funded in part by the Department of Children and Family Services (DCFS).
The views expressed herein should not be construed as representing the policy of the University of Illinois or the Illinois Department of Children and
Family Services.

We want to acknowledge Maria Miller, the Assistant Regional Direc-
tor of the DCFS field office, for her unwavering support of this project.
We also would like to thank Gail Steidl and the staff of the DCFS office for
eagerly giving their time and energy to this project. A special thanks to
Paula McClain for her support, and to Julia Miller, who first began asking
the questions. Thanks also to Sheriff Michael Miller and his staff for their
support of the work of child welfare and their assistance whenever asked.

We are indebted also to the children who welcomed us into their lives
and gave us a child's eye view of methamphetamine misuse, their foster and
biological families, and all of the community members including mental
health and legal professionals, addictions specialists, teachers and principals
who spoke with the research team and provided insight into the methamphetamine problem in rural Illinois.

Contents

Part 1. Methamphetamine Misuse in Sociocultural Context

1. Introduction   3
2. History and Epidemiology   16
3. The Research Program   30
4. Narrative of a Rural Child Welfare Professional   46

Part 2. Methamphetamine-Involved Families

5. Recovering Mothers' Experiences and Perspectives   61
6. Knowledgeable Adults' Experiences and Perspectives   79
7. Children's Experiences and Perspectives   95
8. Children's Psychological Functioning   110
9. Narrative of a Midwestern Psychiatrist   120

Part 3. Meeting the Mental Health Needs of Rural Children in Foster Families

10. Conceptual and Empirical Bases of Life Story Intervention for Rural Foster Children   129
11. Implementing Life Story Intervention   147
12. Children's Responses to Life Story Intervention   178
13. Narrative of a Community Clinician   205

Part 4. Conclusion

14. The Value of the Case in Evidence-Based Social Work   217

References   227
Index   243

Part One

Methamphetamine Misuse in Sociocultural Context

Chapter One

Introduction

In the late twentieth and early twenty-first century United States, the production and misuse of methamphetamine was a growing and urgent public health, criminal justice, and child welfare problem affecting whole families and communities. Methamphetamine, also known as crank, crystal, glass, ice, speed, hillbilly crack, and yaaba, among other names, is a form of amphetamine with strong central nervous system effects (Wermuth, 2000). It gained popularity as a less expensive, more easily available and longer-lasting stimulant than cocaine (Bauer & Olson, 2006). It is highly addictive, and regular use is associated with a variety of serious health and mental heath problems (Lineberry & Bostwick, 2006; Meredith, Jaffe, Ang-Lee & Saxon, 2005; Rawson, Gonzales & Brethen, 2002). Methamphetamine use also contributes to a rising rate of violent crime (Federal Bureau of Investigation, 2006).

Initially limited to the western states and Hawaii, by the late twentieth century, methamphetamine misuse and production had spread throughout the United States (Cretzmeyer, Sarrazin, Huber, Block, & Hall, 2003; Hohman, Oliver & Wright, 2004; Rawson et al., 2002), particularly into rural areas. At the time of our study, a combination of factors fueled the rapid growth of methamphetamine misuse and production in the rural Midwest. Rural poverty contributed to the despair that led some to escape through substance misuse and provided financial incentives for methamphetamine production, just as it had in the past for other illegal cash crops (marijuana and moonshine). Relatively simple recipes for producing methamphetamine could be downloaded from the Internet, and these formulas used ingredients readily available in farming communities, for example, anhydrous ammonia which is a common ingredient in fertilizer, and over-the-counter cold medications containing pseudoephedrine. Although methamphetamine production is a smelly process, toxic waste by-products could be readily concealed in isolated areas (Bauer & Olson, 2006). Furthermore, many rural areas had limited law enforcement resources to deal effectively with multiple clandestine methamphetamine laboratories spread over large geographic areas (Haight, Jacobsen, Black, Kingery, Sheridan & Mulder, 2005).

By the late 1990s, methamphetamine production and misuse had become an urgent problem in rural east central Illinois. Photo by Camilla Black.

Rural areas also had limited social and medical services to deal effectively with the outcomes of methamphetamine misuse, including rising rates of addiction and mental illness. At the time of our study, the highest rates of methamphetamine misuse occurred among 20- to 29-year-olds who often had children (West, McKenna, Stuntz, & Webber-Brown, 2000), and women of childbearing age were the demographic group experiencing the greatest increase in methamphetamine misuse (Hohman et al., 2004). Not surprisingly, rural law enforcement officers and health, mental health, and child welfare professionals increasingly encountered children living in homes where methamphetamine was produced and misused (e.g., Hohman et al., 2004).

Parental methamphetamine misuse poses clear hazards to children. The physical and psychological effects of methamphetamine on the user are formidable obstacles to adequate parenting (e.g., see Joe, 1996; Brown & Hohman, 2006). The initial effect of methamphetamine is a "rush" from the release of high levels of the neurotransmitter dopamine (Rawson et al., 2002). The user experiences euphoria, decreased fatigue and appetite, and increased energy, alertness, and libido that last approximately 10–12 hours (Anglin, Burke, Perrochet, Stamper & Dawad-Noursi, 2000). Eventually, the user "crashes" into a deep sleep that may last for days (Cretzmeyer et al., 2003; Lineberry & Bostwick, 2006). After extended methamphetamine binges, users begin "tweaking," a term used to describe a combination of restless anxiety, irritability, fatigue, and dysphoria. Tweaking is an especially dangerous time for children, because the user is very irritable and miserable, and has impaired cognition. Using more methamphetamine does not improve symptoms during this period, and violence, suicide, jail, or hospitalization are common.

Regular use of methamphetamine is associated with serious health effects including damage to the teeth, lungs, heart, kidneys, and brain (Lineberry & Bostwick, 2006; Meredith et al., 2005). Psychological effects include psychosis, depression, paranoia, rapid mood changes, violent behavior (Anglin et al., 2000; Cretzmeyer et al., 2003; Maxwell, 2005; SAMHSA, 1999) and post traumatic stress disorder (PTSD) (Cohen et al., 2003), as well as deficits in memory, learning, and information processing (Meredith et al., 2005).

The various cognitive and psychiatric symptoms associated with regular methamphetamine misuse may be caused by the lasting neurological effects of methamphetamine. With regular methamphetamine use, the brain adapts, and the user experiences a "dopamine depletion syndrome" in which a normal good mood, energy level, or attention span cannot be experienced (Volkow et al., 2001). In addition, high-resolution magnetic resonance imaging reveals significant structural abnormalities in the brains of individuals who misuse methamphetamine regularly (Thompson et al., 2004). Methamphetamine's ability to disrupt normal brain functioning can be long-lasting; for example, psychotic symptoms may persist for months or years after use of methamphetamine has ceased (Copeland & Sorensen, 2001; Maxwell, 2005; Rawson et al., 2002; SAMHSA, 1999). Cognitive and psychiatric symptoms also may be exacerbated by trauma associated with drug misuse. For example, most individuals who misuse methamphetamine report violent victimization (85% of women and 70% of men) (Cohen et al., 2003).

Parental methamphetamine misuse may first affect children's development through prenatal exposure. Drug misuse during pregnancy generally increases the risk of pregnancy complications and serious medical problems for the neonate (Garcia-Bournissen, Rokach, Karaskov & Koren, 2007), including adverse effects on the developing brain (Merikangas, Dierker & Fenton, 1996). The precise effects of methamphetamine on the fetus are not known, but it does cross the placenta. In addition, women who misuse methamphetamine while pregnant are likely to misuse alcohol and other illegal drugs known to impact the fetus (Garcia-Bournissen et al., 2007). Prenatal exposure to methamphetamine is associated with small-for-gestational-age birth weights (Smith et al., 2006), spontaneous abortion, preterm births, small head circumference, cerebral infarctions, and congenital abnormalities (see Hohman et al., 2004; Stewart & Meeker, 1997). It also may be associated with neurobehavioral outcomes, such as lags in academic and physical development in early adolescence (Cernerud, Eriksson, Jonsson, Steneroth & ZetterStorm, 1996; Wouldes, LaGasse, Sheridan & Lester, 2004). Additional, longitudinal research is necessary, however, to understand any long-term or specific impact of prenatal exposure to methamphetamine on children's development.

Parental methamphetamine misuse also may affect children's physical health and safety in the postnatal environment. Children may have significant medical and dental needs due to neglect and exposure to toxins. Indeed, more than one-third of the children found in homes during methamphetamine laboratory seizures tested positive for illicit drugs because of environmental exposure (Hohman et al., 2004). They also may suffer from burns due to explosions and fire related to methamphetamine production in the home (see Grant, 2007).

The research described in this book focuses on the experiences and psychological functioning of rural children from methamphetamine-involved families. Many children reared by parents who misuse methamphetamine face multiple environmental stressors associated with psychological disturbance in children whose parents misuse other substances, who are maltreated, or who are exposed to violence. Children of substance-misusing parents generally are at risk for the development of substance misuse and mental health disorders (e.g., The National Center on Addiction and Substance Abuse at Columbia University [CASA], 1999; Fals-Stewart, Kelley, Fincham, Golden & Logsdon, 2004; Luthar, Cushing, Merikangas & Rounsaville, 1998; Peleg-Oren & Teichman, 2006), as well as early pregnancy, school failure, and criminal and other antisocial behavior (Millar & Stermac, 2000). Prospective studies show that child maltreatment is associated with conduct problems, disruptive behavior disorders, attention problems, anxiety disorders (including PTSD), and mood disorders (Cicchetti, Toth & Maughan, 2000). Egeland (1997) found that 90% of maltreated children showed at least one diagnosable disorder at age 17, compared to 30% of children who were impoverished but not maltreated. In comparison with other maltreated children, sexually abused children showed more forms of pathology and more extreme forms. Sexual abuse is strongly associated with PTSD and depression (Sroufe, Dougal, Weinfeld & Carlson, 2000). Domestic violence, also common in homes where methamphetamine is misused, is consistently associated with child behavioral and emotional problems (Sroufe et al., 2000).

For professionals working on behalf of children, understanding the impact of parental methamphetamine misuse on children's psychological development is paramount for informing advocacy, substance misuse prevention, mental health care, and other intervention programs. Although parental misuse of any drug poses risks for children, there are a number of reasons why professionals have been particularly concerned about parents' misuse of methamphetamine. First, methamphetamine is one of the few drugs, other than marijuana, that can be produced domestically in the United States.

Methamphetamine produced in and around the home exposes children to toxic chemicals (e.g., Manning, 1999; see Mecham & Melini, 2002 for pediatric protocols), as well as explosions and fires (e.g., Manning, 1999; West & Stuntz, 2000). At the time of our study, such "Mom and Pop" methamphetamine laboratories were prolific suppliers of the drug.

A second reason professionals were concerned is that methamphetamine is highly addictive and, relative to other substances, parents may become rapidly disabled both physically and mentally (Rawson et al., 2002; Substance Abuse and Mental Health Services Administration [SAMHSA], 1999). Rapid parental deterioration can be both frightening and dangerous to children who have little time to adapt—for example, to find other sources of food, safety, and psychological support. Third, parental methamphetamine misuse often was a rural problem and families typically did not have the resources to travel long distances to reach specialized health and mental health services to support children's recovery from any problems related to their parents' methamphetamine misuse (Haight et al., 2005). Finally, parental methamphetamine misuse placed a strain on child welfare systems, as well as criminal justice, mental health care, and educational systems. In a survey from the National Association of Counties, 40% of responding counties reported increases in the number of children entering foster care due to parental methamphetamine misuse, with West Coast and rural areas particularly hard hit (Kyle & Hansell, 2005). Since parents were likely to receive stiff prison terms for methamphetamine misuse and production, many children entering into foster care would remain there for prolonged periods of time. Despite the risks parental methamphetamine misuse poses for children, prior research had not examined the psychological functioning of children from methamphetamine-involved families. Child welfare professionals, social workers, educators, and others working within rural areas had little systematic, descriptive data on which to build effective interventions for the growing numbers of children affected by parental methamphetamine misuse.

We approached the problem of parental methamphetamine misuse not as an isolated event, but as embedded within a complex sociocultural context. The impact of methamphetamine misuse on individuals, families, and communities results from a complex interaction of biological, psychological, social, and cultural factors. Methamphetamine misuse has certain biological effects on the human body, but how the resulting medical symptoms are understood, experienced, and responded to by the individual, family, and community also has strong cultural components. Cultural communities vary in their understanding of addiction (possibly seeing it, for example, as illness or moral failing) and child maltreatment (for example, in determining the degree and type of supervision and physical resources deemed adequate)

(Agathonos-Georgopoulou, 2003; Bamba & Haight, 2007; Fullilove, 1996). These understandings have implications for the design and implementation of culturally appropriate interventions for families affected by parental methamphetamine misuse.

A first step in addressing children's psychological needs is to better understand the physical and social contexts in which they grow, and how those ecologies may impact development. For example, children's experience may include not just parental methamphetamine misuse, but environmental danger, chaos, neglect, abuse, loss, and isolation (Brown & Holman, 2006; Haight et al., 2005). It also is important to underscore the fact that cultural contexts both vary and evolve. The sociocultural context of our research focuses on the rural Midwest from about 2003 to 2006. The extent to which these specific findings are transferable to other cultural contexts, for example, urban communities, is an open empirical question. The extent to which our specific findings are transferable to other historical contexts also is an open empirical question. For example, since approximately 2004, laws limiting access to the precursors for methamphetamine production have reduced small-scale methamphetamine manufacture (Office of National Drug Control Policy, 2006). Since the ongoing demand for methamphetamine remains, the control of the supply has shifted to organized, criminal groups (U. S. Drug Enforcement Agency, 2006), which will introduce new and different risks to rural Midwestern children, families, and communities.

In the remainder of this chapter, we will introduce our sociocultural study of children affected by parental methamphetamine misuse in rural Illinois during the opening years of the twenty-first century. We use this instance as a model to better understand the impact of sociocultural context on children affected by parental substance misuse, and how this understanding can be applied to the design and implementation of interventions.

Methamphetamine Misuse In Sociocultural Context

In Part 1 of this book, we begin with an introductory discussion of the history and epidemiology of methamphetamine. Despite intense publicity in the popular press in the 1990s and early 2000s, methamphetamine was not a new drug, nor were problems with its misuse. Methamphetamine was synthesized more than 100 years ago by a German chemist and was once used to treat a variety of medical conditions including narcolepsy, attention deficit disorder, and obesity (Bauer & Olson, 2006). The drug, however, proved to be highly addictive, and epidemics of methamphetamine misuse arose in diverse cultural contexts from urban Japan to the rural Midwest. The social impact of various methamphetamine epidemics were related to the quality of the drug, its means of distribution, population of users, methods of administration, and legal sanctions, all of which have varied widely across time and place. For example, surplus stockpiles of methamphetamine used to keep pilots and factory workers alert were released as over-the-counter medications to the Japanese public following World War II and led to widespread stimulant misuse (Anglin et al., 2000). In rural Illinois, as summarized earlier, easy instructions for producing highly potent crystal methamphetamine at home were available from the Internet, leading to widespread misuse by rural adults with children.

Part 1 of this book also introduces our research strategy. Rural Illinois in the early twenty-first century is an important case because of its growing and urgent methamphetamine problem. In 1997, police seized only 24 clandestine methamphetamine laboratories in Illinois. During 2003, the first year of our study, Illinois had 760 clandestine methamphetamine laboratory seizures by state police, ranking the state seventh highest in the United States for such seizures. In 2005, 1200 labs were seized by the Illinois State Police, and Illinois surpassed all states but Missouri in number of methamphetamine laboratory seizures. (U.S. Drug Enforcement Agency, n.d.). The majority of these labs (66%) were in rural areas. Other indicators also reflected the growing and urgent methamphetamine problem in rural Illinois. For example, between 1994 and 2005, reported cases of substance-exposed infants decreased 80% in Cook County, which includes Chicago, and 41% in other urban counties. In contrast, a 55% increase in substance-exposed infants occurred in rural counties, largely attributable to the growing methamphetamine problem (Bauer & Olson, 2006).

The site of our research was a rural, predominantly white, working-class, seven-county area served by a field office of the Illinois child protection agency (Department of Children and Family Services, or DCFS). This region was experiencing an increasingly serious drug problem, and large numbers of families were entering the child protective system because of parental methamphetamine misuse and production. We began our study with extensive participant observation in the area. We attended Illinois state methamphetamine task force meetings, at which community members and politicians discussed the methamphetamine problem and possible public policy responses. We attended drug court, where individuals convicted of crimes related to their addictions were diverted from prison and into treatment. We visited rural schools, substance misuse treatment facilities, and families fostering children from methamphetamine-involved families. We also spent over 90 hours shadowing rural child welfare investigators. Systematic field notes recorded our conversations, community reactions, and responses to the methamphetamine problem, as well as the living conditions of rural families involved with methamphetamine.

In conjunction with our participant observation, we conducted in-depth, audiotaped, individual interviews with knowledgeable adults: four recovering mothers with children in foster care because of their methamphetamine misuse, 28 professionals who dealt with the problem of methamphetamine on a regular basis (child welfare professionals, law enforcement professionals, educators, substance misuse treatment providers, and counselors), and seven foster caregivers of children from methamphetamine-involved families. Mothers described their experiences of methamphetamine addiction and recovery, and its impact on their lives and children. Other knowledgeable adults discussed their experiences with families involved with methamphetamine, beliefs about the effects of parental methamphetamine misuse on school-aged children, and appropriate strategies for intervention.

We also visited 29 children in and around their homes and communities. They were between the ages of 6 and 15 years, and were involved with the rural field office because of parental methamphetamine misuse. We focused on school-aged and young adolescents because they are at risk for initiating substance misuse and because they have the verbal ability to describe their perspectives. We focused on children involved with child protective services because, given the illegal and hidden nature of parents' methamphetamine misuse, we reasoned that they would be more representative than children not in foster care of those children most likely to present for services to social workers and other service providers. We also anticipated that these children would be among our most vulnerable. Indeed, for most of the children in our study, both parents not only misused methamphetamine, but misused other substances such as alcohol and marijuana, and were involved in criminal activities including the production of methamphetamine.

As part of a semistructured interview, we engaged with children in a variety of leisure and play activities, or just talked, during which time we invited them to discuss their experiences and perceptions of their families, including methamphetamine and other substance misuse. In addition, we were able to review children's case records and to conduct a variety of standardized assessments of children's development and mental health, including the Peabody Picture Vocabulary Test (PPVT) (Dunn & Dunn, 1997), Childhood Behavior Checklist (CBCL) (Achenbach & Rescorla, 2001), and Trauma Symptom Checklist for Children (TSCC) (Briere, 1996). As part of the mental health intervention (described in Part 3), we followed 17 of these 29 children for 12–18 months. During this period, we readministered interviews and standardized assessments, and collected information on their responses to the intervention.

Several key characteristics of the data set are worth highlighting, as they enhance the rigor and credibility of the research:

- We participated, observed, and interviewed participants within routine contexts familiar and emotionally meaningful to them: their homes, schools, communities, and places of employment. We anticipated that children, and adults too, would behave in a more natural manner and more fully express their perspectives in these contexts than in a laboratory or clinic.

- We engaged in sustained community contact over a period of 3 years and spanning approximately 650 hours of direct contact. Gaining access to, and understanding the perspectives of others, as well as delivering meaningful interventions, requires an investment of time to avoid a superficial and ultimately unhelpful characterization of a complex human problem.

- We drew upon the perspectives of a variety of individuals, including children and adults. The diverse and overlapping perspectives and experiences of individuals occupying various social vantage points provide a rich and nuanced account of beliefs and practices related to methamphetamine misuse.

- We drew upon multiple contexts of observation, for example, homes, schools, and community meetings, to allow for a more complete account of practices and beliefs.

- The data reflect a variety of research methods, including direct observation, standardized assessments, and clinical interviews to balance the inherent limitations of any one strategy and to provide multiple checks on interpretations.

- Rapport building was emphasized throughout. It was essential that participants felt comfortable with us. Establishing trusting relationships is necessary to obtaining ecologically valid observations and conducting meaningful interviews.

- The development of thematic codes describing beliefs incorporated independent analyses from multiple members of the interdisciplinary team, peer audits, and member checks.

- Reliability checks were conducted to enhance the consistency of our qualitative coding.

Our project overview concludes with a portrait of the impact of parental methamphetamine misuse, as seen through the eyes of Linda Kingery, a child welfare professional with over 25 years experience working with children and families in rural Illinois. A master's-level social worker and natural story-teller, Ms Kingery recounts how methamphetamine's influx, beginning in the mid 1990s, affected rural Illinois. She describes the impact on rural communities, child welfare services, and individual children and families. In many respects, Ms Kingery's account parallels the literature: For example, she describes the strain on rural communities and the devastation of individuals and families. Ms Kingery's contribution makes concrete the human experiences of methamphetamine misuse: the endangered child welfare professionals, devastated parents and traumatized children, and also their resilience and resourcefulness.

Methamphetamine-Involved Families

Part 2 of this book considers the contexts in which children whose parents misuse methamphetamine are reared, as well as their psychological functioning. Clinicians working in the area of substance misuse, especially those with a family systems perspective, report that when parents who misuse drugs become increasingly dysfunctional, the entire family is affected as members attempt to adjust in a variety of ways. Children, for example, may take on parental roles, adjust to an increasingly chaotic living situation, act out, or strive for perfection in school. These strategies can interfere with development in other areas; for example, the extremely responsible child may take little opportunity to play with peers and create friendships. Often, there is an unspoken rule within the family that substance misuse is not directly discussed, and clinicians report that even when substance misuse dominates family life, denial of family problems, repression of feelings, shame, and mistrust are common. (See, for example, Black, 2001; Bradshaw, 1995; Freeman, 1993; Kroll, 2004; McRoy, Aguilar & Shorkey, 1993).

A growing body of empirical literature addressing parental misuse of illicit drugs (not specifically methamphetamine) also suggests a variety of specific risks deriving from the postnatal, family contexts in which children are reared (e.g., Johnson, Dunlap & Maher, 1998. Also see Gruber & Taylor, 2006, for a review on the impact of substance misuse from a family systems perspective). These contexts may include exposure to criminality associated with drug-seeking behavior, family attitudes accepting of substance misuse (Hawkins, Catalano & Miller, 1992; Kumpfer, Olds, Alexander, Zucker & Gary, 1996), and the ready availability of drugs (Merikangas et al., 1996). Parental substance misuse also may co-occur with other risk factors for children, such as parent psychopathology (Hans, Bernstein & Henson, 1999) and compromised parenting (Kandel, 1990; Mayes, 1995) including punitive (Miller, Smyth & Mudar, 1999) and inconsistent discipline, inadequate monitoring of children's activities (Hawkins et al., 1992; Dishion & McMahon, 1996), and maltreatment (CASA, 1999; Walsh, Macmillan & Jamieson, 2003; Yampolskaya & Banks, 2006). Some estimates indicate that children whose parents misuse drugs are almost three times as likely to be physically or sexually abused, and more than four times more likely to be neglected than children whose parents do not misuse drugs (CASA, 1999). Unsurprisingly, parental substance misuse is the most common factor when children come to the attention of the child welfare system (see Suchman, Pajulo, DeCoste & Mayes, 2006), and is a significant obstacle to family reunification (Ryan, 2006).

It is important to note that prior research also suggests variation in families involved with substance misuse. For example, some parents who are chemically dependent provide environments that meet children's basic needs (Baker & Carson, 1999; Hans, 2004), are concerned about their children's exposure to adult substance misuse (Woodhouse, 1992), and attempt to protect their children from such exposure with varying degrees of success (Kearney, Murphy & Rosenbaum, 1994).

Chapter 5 focuses on the perspectives and experiences of four mothers in recovery from addiction to methamphetamine, and Chapter 6 on that of other knowledgeable adults. Chapter 7 explores children's perspectives and experiences, and Chapter 8 their psychological functioning. Throughout Part 2, we attend to individual variation as well as group trends. Recognizing diversity in family and child functioning can suggest protective processes that may be enhanced through preventive and interventional services, as well as counteract negative stereotyping that can be an impediment to services. Part 2 concludes with a discussion of the rural methamphetamine crisis through the eyes of a Midwestern psychiatrist. James Black has over 15 years of experience working with diverse individuals affected by methamphetamine misuse.

Meeting the Mental Health Needs of Rural Children in Foster Care

Part 2 reveals that many children placed in foster care whose parent misuse methamphetamine experience high levels of trauma symptoms and behavior problems. Part 3 of this book describes Life Story Intervention, a mental health intervention we designed specifically for rural children from methamphetamine-involved families. We discuss the conceptual and empirical bases of Life Story Intervention, as well as implementation issues from a sociocultural perspective that tailors services to individual children within the context of their homes and communities.

Many families involved with methamphetamine live in rural, predominantly white areas (e.g., Bauer & Olson, 2006). Much of the research examining the impact of parental illicit drug misuse on children, however, has focused on urban settings, often low-income Hispanic or African-American communities. Rural communities have particular cultural strengths and vulnerabilities, and members have particular socialization beliefs and practices, that must be considered when developing and implementing mental health interventions for children living in those areas. Furthermore, mental health interventions may need to address not only parental methamphetamine misuse per se and its associated traumas, but ongoing psychological distress. By the time children enter into mental health care, many will be living away from one or both parents. Family disruptions, especially if the child is placed in foster or other substitute care, often result in additional, ongoing psychological stress (Haight et al., 2006).

There are likely to be a variety of barriers to the implementation of quality mental health care services to rural children whose parents misuse methamphetamine. In rural areas, mental health care providers may be in short supply, and caregivers may not have the resources to travel long distances and to pay for costly care. More basically, parents and substitute caregivers may hold a variety of beliefs regarding children's responses to and recovery from psychological trauma that may undermine mental health intervention; for example, they may deny children's problems, or believe that children will just "forget" traumatic events and move on with life.

Our collaboration with the rural field office of DCFS extended beyond the collection of descriptive and mental health data to the design, implementation, and evaluation of a culturally sensitive mental health intervention for rural children involved in the child welfare system. Life Story Intervention is a 6- to 8-month-long, individual program for children (ages 6–16). It is evidence-based and draws upon the American Association of Child and Adolescent Psychiatry guidelines for intervention with children who have experienced trauma (Cohen, Deblinger, Mannarino & Steer, 2004), clinical discussions of substance-involved families (e.g., Black, 2001), narrative therapy (e.g., Freedman & Combs, 1996), and research on community- and relationship-based interventions for at-risk children, including foster children (e.g., Rhodes, 2002). It also draws upon indigenous, oral narrative traditions in rural Illinois. It provides children with an opportunity to develop a supportive relationship with a healthy, reliable adult, who can help them to express their feelings, and interpret and contextualize their experiences, including troubling or traumatic memories. The overarching goal is to enhance the mental health and overall well-being of struggling rural children who are in foster care following parental methamphetamine misuse.

Life Story Intervention also addresses the problem of accessibility of mental health services to rural children. Similar to other rural communities, the region in which we conducted our research had few services for children, and professionals lacked specialized training in addressing problems related to trauma. Life Story Intervention is delivered to children in their homes and communities by local professionals (e.g., retired child welfare workers, educators, social workers). Each local professional takes on one or two children. They receive intensive, weekly supervision from an experienced PhD- or MD-level mental health professional located in adjacent, urban communities. In addition to addressing issues of accessibility, providing services to children in their homes and communities has a variety of benefits. The adult obtains rich information about the child's interactions with family, friends, and other community members. Foster parents are well-informed, can receive any psychological education as needed, and are not unduly inconvenienced by long car rides to town. Finally, the natural contexts of home and community provide the child with scaffolding for oral narrative. For example, children have produced rich narratives while driving by former foster homes, visiting a parent's grave, and visiting the elementary school they attended before foster care placement.

Evaluation of Life Story Intervention using a quasi-experimental, longitudinal design is ongoing. Part 3 describes the intervention's pilot tests, and presents several contrasting case studies of children's responses to Life Story Intervention. It concludes with Linda Kingery's account of her experiences in conducting Life Story Intervention with two young boys.

Conclusion

Our research presented in this book is undergirded by a sociocultural model of human development in social work practice (Haight & Taylor, 2007). Our aim is to create a more culture-sensitive understanding of human development, and to use that knowledge to better the lives of vulnerable children. Following scholars such as L. Vygotsky, U. Bronfenbrenner, B. Rogoff, P.J. Miller, and R. Shweder, we view development as intrinsically embedded in a social, cultural and historical context, in which the individual and other aspects of the context mutually shape and jointly define one another within specific, localized communities to create distinctive developmental pathways. The context of development for many children involved with child protective services whose parents misuse methamphetamine includes exposure to family violence, disrupted relationships with parents, adult poly-substance misuse, and poverty. At the same time, developmental contexts also may include positive features such as supportive educators, extended family members, and church communities. Understanding the contexts in which children are reared, as well as participants' (children's, parents', professionals') experiences and perceptions of those contexts, provides models for the design of culturally and developmentally sensitive interventions.

Chapter Two

History and Epidemiology

Methamphetamine misuse has been a persistent problem worldwide, demonstrating an interaction frequently observed in addiction medicine between the biology and cultural context of addiction. Examination of the cultural and historical contexts of methamphetamine misuse reveals some common themes related to the biology of addiction, with variations in associated medical and social problems due to changes in the quality of the drug, methods of administration and distribution, population of users, and legal sanctions. The study of cultural similarities and variations in methamphetamine misuse can enhance our understanding of the vulnerabilities of certain groups and individuals, and has implications for societal responses likely to be effective. By considering the biology of addiction in relation to the broader historical and cultural context, this chapter examines the question of why methamphetamine misuse has been a persistent and widespread problem.

Worldwide, amphetamine-related drugs are the most commonly misused illicit drugs after cannabis. The World Health Organization (WHO) estimated that over 35 million people misuse amphetamine-related drugs (WHO, 1997), and amphetamine-related stimulants are the most widely used illicit drugs in the United States (Pach & Gorman, 2002). Since World War II, methamphetamine misuse has occurred in such culturally diverse contexts as South Africa (Kiley, 2007), Japan (e.g., Tamura, 1989), and the United States (e.g., Anglin, Burke, Perrochet, Stamper & Dawud-Noursi, 2000); and in regions within the United States such as Hawaii, the South, and the Midwest. In the United States alone, methamphetamine misuse has occurred in such diverse groups as medical students studying for exams during the 1960s; outlaw motorcycle gangs generating income in California in the 1970s; long-haul truck drivers maintaining alertness in the 1980s; urban gay men seeking sexual enhancement in San Francisco in the 1990s; and rural Kentucky women self-medicating for depression in the 2000s.

At the time of our study, the Drug Enforcement Administration (DEA) identified methamphetamine as the most prevalent clandestinely produced

The woods of east central Illinois provided concealment for methamphetamine production. Photo by Carl Kingery.

and lethal controlled substance in the United States since 1979 (reported in Wermuth, 2000). Figure 2.1 shows the rapid increase, in kilograms, of methamphetamine seized by the DEA from the mid 1980s through 2005, particularly in rural counties. (Data retrieved on 2 April 2008 from http://www.usdoj.gov/dea/statistics.html#seizures.) According to the 2000 National Household Survey on Drug Use, an estimated 8.8 million people (4% of the population) had tried methamphetamine (reported in Wermuth, 2000). Data from the 2000 Drug Abuse Warning Network (DAWN), which collects information on drug-related episodes from hospital emergency rooms in 21 metropolitan areas, indicated that methamphetamine-related episodes increased by 30% from approximately 10,400 in 1999 to 13,500 in 2000 (Wermuth, 2000). In 2006, a total of 6435 clandestine laboratory incidents (including investigation of labs, dumpsites, chemicals, and glassware) were reported by the DEA. Missouri ranked number 1 with 1268 incidents, and Illinois ranked number 2 with 751 incidents. At the time our study began in 2004, Illinois ranked fourth in the nation, with 1058 incidents (up from 124 incidents in 1999) (Department of Justice, 2008).

The Biology of Addiction

Methamphetamine is one of many stimulants (e.g., amphetamine, cocaine, caffeine, nicotine) with a wide variety of molecular structures and chemical mechanisms. What the various stimulants have in common are effects that

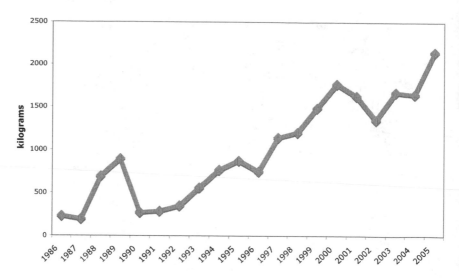

Figure 2.1 U.S. Drug Enforcement Agency (DEA) seizures of methamphetamine from 1986-2005.

mimic those of the sympathetic nervous system, both peripheral and central nervous system components, to produce arousing effects similar to epinephrine. The peripheral nervous system effects include vasoconstriction, increased muscle tone, increased heart rate, higher blood pressure, and anesthesia. In medical settings, stimulant medications can be used to control bleeding, rescue patients from shock, numb a sore throat, relieve asthma, or clear a stuffy nose. Incorrect use of the same stimulant medications, however, can kill patients by causing fatal elevations of temperature, irregular heart rhythms, stroke, or heart attacks. Central nervous system effects include increased alertness and energy, and decreased appetite. Stimulants are especially helpful in specific disorders such as narcolepsy, attention deficit disorders, HIV, and aspects of depression. Incorrect use of stimulants, however, is associated with seizures, psychosis, anxiety, depression, and suicidality. Chronic use can also aggravate anorexia, involuntary movements, and skin-picking.

Whether the effects of stimulant use are toxic or therapeutic is determined by three dimensions of pharmacology (Preskorn, 1996), each of which plays an important role in understanding the rural, Midwestern methamphetamine crisis of the late twentieth and early twenty-first centuries. First, a drug's effect is partly determined by its molecular structure and how it binds to its target. Various stimulants have a range of effects due to their molecular structures. Cocaine, for example, produces a much shorter effect than the amphetamines because of a very different mechanism of action at the level of the synapse. Methamphetamine differs from its parent drug amphetamine in that it crosses the blood–brain barrier more readily (i.e., with comparable doses, much higher levels of drug get into the brain, and it produces more potent effects). It also appears to produce a much longer-lasting and more harmful effect on the central nervous system (National Instiue of Drug Abuse (NIDA), 2006). Thus, the molecular structure of methamphetamine contributes to relatively higher rates of addiction and psychiatric morbidity (discussed later) than other forms of amphetamine.

Second, a drug's effect depends on its availability or concentration in the blood and brain. Drugs like cocaine, amphetamine, and methamphetamine readily cross from the blood into the brain, making them very psychoactive. The subjective euphoria associated with stimulant misuse is very closely related to the binding of the drug to receptors on dopamine neurons in the brain (Schlaepfer, Pearlson, Wong, Marenco & Dannals, 1997). If the stimulants are delivered to a person very slowly, as in a person chewing coca leaves (which produce the undistilled precursor to cocaine) or a patient getting timed-release amphetamines for attention deficit-hyperactivity disorder (ADHD), no perceived "buzz" occurs, and there is very little misuse potential. In fact, providing low-dose, timed-release stimulant medications to children with ADHD apparently protects them to some degree from the risk of later substance misuse (Wilens, Faraone, Biederman & Gunawardene, 2003). On the other hand, if these same drugs are sent directly to the brain, so as to quickly elevate brain concentration, then the person will sometimes feel a subjective euphoria or "high."

One way of rapidly getting drugs that cross the blood–brain barrier into the brain is to inject them directly into the blood (i.e., through intravenous administration). Alternatively, if the product can be smoked, it may dissolve across the alveolar membranes, then enter the pulmonary blood supply and pass directly to the brain. The cocaine problem in the United States was greatly transformed by the invention of "crack," which allowed cocaine to be smoked and delivered to the brain rapidly to obtain a rush. The crack form of cocaine was thus much more addictive than the powder form inhaled through the nose. Similarly, methamphetamine taken in tablets or powder form can produce desired results (e.g., weight loss, extra energy, alertness), but it becomes quite addictive if injected or if used in the smokable form of crystal methamphetamine and delivered rapidly to the brain. Thus, the new methods of administering methamphetamine emerging in the 1990s contributed to increasing rates of methamphetamine addiction.

Third, a drug's effect is partly determined by individual variation. Preskorn (1996) emphasizes genetic variation in response to medications, and certainly people do differ in their vulnerability and tolerance to drugs of abuse. People also are greatly affected by their personal history, which affects brain structure. The response of stressed, depressed, or traumatized individuals to addictive drugs is shaped by their histories. In considering variability, we also recognize what, essentially, are *cohort effects*. Entire communities and generations are affected by cultural values, historical changes, and economic disasters. Adolescents' attitudes toward drugs can affect their potential risks of addiction. Similarly, pressures on a community may be important in either positive or negative ways, by affecting the support for individuals struggling with addiction (Fullilove, 1996). In the rural Midwestern site of the current study, grinding rural poverty and limited opportunities may have contributed to depression and despair, which can lead groups of people to turn to substance misuse. At the time of our research, crystal methamphetamine was cheap, easily available, and highly addictive.

A Brief Overview of Cultural and Historical Contexts

The persistent and widespread problem of methamphetamine misuse is shaped not only by the biology of addiction, but by historical and cultural contexts. Methamphetamine is a methylated derivative of amphetamine, which was first synthesized in 1887, by a German chemist. It was first synthesized from ephedrine in 1893, by a Japanese chemist. In 1919, methamphetamine was synthesized in Japan via reduction of ephedrine using red phosphorous and iodine (Suwaki, Fukui & Konuma, 1997). The first medical use for methamphetamine was marketed by Smith-Kline-French in 1928 as Benzedrine, used in inhalers sold over-the-counter for treating asthma. (Benzedrine led to the street name of "bennies."). Amphetamines were subsequently found to be effective in treating narcolepsy, nasal congestion, weight gain, and attention deficit disorder, and for providing extended periods of wakefulness (Bender & Cottington, 1942). In the 1930s and 1940s, amphetamines were prescribed for schizophrenia, morphine addiction, and low blood pressure. During World War II, the armies of Japan, Germany, and the United States all provided amphetamines to military personnel to fight fatigue and enhance performance. Amphetamines also were used in Japan to improve the productivity of civilian factory workers in the war industries (Anglin et al., 2000; NIDA, 2006).

Problems with the misuse of amphetamines quickly emerged in diverse cultural contexts. Although cultural contexts shaped amphetamine use, certain common patterns also are discernible. When problems with addiction became apparent, governments typically attempted to regulate the use of amphetamines, primarily through criminal penalties. Without concurrent efforts in treatment and prevention, strong consumer demand for amphetamines remained. Criminal enterprises quickly moved in to exploit this demand, resulting in additional problems for communities.

The Japanese Case

The case of methamphetamine misuse in Japan is important because it was recognized early as a social problem, hence the various governmental interventions undertaken (as well as changes in distribution) may be considered over time. Examination of the more extended trajectory of methamphetamine misuse in Japan, a modern and technologically advanced society, reveals some similarities and differences to the U.S. case, possibly relevant to U.S. policy. The history and epidemiology of methamphetamine misuse in Japan reflects a complex interaction of widespread addiction due to lack of knowledge about the health risks, followed by partially successful attempts by the government to control resultant problems through criminalization of stimulant misuse, and the subsequent exploitation of persisting demand for stimulants by criminal syndicates.

In 1941, there were no restrictions on the sale of methamphetamine, which was initially sold under the trade name Philopon in Japan. It was sold over the counter to fight sleepiness and enhance vitality. Widespread misuse of methamphetamine occurred after World War II, as methamphetamine from surplus army stocks flooded the market. From 1946 to 1956, Japan experienced a serious stimulant epidemic. In 1950, an ordinance from the Ministry of Health banned all stimulant production. Nonetheless, many pharmaceutical companies illegally produced stimulants and made them available on the black market. In addition, clandestine laboratories produced their own versions of Philopon.

In 1951, enactment of the Stimulants Control Law criminalized stimulant misuse, punishable by up to 3 years imprisonment. By 1954, there were approximately 550,000 chronic stimulant users in Japan, about 10% of whom experienced methamphetamine-induced psychosis. The Stimulant Control Act was amended in 1954 and rigorously enforced to permit harsher penalties for stimulant offences, with terms of up to 5 years imprisonment for the first offense and 7 years for recidivists and traffickers. The Mental Hygiene Law was amended to place drug-addicted persons with symptoms of psychosis in treatment programs in mental health care facilities.

The relatively harsh penalties for stimulant misuse have been credited with largely eliminating the first epidemic of methamphetamine misuse in Japan. From 1954 to 1958, the number of people arrested for violating the Stimulant Control Law decreased to 271. From 1957 to 1969, stimulant misuse was relatively stable in Japan, with approximately 500 persons arrested annually for stimulant use–related offenses.

Since 1970, Japan has experienced a period of economic growth and prosperity. It also has experienced a second stimulant epidemic, as methamphetamine misuse has spread, for example, to students, office workers, and blue-collar workers such as truck drivers. Japan has a strong work ethic and a competitive system of education. For some, methamphetamine may be at-tractive because it enhances energy and wakefulness, and hence the ability to work and study for long hours.

From 1970 to 1974, the number of people arrested for stimulant use–related offenses doubled each year. In 1973, a harsher criminal penalty was introduced through amendment of the Stimulant Control Law. This legisla-tion was credited with a significant reduction in the problem, but the effect only lasted for 1 year. Over 10,000 people were arrested in 1975 for stimu-lant use–related offenses. Since 1981, arrest figures have remained at over 20,000 per year.

Methamphetamine misuse has become highly stigmatized and associ-ated with the Japanese underworld. Japanese organized criminal syndicates called *bouryokudan* or *yakuza* have come to dominate stimulant supply, a development not characteristic of the first epidemic. In the early 1970s, many gang members and their leaders who had been imprisoned in the 1960s were released, and criminal syndicates expanded their operations throughout Japan. Today, relatively few arrests occur in Japan for production. Rather, stimulants are imported illegally from other Asian countries through organized Japanese gangs, thus introducing other social problems (Anglin et al., 2000; Tamura, 1989).

The South African Case

The South African case demonstrates interactions among the biology of ad-diction, market economics, and cultural context similar to the Japanese case. Crystal methamphetamine, commonly called *tik*, is impacting black South-African youths in the impoverished Cape Flats area. South African organized criminal syndicates have a demand for the pseudoephedrine precursor of methamphetamine, as well as illegally manufactured methaqualone (sedative Quaaludes). The Chinese gangs have, in turn, a huge demand for a South-African seafood delicacy, abalone, an endangered and protected species that can eventually be sold to Chinese buyers in Hong Kong for over $200 per pound (Kiley, 2007). In a cash-free black-market transaction, the Chinese Triad gangs and Western Cape drug lords trade abalone for the ingredients to make methamphetamine. Hundreds of tons of abalone are smuggled out of the Cape every year, bringing wild abalone to the brink of extinction in little more than a decade (Steinberg, 2005). The South-African drug lords who gained control of significant volumes of abalone also captured a mo-nopoly over cheap crystal meth and illegal Quaaludes. The result is that every serious player in the drug industry must obtain abalone to stay in business. The widespread use of *tik* among South-African youth has caused an increase in crime and social breakdown, thereby putting enormous stress on already limited social services throughout the Cape. The high-risk sexual behavior associated with *tik* may cause the HIV epidemic in southern Africa to return (Morris & Parry, 2006).

The U.S. Case

The interaction among the biology of addiction, market economics, and other aspects of cultural context also has been observed repeatedly in the United States. In the years after World War II, over-the-counter drugs containing methamphetamine were widely available in the United States. Amphetamine tablets were available without prescription until 1951, and amphetamine-containing inhalers were available over the counter until 1959. During the 1950s, persons in various walks of life including college students, long-haul truck drivers, individuals trying to lose weight, and athletes trying to enhance their performance used methamphetamine in legal tablet form for nonmedical purposes. Amphetamines were extremely popular with the general public as dieting and "pep" pills. Benzedrine was available without a prescription and was regarded as harmless. Famous musicians, film stars, and writers believed that their talents would be enhanced with amphetamine use. W.H. Auden, James Agee, Graham Greene, Philip K. Dick, John-Paul Sarte, and Jack Kerouac all used stimulants to improve their stamina and literary output.

As the use of the drugs expanded, so did the number of people who became addicted (Anglin et al., 2000; Kyle & Hansell, 2005). The relaxed cultural attitude toward amphetamine use shifted during the 1950s with the recognition of amphetamine addiction and psychosis. The media began warning of "dope fiends," and the government moved in with restrictive legislation. In 1959, Benzedrine was made available as a prescription-only drug by the U.S. Food and Drug Administration (FDA). In 1963, the American Medical Association (AMA) Council on Drugs initially stated that "compulsive use of the amphetamines (appears to be) a small problem." But 3 years later, the AMA Committee on Alcoholism and Addiction became worried about the vast amounts of uncontrolled amphetamines in the United States and recommended that only physicians were qualified to control this dangerous drug. During the 1960s, amphetamine was prescribed to treat depression and obesity, with use reaching its peak in 1967, when 31 million prescriptions were written.

When over-the counter stimulants became unavailable, prescriptions for amphetamines increased in value. From 1968 to 1971 "script doctors" (corrupt or inept doctors who wrote phony prescriptions for narcotics) and burglaries of drugstores to obtain pills increased. (The well-regarded film "Drugstore Cowboy" is about the drug culture of this period.) The law enforcement response from 1970 to 1973 was to target script doctors and increase drugstore security.

New forms of administration also impacted methamphetamine addiction in the 1960s. In the 1960s, a liquid form of methamphetamine became widely available as a treatment for heroin addiction. The liquid form quickly contributed to a new misuse pattern, involving intravenous injections of methamphetamine, either alone or with heroin (i.e., the "speedball"; Ray & Ksir, 2004). This form of administering methamphetamine was much more addictive than the oral tablet form common in the 1950s.

In the 1960s, governmental regulations impacted the production and distribution of methamphetamine. After withdrawal of Desoxyn, Benzedrine, and methedrine from the pharmaceutical market, illicit methamphetamine laboratories emerged in San Francisco in 1962. The drug was synthesized using P-2-P (phenyl-2-propanone) and methylamine as precursors. The resulting product (called "crank") was a mixture of two isomers (levo- and dextro-methamphetamine), which yielded a less potent form of the pharmaceutical product. The resulting product was inexpensive and could be snorted, made into pills, or injected, but it could not be smoked due to toxins produced when heated. By the mid 1960s, crank dominated the "speed" market as Bay Area motorcycle gangs took over the manufacture and distribution of methamphetamine, spreading methamphetamine north and south along the Pacific Coast (Miller, 1997). Outlaw motorcycle gangs such as the Hell's Angels dominated the market and received considerable attention from law enforcement. (The bikers sometimes smuggled their product in motorcycle crankcases, hence the slang term for methamphetamine: "crank.")

By the 1970s, the dangers associated with the use of amphetamines were better understood, and additional restrictions were placed on the amount that could be legally produced and how it could be distributed. Increased levels of illicit production ensued, originally limited to motorcycle gangs and other independent groups (Lucas, 1997). At the same time, the typical user population expanded from Caucasian blue-collar workers to include college students, young professionals, minorities, women, and professional athletes. For example, Dr. Arnold Mandell, a professor of psychiatry at the University of California at San Diego, consulted with the San Diego Chargers football team and found many players using illicit amphetamines, obtained from Tijuana, Mexico, and other unsafe sources. In an attempt to get team members off of street "speed," he prescribed pharmaceutical amphetamines for them and reported his concerns regarding the issue of player drug use to the National Football League (NFL) (Mandell, 1976). Instead of addressing the problem directly, the NFL officials held a press conference and announced that the team manager, and eight players would be fined. Dr. Mandell was banned from further contact with players. The involvement of professional sports with performance-enhancing drugs, and the failure to realistically deal with it, is a theme familiar to modern readers.

California. In the 1980s, intensified law enforcement efforts targeting the biker groups shifted the center of methamphetamine production toward San Diego. Once again, technology and cultural opportunity combined to produce a new wave of methamphetamine misuse. The technology in this case was a variation on the ephedrine reduction-based method of production, imported from the Pacific and popularized in Southern California, resulting in crystal methamphetamine. The cultural shift was the federal government's successful targeting of biker gangs, subsequently causing Mexican traffickers to move in and take over distribution routes (Morgan & Beck, 1997). Large quantities of illicitly produced "crystal meth," as well as precursor chemicals, were smuggled from Mexico into California and were distributed not only in the traditional regions of use, but also were increasingly directed toward the southwestern and midwestern states.

This new product and its distribution network enjoyed several advantages similar to those following the transformation from powder cocaine to crack. The quality of illicitly produced methamphetamine improved with crystal methamphetamine, which was an addictive, smokable form. The organized criminal distribution network was widespread, but this time made use of preexisting routes for smuggling marijuana and illegal aliens, and it stayed out of the inner cities. The product was very cheap, relatively pure, and could be purchased in small quantities. This marketing similarity, as well as the higher addiction potential of a smokable product, was similar to that of crack cocaine. The crystal meth epidemic, however, spread along the West Coast to Hawaii, flooding substance misuse treatment centers and increasing methamphetamine-related crime.

Texas. Methamphetamine misuse also has been problematic in the southern regions of the United States. For example, Zule and Desmond (1999) described dramatic historical and cultural changes in methamphetamine use in West Texas over the course of four decades. In the 1950s, it was relatively common for Austin college students, housewives, and others to use amphetamine pills, but needles were a psychological barrier and intravenous use was rare. When the counter-culture of the 1960s began to influence Austin and surrounding communities, especially its attitudes toward recreational drug use, a large increase in methamphetamine misuse occurred, along with an increase in needle experimentation. Law enforcement recognized an initial crisis and responded with a slogan "Speed Kills." Nonetheless, a stable community of intravenous methamphetamine users grew. From the 1970s to late 1990s, methamphetamine misuse stabilized and remained endemic.

As is common in heroin subcultures, experienced users mentored new users including heterosexual blue-collar workers, motorcycle riders, musicians, and criminals. In contrast to the current methamphetamine crisis, rural users were rare, as most users were located in Austin. Some users would go on week-long binges, while others transitioned into more stable patterns of using, with a small amount in the morning before work and heavier use on the weekend. Some users eventually quit or moved on to other habits, such as alcohol or heroin. The outcome for some included prison and health effects such as Hepatitis C.

Hawaii. Hawaii's crystal methamphetamine problem has been especially serious. In the 1980s, large quantities of a smokable, highly pure form of crystal methamphetamine ("ice") became available in Hawaii from Far East sources in the Philippines, Japan, Korea, and Taiwan (Laidler & Morgan, 1997). During the 1990s, use of ice became epidemic in the Hawaiian Islands, and distribution of the drug was dominated by Mexico- and California-based trafficking organizations. These transnational organized crime groups were supplemented in Hawaii by extended kinship networks that played a major role in initiating and spreading methamphetamine/ice use. These kinship networks included entire families, coworkers, and neighborhoods (Laidler & Morgan, 1997). Some of these networks extend back to the mainland through kinship groups and criminal connections (Shinn, 2000).

Wyoming. Methamphetamine misuse also has been a serious problem in the intermountain west, including Utah, Montana, Idaho, and Wyoming. In Wyoming, the least populated state in the country, methamphetamine misuse was more than twice the national average in 2004. Local experts viewed methamphetamine misuse as a symptom of rural decline, as people gave up on faltering farms and factories. This rural decline is reflected in Wyoming's profound demographic changes. In 2004, the state's population was older than that of any other state, and, for the first time, most people were aged 35 and older. People in their 20s and 30s, left behind in places like Lovell, tended to be less educated, often high school drop-outs, and working at low-paying jobs or not at all. Most of those convicted of methamphetamine misuse and production in this area fit this description.

Local experts also viewed methamphetamine misuse as a cause that made the rural decline worse. From 2002 to 2004, approximately 70 people in Lovell (population approximately 2300) were convicted of buying or selling methamphetamine. Methamphetamine-related crimes consumed half of the time of Lovell's seven-officer police force. Methamphetamine was easy to produce in Audubon County, because only 10 law enforcement officers patrolled 450 square miles, and because one of the drug's main ingredients, anhydrous ammonia, was available in bags from isolated farm fields (*Deseret News*, Salt Lake City, January 5, 2004).

Midwest. By the 1990s, methamphetamine misuse had spread across the country to the Midwest. Rural communities in the Midwest were vulnerable for some of the same reasons as those in the intermountain west: rural decline, easy accessibility to ingredients and isolated areas for production, and relatively little police presence across large geographic areas. In the 1990s, a growing number of methamphetamine labs began operating in midwestern states. In response to the growing public health threat posed by the use and production of methamphetamine (and especially environmental hazards associated with the toxic compounds used in clandestine labs), and consistent with the U.S. Congress and Justice Department's "War against Drugs" approach to substance misuse, the Comprehensive Methamphetamine Control Act was enacted in 1996 (Anglin et al., 2000). This act more than doubled the maximum criminal penalty from 4 to 10 years for possession of manufacturing equipment, and established new penalties and controls for distribution of chemicals involved in the production of methamphetamine, including the precursor chemicals of iodine, red phosphorous, and hydrochloric gas. In addition, the law made large purchases of pseudoephedrine (a substitute for ephedrine in the production of methamphetamine) more traceable under the Controlled Substances Act (Wermuth, 2000).

The decline in the number of "Mom and Pop" methamphetamine laboratories in the early twenty-first century has been attributed, in part, to the success of the Comprehensive Methamphetamine Control Act. An unintended effect of the act, however, also seems to be an increase in criminal trafficking of methamphetamine in the rural Midwest (U.S. Drug Enforcement Agency, 2006), which introduces a whole new set of challenges to vulnerable rural communities.

Figure 2.2 shows the increase in the mean number of methamphetamine laboratories raided by police from 1997 to 2005, the predominance of raids in rural counties, and the apparent decrease in police raids in the early 2000s. Data are from the U.S. Census (accessed on 2 April 2008 from http://www.census.gov/geo/www/ua/ua_2k.html). Urban counties were those with some census block densities of 1000 residents per square mile and surrounded by other relatively dense census blocks. Most of these urban counties are in northern Illinois.

Conclusion

In conclusion, historical and cultural analyses facilitate a greater understanding of the larger social forces shaping some groups' and individuals' vulnerability

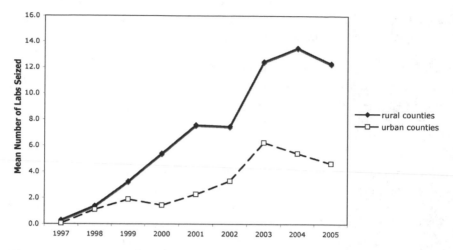

Figure 2.2 Mean number of Illinois urban and rural county clandestine methamphetamine laboratory seizures.

to methamphetamine addiction, as well as highlight societal interventions likely to be effective. Methamphetamine misuse is not a new problem. It has been a problem among various groups in the United States, Japan, and other countries since World War II. Over time, however, more potent and addictive forms of the drug have been manufactured. In competitive cultural contexts including Japan and the United States, methamphetamine may be attractive to individuals seeking to enhance their work and study performance. In contexts of fewer resources—for example, impoverished rural communities in the United States—methamphetamine may be attractive to individuals needing energy to combine multiple jobs and family responsibilities. In impoverished, rural communities with few resources for mental health and few job opportunities, methamphetamine production also may be attractive as a source of subsistence-level income and/or self-medication for depression and boredom. In urban communities, methamphetamine misuse has been attractive as a club drug.

As methamphetamine misuse has spread throughout the United States, smaller towns and rural areas have been especially vulnerable. Historically, rural youth have shown a pattern of attraction to stimulants. When methamphetamine enters a rural community or small town with limited resources for law enforcement and substance misuse and mental health treatments, the effects can be devastating. Small communities, as well as urban areas in which methamphetamine has become popular, have seen increased hospital emergency department episodes, surges in crime, and explosions and fires from the methamphetamine production process. In addition, clean-up of toxic laboratories is dangerous and very expensive, although the Federal government offers some assistance to communities unable to manage it by themselves (Wermuth, 2000).

Japanese and U.S. governments have largely responded to increasing methamphetamine misuse by increasing penalties. This response does co-occur with the reduction of methamphetamine misuse. Concurrent with the criminalization of methamphetamine misuse, however, organized criminal groups increasingly have taken over the production and distribution of methamphetamine, thus leading to additional problems for struggling rural communities. This brief historical and cultural analysis suggests that an optimal societal response will decrease the demand for methamphetamine, in addition to providing for the criminalization of its use and production. In rural areas, this complex challenge may require an increase in the availability of effective prevention and substance misuse and mental health treatment resources, as well as economic stimulus programs for impoverished communities. Without such a comprehensive approach to combating the methamphetamine problem, isolated societal responses are likely to fail.

Chapter Three

The Research Program

In approaching the problem of parental methamphetamine misuse, we chose a mixed-methods research strategy. This choice reflects our underlying interest in understanding human development as an outgrowth of cultural life, and in using such knowledge to inform the design and evaluation of interventions with vulnerable children. Our research strategy integrates developmental, ethnographic, and clinical methods. The intent of such methodological pluralism is to strengthen each approach, to better understand development in its sociocultural context (see Jessor, Colby & Shweder, 1996). Developmental methods include the systematic description of children's participation in various activities and changes over time. Ethnographic methods include the description and interpretation of social behavior and its meanings from participants' perspectives through analysis of the broader context of beliefs and practices. Clinical methods include the use of in-depth interviews and culturally appropriate assessments of mental health. The intertwining of developmental, ethnographic, and clinical methods allows identification of the regularities inherent in everyday life within particular communities, an interpretation of what such regularities may mean to the participants themselves (Gaskins, Miller & Corsaro, 1992; Sperry & Sperry, 1996), and a broader contextualization of participants' psychological functioning.

A mixed-method approach also is widely recognized as critical for understanding children from diverse cultural communities (e.g., Heath, 1996; Miller, 1982; Ogbu, 1974; Phillips, 1983), including children who grow up in contexts that place them at risk (e.g., Jessor et al., 1996). Moore (1991) argues that inclusion of ethnographic methods is particularly important when those involved—the children and their parents, mental health professionals, and researchers—come from different cultural communities, for example, urban and rural. The ethnographic approach is a "dialectical, or feed-back (or interactive-adaptive) method" (Hymes, 1982) in which data, research questions, and analytic categories interact as the study evolves. Incorporating such ethnographic methods into more traditional developmental and clinical approaches forces mental health professionals and researchers to understand

Participant observation included shadowing a child welfare investigator to rural properties. Photo by Sheriff Michael Miller.

the meaning of observed behavior from categories emerging from the community being studied, not their own communities.

More generally, a mixed-method approach is necessary to context-specific conceptualizations of children's development (see Shweder, Goodnow, Hitano, LeVine, Markus & Miller, 2006). In recent decades, there has been a move away from defining developmental sequences or trajectories in universal terms, abstracted from the particular practices within which children develop, toward the identification of various kinds of expertise that emerge within specific cultural contexts and then charting developmental progress in relation to these locally defined goals or types of expertise (Rogoff, 1990). From this perspective, development can be characterized as a process of children's increasing participation with adults and peers in the routines and communicative events through which culture is maintained and elaborated (e.g., Corsaro, 1996; Lave & Wenger, 1991; Rogoff, 1990). Understanding development, then, requires diverse methodological tools to describe children's emerging competencies in relation to their complex sociocultural contexts.

Such context-specific conceptualizations of development are at the heart of culturally sensitive interventions. Many mental health and child welfare interventions for children are based upon European-American, middle-class preferences for child-centered, verbal, emotionally positive, stimulating, and sensitive adult–child interactions. Comparative research, however, indicates that adults in many other cultural communities exhibit these behaviors less frequently than do middle-class European Americans, and that such differences reflect a commitment to other socialization goals, values, and understanding of the world (Shweder et al., 2006). Understanding the socialization beliefs and practices of the community within which the child is being reared, then, is prerequisite to the design of an effective intervention that is comprehensible to and accepted as relevant by the child, the child's family, and the community.

The first phase of our research reflects a long tradition of descriptive research in developmental psychology combined with ethnographic approaches in anthropology and assessment approaches from clinical psychology. A keystone of this empirical approach is to describe development based on observations of everyday behavior. These naturalistic observations are supplemented by structured observations and contextualized by in-depth interviews focusing on adult beliefs that frame and inform socialization practices, as well as children's experiences and perceptions. The first phase of the research described in this book also includes the use of standardized assessments of children's mental health. These assessments can be valuable in the identification of clinical symptoms of psychological distress, such as post-traumatic stress disorder, and in placing children's psychological functioning within a broader context of children from diverse communities. Such assessments, however, typically assume universalism in human functioning and are used with caution. We have chosen widely used assessments that can be administered individually and that allow children to provide narrative elaborations of responses to questions about basic emotional and behavioral responses. We also interpret these instruments in the context of data from a variety of sources, for example, foster parent reports, child interviews, and case records.

In the second phase of our research, these descriptive data are used in conjunction with existing clinical research to inform the design of culturally sensitive and evidence-informed interventions. In the third phase of our ongoing research, interventions are empirically assessed, typically using experimental and quasi-experimental designs and a combination of qualitative and quantitative methods.

Phase 1: Ethnographic–Developmental Overview of Parental Methamphetamine Misuse and Children's Psychological Functioning

Part 2 of this book provides an in-depth description of the problem of parental methamphetamine misuse in the cultural context of rural Illinois and a description of affected children's psychological functioning. We attempt to understand, in depth, the socialization beliefs and practices of adults, as well as children's experiences and psychological functioning. We seek to characterize, as opposed to simplify, the complexities of socialization beliefs and practices to obtain a more complete, accurate understanding of community members' points of view (Becker, 1996). This task is challenging, given the heterogeneity of rural Illinois, including potential within-group variation in the socialization beliefs and practices of children's families of origin and foster families. Some biological parents who lead more conventional lives may resemble their children's foster parents. Others, especially those who have been raised in families affected by generations of substance misuse, may hold divergent socialization beliefs and practices.

Research Site

The site of the study was the seven-county areas served by a rural field office of the Illinois Department of Children and Family Services (DCFS). This area is predominantly rural, white, and working-class with an average yearly family income of $38,000 (e-PODUNK, 2004). It was an excellent site for this case-based research for a number of reasons. First, it was a center of the growing methamphetamine problem in Illinois. One of the small, rural counties served by the rural field office had 220 drug crime arrests in 2001, more than a 100% increase over the previous year's arrests, and 97 methamphetamine laboratory seizures by state police. The area served by the rural field office continued to experience significant numbers of methamphetamine lab seizures and drug arrests throughout the period of our study. Second, as in other areas of rural American, methamphetamine misuse had taken a toll on children. At the time of the study, the rural field office was handling between 95 and 100 cases of child maltreatment per month. Administrators estimated that approximately 25% of those cases involved parental methamphetamine misuse. Indeed, the most frequently cited reason for opening a case in the rural field office was parental substance misuse. Most cases involving protective custody; that is, when children were actually removed from their parents' care and placed in foster care, were from families involved with methamphetamine. Finally, the rural field office was an effective organization. The year prior to the initiation of our study, it was the subject of an in-depth federal review. It was specifically cited as excellent on achieving a variety of safety, permanency, and well-being goals for children. Turn-over of staff in the field office was low. Most were members of surrounding rural areas and had long-standing relationships in the community and with one another. Administrators emphasized teamwork, support, and cooperation, and actively sought new information to improve their practice. This atmosphere afforded us an unprecedented opportunity to study highly vulnerable children within a unique historical period.

Participants

Participants included knowledgeable adults ($N = 35$), mothers recovering from methamphetamine addiction ($N = 4$), and school-aged children involved with the rural field office because of parental methamphetamine misuse ($N = 29$). Knowledgeable adults had regular contact with children from methamphetamine-involved families. Child welfare workers were recruited by word of mouth. All child welfare workers invited to participate agreed ($N = 18$). There were 14 women. Six had master's degrees in social work or a related profession, three were enrolled in a master of social work (MSW) program, and the remaining nine had bachelor's degrees. They had a mean of 13 years of experience in child welfare (range = 5–22 years), and 6 years at the rural field office (range = 1–16 years). As will be elaborated in Chapter 4, rural child welfare workers are called upon by police to take protective custody of children when their parents are involved with methamphetamine, to respond to and investigate hotline reports of child maltreatment by parents who misuse methamphetamine, and to follow-up and monitor services to children and families.

Our research also included seven foster caregivers (six were women). These individuals observe, live with, and nurture children in protective custody because of parental methamphetamine misuse. They were referred by child welfare workers at the rural field office as experienced and knowledgeable in dealing with children whose parents misuse methamphetamine. Ninety percent of caregivers approached agreed to participate.

There were 10 professionals from community agencies and schools that routinely provide services to families involved with methamphetamine. They were referred by workers at the rural field office as knowledgeable colleagues with whom they routinely work. They were counselors from a private social service agency, a state's attorney, a police officer from the drug task force, a local substance abuse counselor, school counselors, and an elementary school principal. Ninety percent of community professionals invited agreed to participate.

Parents who misuse methamphetamine are difficult to recruit, and only a fraction agreed to participate. They were four, rural, white, single mothers in their 30s who were recovering from methamphetamine addiction. Recruited through community contacts from different villages and small towns in the rural Midwest, they were each the mother of from three to five children, ranging in age from 3 to 18 years. All of the women were in recovery from methamphetamine addiction. All identified methamphetamine as their drug of choice, but they also had misused other drugs. Each woman had experienced separations from her children, and only one was actively parenting at the time of the interview. The women had been drug-free from 6 months to 2 years. Only one woman (Amy) reported a formal psychiatric diagnosis (bipolar disorder) in addition to substance addiction. All but one woman (Mary) grew up in poverty and reported substance misuse in her family of origin.

Twenty-nine children also participated in phase one of the research. The rural field office responsible for the seven-county region referred all children between the ages of 6 and 16 years from families with a substantiated report of maltreatment or risk of harm due to parental methamphetamine misuse. Children were referred from April to August, 2004, and from April to June, 2006. Ninety-four percent of eligible children agreed to participate.

The mean age of the 17 participating boys and 12 participating girls was 9.8 years, with a range of 6–14.6 years. Table 3.1 describes the type and extent of children's exposure to parental substance use and criminality, as indicated by case records and/or caseworker reports. Note that most children's exposure to parental methamphetamine misuse was intense, involving both parents ($N = 19$), methamphetamine misuse lasting more than 3 months ($N = 26$), and methamphetamine production at home ($N = 25$). In addition to their parents' misuse of methamphetamine, most children were exposed to parents' involvement in the criminal justice system because of methamphetamine misuse ($N = 22$) and parents' misuse of alcohol or other illegal drugs for more than 3 years ($N = 24$). At study onset, four children (14%) were residing with non–substance-abusing family members. Twenty-five (86%) were residing in traditional foster homes. These children had been in foster care for a mean of 15 months (range, 0–39 months). The mean number of foster placements was 1.5 (range, 0–5). One child had been seen by a psychiatrist.

Table 3.1 Children's ($N = 29$) exposure to parental substance misuse and criminality as indicated by case records or caseworker reports[a]

Exposure	Percentage (number) of children
Both parents[b] misused meth	66% (19)
Parent misused meth for >3 months	90% (26)
Parent produced methamphetamine at home	86% (25)
Parent in jail/prison for meth-related offense	76% (22)
Both parents misused alcohol	48% (14)
Both parents misused other illegal drugs	66% (19)
Parents misused alcohol or other illegal drugs for >3 years	83% (24)

[a]Note that several siblings participated, so that data pertain to 29 children from 18 separate families.
[b]For most children, "parent" refers to biological mother and father, but for at least three children "parent" refers to biological mother and her live-in partner.

We chose to focus on children between the ages of 6 and 16 years because children in this range are at especially high risk for the development of problems with substance misuse (Oetting, Edwards, Kelly & Beauvais, 1997). They also constitute the largest number of children who are involved with the child welfare system (Administration for Children and Families, 2003). In addition, children in this age range can complete standard assessment tools and respond to interview questions, allowing us to understand their perspectives on their experiences and families. The requirement that the families be involved with child protective custody was included because families involved in illegal methamphetamine production and misuse were not likely to allow their children to participate in this study before detection by the authorities. In addition, these children are arguably among our most vulnerable and in need of advocacy and intervention. From a pragmatic perspective, they also are those most likely to present to social workers and other professionals for services.

The study was approved by the University of Illinois and child protective services institutional review boards. The children's legal guardian provided formal permission, and children provided verbal assent.

Procedures

Entering the Community. Professionals from the rural field office and their colleagues (educators, law enforcement personnel, and substance abuse counselors) were very concerned about the significant and growing problem of methamphetamine in their communities and how it impacts the children and families they served. Child welfare workers from the rural field office who were studying for their MSW degrees at the University of Illinois at Urbana-Champaign asked for our help in collecting information that would be relevant to the development of interventions. Linda Kingery, a child protective worker with deep roots in the community and generally excellent relations with other professionals, as well as clients, then facilitated our access by identifying adults and children and introducing the project to them.

Participant Observation. Two of us (Haight, Ostler) each participated in approximately 90 hours of fieldwork over a 6-month period from April 2004 through September 2004. Field notes concentrated on descriptions of investigations of rural homes visited during 17 mornings or afternoons spent "shadowing" a child welfare investigator. Field notes also included observations of a staffing of investigators, supervision of an investigation, court appearances of methamphetamine-involved parents, two Illinois state legislative methamphetamine task force meetings, three visits to rural schools, and multiple visits to rural field offices.

Record Reviews. Record reviews included newspaper articles, materials from local substance-misuse counseling services and law enforcement, other documentation of methamphetamine misuse in rural Illinois, and several state websites. We also obtained information on individual children from review of their DCFS case records.

Adult Interviews.

Mothers. The women described their life experiences through individual, face-to-face, in-depth, semi-structured interviews. They were interviewed in their homes by two social work PhD students with MSW degrees and practice experience, or at a homeless shelter by a social work professor with over 20 years of practice experience. The women had met with and interacted with the interviewers prior to the formal interviews. The interviews probed women's histories, initial misuse of methamphetamine, active use and addiction, impact on parenting, treatment and recovery, and any lasting effects on them or their children. Interviews lasted approximately 2–3 hours. They were tape recorded and transcribed verbatim. A description of the cases was constructed through multiple readings of the transcripts.

Other Adult Interviews. Other adult informants participated in individual, semi-structured, audiotaped interviews that were approximately 1 hour long. These interviews focused on the individuals' experiences with methamphetamine-involved families, and their beliefs about the effects of parental methamphetamine misuse on school-aged children and appropriate strategies to promote children's psychological development and mental health. Interviews were conducted by PhD-level psychologists.

Child Interviews and Assessments. Children's interviews and assessments were conducted by an experienced psychiatrist, developmental psychologist, clinical psychologist, or master's level social worker and audiotaped for later verbatim transcription. They were conducted in a private location, typically a room in the children's home. Testing and interviews were completed on the same day and took approximately 2 hours. With the exception of the Peabody Picture Vocabulary Test (PPVT), the order of administration of the test and interviews were counterbalanced. Children were given breaks as needed.

The Peabody Picture Vocabulary Test. The interviews and assessments are dependent on verbal ability. Therefore, we first screened for children's significant language delays using the PPVT-3, a norm-referenced, individually administered measure of receptive vocabulary for individuals from age 2-1/2 to adult (Dunn & Dunn, 1997). The PPVT-3 takes approximately 11–12 minutes to administer and requires that children point to pictures. It has excellent reliability and validity. It is related to measures of general intellectual functioning such as the Wechsler Intelligence Scale for Children. Children appeared to enjoy the PPVT, so that it also served as a warm-up task.

The PPVT-3 established that the children could participate in age-appropriate standardized assessments and interviews. Children's mean score on the Peabody was 98.5, with a standard deviation of 13.7. Two children scored one standard deviation above the mean on the PPVT; one scored one standard deviation below.

The Trauma Symptom Checklist for Children. Children completed the Trauma Symptom Checklist for Children (TSCC). This 44-item checklist provides information on posttraumatic distress in children who have experienced traumatic events. Items describe what children may feel, think, and do, such as "feeling like I'm not in my body" and "getting mad and can't calm down" (Briere, 1996). Children respond using a four-point Likert-scale ranging from "never happens" to "happens almost all of the time." The TSCC has two validity scales (Under-response, Hyper-response) and five clinical scales (Anxiety, Depression, Anger, Posttraumatic Stress, and Dissociation). Standardized scores are available for different age groups and by gender. The TSCC has moderate to high reliability and good concurrent and construct validity (Briere, 1996). The TSCC was read to the children to ensure understanding.

Experience in family of origin. A semi-structured, individual interview provided information on children's perspectives of their families and parents' methamphetamine misuse. This interview was embedded within a larger protocol, including standardized assessments and enjoyable activities of the child's choice, for example, puppet play. Children were first asked to talk about a time in their family that was happy, followed by a time in their family that was sad or scary. Probes explored what happened, how the child felt, and what the child thought and did, including when parents misused methamphetamine and other drugs. The interview concluded with an invitation for children to "Tell me about a time in your family that was fun."

Children's attitudes about drugs and alcohol. The American Drug and Alcohol Survey – Children's Form (ADAS) was administered to provide supplementary information on children's beliefs and attitudes about methamphetamine, alcohol, and other substances. This paper-and-pencil measure asks questions about children's attitudes about substance use, including their perception of the harmfulness of drugs, their intention to use in the future, and any current use. We read the forms to all children, as it provided an opportunity to clarify responses and understanding. It is generally completed in about 20 minutes, and is reliable when used in the general population and with rural children (Oetting, Edwards & Beauvais, 1985; Oetting et al., 1997).

This instrument, however, was problematic for our participants, and so we will not present results in this book. The majority of the children in our study had been strongly socialized against discussing substance misuse. Typical responses of the children were to refuse to answer the questions, or simply respond in the negative to all items without reading them or before we had read them. These responses are consistent with reports of clinicians in the addictions field that secrecy and denial are typical responses in families involved with addictions (e.g., Black, 2001).

Foster Parent Child Behavior Checklist. We obtained additional information on the children's behavioral functioning from foster parents. Foster caregivers completed The Child Behavior Checklist (CBCL) for ages 6–18 (Achenbach & Rescorla, 2001) in a private location on the day children were interviewed. Each of the 112 items on this questionnaire are rated on a three-point scale (not true = 0, somewhat or sometimes true = 1, very often true = 2). It yields a total score, two "broad-band" scores representing externalizing and internalizing dimensions of behavior and emotional problems, and scores for eight "narrow-band" scales (withdrawn/depressed behavior, somatic complaints, social problems, anxious/depressed, thought problems, attention problems, rule-breaking behavior, aggressive behavior). The CBCL has excellent reliability and validity (Achenbach & Rescorla, 2001), and standardized scores are available for different age groups and by gender.

A scale representing dissociative and posttraumatic symptoms was derived from the CBCL by Ogawa and colleagues (Ogawa, Sroufe, Weinfield, Carlson & Egeland, 1997). This scale is based on CBCL items that are similar in content to items assessed by the Children's Dissociative Checklist (Putnam, Helmers & Trickett, 1993). The 12 items comprising this scale (e.g., "stares blankly," "sudden changes in mood or feelings," "confused or seems to be in a fog," "acts too young for his/her age," "hears sounds or voices that aren't there") were summed (scores range from 0 to 24) for each child, with higher scores indicating more dissociative symptoms. Items from this and similar scales have good structural coherence (Cronbach's alpha = .63–.68) and can provide valid information on dissociative symptoms in children and adolescents (Carlson, 1998, Malinowsky-Rummel & Hoier, 1991; Ogawa et al., 1997). Following prior research (Carlson, 1998; Malinowsky-Rummel & Hoier 1991; Ogawa et al., 1997), we chose a clinical cutoff (6) based on evidence that the child was displaying a cluster of posttraumatic and dissociative symptoms (cf. American Psychiatric Association, 2000).

Transcription and Analysis of Interviews

Adult and child interviews were transcribed verbatim. Emic codes, which focus on the meanings ascribed by the participants to their experiences, were developed through repeated readings of the transcribed interviews (Schwandt, 2001). All interviews were read by two individuals who independently, and through discussion, generated a list of descriptive codes characterizing participants' responses. Peer debriefing was utilized as we sought feedback regarding coding from knowledgeable colleagues. Member checks also were conducted to ensure that descriptive codes characterized the meanings informants intended to convey through their responses (see Denzin & Lincoln, 2000; Lincoln & Guba, 1985; Miles & Huberman, 1994).

Following training, transcribed adult and child interviews were coded independently by two additional coders. Coders for child interviews were blinded with respect to children's performance on standardized mental health assessments. Percent agreement on a randomly selected 15% of interviews not used in training was adequate (details available from authors). Disagreements were resolved through discussion. The descriptive codes are presented in the following chapters, in which we focus on interview themes emerging from multiple informants.

Phase 2: Design of a Culturally Sensitive, Evidence-Based Intervention

Part 3 of the book focuses on integrating findings from phase one with evidence-based clinical research and clinical experience in the mental health and addictions fields to design a culturally and developmentally sensitive intervention for rural children in foster care whose parent's misuse methamphetamine. The result was the Life Story Intervention. Our aim was to harness potential protective factors to address risks to children's mental health. Our phase 1 data revealed that many children were challenged by a high rate of trauma symptoms, as well as lack of social support for understanding what had happened to them in their families. At the community level, no specialized services were available for children experiencing trauma symptoms, and the nearest child psychiatrists were located in urban areas at considerable distances from the children's homes. We also discovered, however, a rich tradition of rural storytelling and rural professionals accustomed to serving in multiple roles in children's lives. For example, in one of the rural schools we visited, educators routinely provided young adolescents from methamphetamine-involved homes with food, toiletries, and clean clothing.

We reviewed the literature on evidence-based approaches to helping children cope with trauma. We drew upon the American Association of Child and Adolescent Psychiatry guidelines for intervention with children who have experienced trauma (Cohen, Deblinger, Mannarino & Steer, 2004).

We also considered narrative therapy (e.g., Freedman & Combs, 1996), clinical literature on families and addiction using family system theory (e.g., Black, 2001), and research on community- and relationship-based interventions for at-risk children in foster care (e.g., Rhodes, 2002). We also considered the extensive clinical expertise of research team members with practice experience treating Illinois children in foster care suffering from trauma symptoms and children from substance-involved families.

These sources of evidence were combined to design the Life Story Intervention described in Part 3 of this book. The overarching goal was to enhance the mental health and overall well-being of rural children in foster care whose parents misuse methamphetamine through a narrative- and relationship-based intervention. We drew upon rural professionals, such as child welfare workers, social workers, retired counselors, and educators, to implement the Life Story Intervention with one or two children each in their rural area. We provided them with weekly supervision from experienced clinicians on our research team who were located in an adjacent urban area.

Phase 3: Evaluation of Life Story Intervention

Phase three of our research program will be foreshadowed in Part 3 of the book, in a presentation of the pilot-tested intervention. We describe the conceptual and empirical bases of Life Story Intervention, as well as implementation issues. We also present case-based descriptions of various child responses to the intervention over a 12- to 18-month period. Additional evaluation of the intervention using an experimental design and a combination of qualitative and quantitative methods to describe children's functioning over a period of 12–18 months will be forthcoming in future publications.

Key Characteristics of the Research Program

The design and methods employed in this research program combine several features worth highlighting that are designed to maximize the cultural validity and trustworthiness of the findings.

Case-based Research Strategy. The focus of this research is on understanding parental methamphetamine misuse and their children's psychological functioning within the cultural context of rural Illinois. In the short run, our case-based research strategy suggested strategies for intervention within this rural area. In the long run, the complex and differentiated portrait emerging from this case-based research strategy can provide a model and basis for meaningful comparisons with other areas.

Strong Practitioner–Researcher Collaboration. Developing productive practitioner–researcher collaborations that allow relevant research to be integrated into practice has been a perennial problem in a variety of fields, including social work. Researchers are criticized for conducting esoteric studies of questionable utility to solving social problems, and practitioners have been criticized for failing to utilize evidence from social science research to improve practice. The research program described in this book was initiated by social work practitioners. It was conducted in collaboration with researchers who have keen interests in using the tools of social science to address pressing social problems, and who have practice experience. Thus, the relevance of this research to social work practice was enhanced by a practitioner–research team involved in all stages of the research program.

Transdisciplinary Research Team. In addition to practitioners, researchers representing diverse fields (developmental psychology, social work, child welfare, psychiatry, and child clinical psychology) were involved in all phases of the development of this research program. The project thus benefited from a transdisciplinary perspective throughout all phases, from the development of the research questions, to the collection and analysis of the data, to the design and assessment of the intervention.

Mixed-method Research Program. Our three-phase research program utilizes a mixed-method design, in which we begin with a rich description of the context in which children are reared and their psychological functioning, emphasizing qualitative methods, but including some quantitative assessments. Only after we obtain a rich understanding of the cultural context and children's psychological functioning do we design and then evaluate an intervention using qualitative and quantitative methods.

Multiplism. Our research program includes multiple informants, contexts of observation, and methods. We draw upon the diverse perspectives of a variety of individuals knowledgeable about parental methamphetamine misuse, including professionals, children, and parents who have been addicted to methamphetamine. These perspectives and experiences, emerging from diverse social positions, provide a more complete account of beliefs and practices relevant to understanding parental methamphetamine misuse.

Our research program also draws upon multiple contexts of observation. Field notes were collected in diverse contexts, including children's homes, schools, communities, and political task force meetings. These observations allow for a more complete account of beliefs and practices relevant to parental methamphetamine misuse. Observations in multiple contexts can discipline emerging interpretations, provide counter examples, and motivate re analyses.

For example, observations of discussions during an Illinois methamphet-amine task force meeting suggested a generally angry and punitive stance to-ward individuals addicted to methamphetamine that was contradicted by private, individual interviews in which adults also expressed grief over fam-ily members and friends involved with methamphetamine.

The research program also employs a variety of research methods. The use of multiple methods balances the strengths and limitations of various strategies and provides multiple checks on interpretation. Multiple methods allow participants a variety of options for responding. For example, in de-scribing children's mental health functioning, we employed both standard-ized assessments and semi-structured, in-depth interviews. Some children were reluctant to talk about their families, but readily responded to paper and pencil measures. Other children under-reported symptoms on the stan-dardized assessments, but detailed trauma symptoms during the interview. Multiple methods also allowed us to triangulate, for example, caregiver ver-sus child reports of the child's mental health.

Rapport Building. Rapport building with community members was facili-tated by the prior positive working relationships practitioners from the rural field office had established with community informants. On a typical day, we would arrive at the rural field office and be handed a schedule of inter-views with knowledgeable adults already arranged by Linda Kingery and colleagues. Since we were friends of Linda, then our participants welcomed us, generously shared their perspectives, and patiently answered our many questions.

Rapport building with children was enhanced by the clinical experi-ence of the researchers. It was essential that children felt comfortable with us, both to meet our ethical requirements and to collect meaningful data. Taking the time to establish a trusting relationship was a prerequisite to ob-taining children's willingness to participate and ability to provide elaborated answers. This process was facilitated by our willingness to meet with chil-dren in and around their homes and communities.

Sustained Involvement. Our description of parental methamphetamine misuse is based on sustained community involvement spanning a 3-year period and approximately 650 hours of direct contact. Gaining access to and un-derstanding the perspectives of others is time intensive. Although this book focuses on the cross-sectional analyses in phase 3 of the study, children were followed for 12–18 months with 6–8 months of weekly home visits. This strategy of prolonged engagement was designed to avoid what Richard Shweder (1996a) described as "superficialism": the fallacious assumption that others can "upon demand and 'off the tops of their heads' . . . tell what they know, know what they are talking about, and keep their answers short" (p. 21).

Clinically Sophisticated Researchers. To enhance the validity of the data, as well as reduce harm to participants, interviews and assessments were conducted by experienced clinicians. Discussing potentially traumatic events with children and their parents can be retraumatizing if not done with skill and care. Interviewers spent time to establish rapport before beginning the assessments or interviews, and they moved at the participant's pace, taking care to provide psychological support. They also spent time with participants, engaging in positive or neutral conversation or activities following data collection—for example, playing a board game with a child.

Credible Analyses. To enhance the credibility of our qualitative coding, all transcribed interviews were read by two independent readers, and we made use of peer debriefing and member checks (as described earlier). Although not typical of many qualitative analyses, we include reliability checks to enhance the consistency of our analyses of interview data.

Limitations

As with all research program, ours also has several limitations worth highlighting here.

Limited Parental Participation. Methamphetamine misuse is a highly stigmatized, illegal activity. We had many difficulties recruiting parents. Although most children came from two-parent families, no fathers participated. The four mothers who participated were invaluable to our understanding, but our understanding of parental methamphetamine misuse would have been enhanced by greater participation by parents. Although their accounts shared many common themes, discussed in Chapter 5, it is unlikely that all important themes were illuminated (i.e., we probably did not achieve saturation).

Greater parental participation also would have allowed us to gain important information on topics such as children's prenatal exposure to any drugs or alcohol, their early development, and contexts of rearing in infancy and early childhood.

Limited Systematic Information on Children's Development. Ideally, we would have preferred to obtain more systematic information on children's language, cognitive, social, and emotional development. We also would have preferred to obtain more systematic information on children's functioning in diverse contexts, especially school.

No Contact with Children Prior to Their Entrance into Foster Care. Methamphetamine misuse is a hidden activity. Children whose parents are actively misusing methamphetamine tend to be an invisible group. When authorities do become aware of parents' involvement, children are placed in the care of extended family members or foster parents. Thus, our direct observations of children's socialization contexts and functioning at their family homes were restricted to field notes taken while shadowing child welfare investigators. Once children enter foster care, they experience a variety of additional stressors, for example, long-term separation from their parents and friction with foster family members, which impact their psychological functioning beyond any traumatic experiences in their families of origin. Furthermore, the accounts they provide us are retrospective.

Conclusion

Our mixed-methods approach to the problem of parental methamphetamine misuse reflects our sociocultural perspective of children's development. In a three-phase research program, we first examine the problem of parental methamphetamine misuse in the context of families living in early twenty first-century, rural Illinois; as well as the mental health functioning of their children. In the second phase, this information is combined with empirical research on effective interventions for children experiencing trauma symptoms, clinical discussions with children from substance-involved families, and the clinical experience of team members in providing services for rural children in foster care and from substance–involved families. The third phase of the research program is to implement and evaluate the resulting intervention: Life Story Intervention.

Chapter Four

Narrative of a Rural Child Welfare Professional

Our research program grew from a collaboration between practitioners and university professors. This partnership has been invaluable in designing a transdisciplinary research program to address a pressing social issue in rural America. It also allows us to bring to the fore those perspectives of practitioners that are too often ignored by researchers. In this chapter, we depart from a traditional academic presentation to provide a glimpse of rural Midwestern storytelling. Linda Kingery, a master's level social worker and child welfare professional with over 20 years of experience in rural area substance misuse, provides a first-person account of child welfare practice in contemporary rural Illinois. Her discussion illustrates some general principles of a child abuse/neglect investigation in rural Illinois, as well as a description of a case involving parental methamphetamine misuse.

My early years of work in child welfare seemed to be business as usual. Most of the families who were involved in child abuse/neglect investigations at that time were dealing with alcohol misuse and sometimes marijuana misuse. There was no mention of methamphetamine. Sometime in 2003, it became painfully apparent throughout the child welfare office where I am employed that methamphetamine use was increasing in our rural area, and the effects on children were devastating. As an advanced child protection specialist, I am involved in gathering information that helps in assessing the safety of children and making a decision as to whether or not an incident of child maltreatment has occurred. These responsibilities brought me into frequent contact with methamphetamine-affected families.

Child Abuse/Neglect Investigation in Rural Illinois

The Report

All suspected cases of child abuse/neglect are reported to the state's central registry, where calls are screened for eligibility for investigation. If the caller

Investigating child maltreatment cases often takes child welfare workers into impoverished and isolated areas. Photo by Carl Kingery.

provides information that a child under the age of 18 is suspected of receiving maltreatment from a caretaker, or that a situation of significant risk for maltreatment exists, a report is generated and an investigation specialist is assigned to begin the investigative process. The first step in this process is to "initiate" the investigation, in other words, to assess the safety of the children. The initiation typically is the most intense part of the investigation.

The Initiation

To initiate a child abuse/neglect investigation, the child welfare worker is mandated by law to see the children named in the report, or make a good faith attempt to do so, within 24 hours of receiving the hotline report. Workers sometimes see children at school, but often a visit to the home is how this first contact with children occurs. The law requires that a visit to the home occur at some point in the investigation.

Entering someone's home to discuss allegations of child abuse/neglect can be frightening to everyone. One need only think for a moment of what it would feel like to have a state official question your parenting abilities to begin to understand the defensive posture that many parents quickly assume. This defensive posture increases the potential for violence. It is common to be called to a residence that is located 20 to 30 minutes from the nearest town, and the investigator may then find that cell phone service is unavailable.

Law enforcement assistance is available upon request, but it is difficult to predict when such assistance will be necessary. It is not feasible for workers to request law enforcement personnel to accompany them on every investigation. If every report came in with details as to the propensity for violence or other dangers, it would be an easier decision.

I recall a time when I received a report alleging suspected "substantial risk of physical injury" to two adolescent children in the home, but the directions to the home were unclear. As is customary for child protection investigators, I contacted our county sheriff's office for assistance in finding the home of the involved family. It is important to note that I have a long-standing relationship with law enforcement personnel in the county where I work, because I have been working in this county for several years. We have worked together often on cases involving child abuse/neglect situations that have led to criminal prosecution. As we have worked together, bonds have formed and trust has developed.

On this particular case, the deputy I contacted was familiar with the family I sought and was able to provide explicit directions to the home. Keep in mind that directions in the rural Midwest can be quite interesting, some might even say, colorful. The deputy said, "You need to head west out of town and turn south when you get to Coon Chase Road." He then asked, "Now, do you know where the coon huntin' clubhouse is?" I responded that I thought I might have been by there before, so the deputy gave a few more details such as the old blue house with the broken cars in the yard along with several dogs. This helped me to identify the surrounding area a bit more specifically. The deputy explained that the home I was searching for was down a lane to the right, about a mile past the "coon huntin' clubhouse." He then added, almost as an afterthought, "You might want to be careful, Linda. This guy is a little odd." I thanked him for the information, which did not seem especially concerning, and continued on with my work.

I found my way to Coon Chase Road quite easily and drove my car down the lane, which was about a half-mile in length. At times like this, it is impossible not to think about the possibility that a situation could get out of hand. The nearest help is at least 30 minutes away, and it might not even be possible to make that call for help. On this particular day, the sun was shining (which somehow seems less threatening), and the report did not contain any information that would lead me to believe violence was a concern. In fact, my information was that the involved family was living with maternal grandparents, who were reportedly in their late 60s. Since I was 50 at the time, I figured I could deal with a couple of elderly grandparents and any resistance they might bring to the situation. The only subtle hint of needed caution was from my deputy friend, "This guy is a little odd." So,

I continued down the lane with my thoughts mainly focused on how the rocky terrain was affecting my brand-new car.

I approached the residence and found a kind and welcoming middle-aged woman. I said, "Hello, I'm Linda Kingery with the Department of Children and Family Services," as I presented my identification badge. "I'm looking for Jen."

The lady responded, "Oh, she and the girls went in town, but I'm expecting them back at any time. Why don't you have a seat here on the patio. They'll most likely be here any minute."

While observing the beautiful surroundings, I noticed a flower garden nearby and commented, "Your garden is lovely. It must take a lot of work." The woman proceeded to tell me about her garden with great pride, commenting, "The tulips are my husband's favorites."

As small talk often does, it distracted from my original purpose and allowed me, for a brief moment, to lapse into a sense of security. The serenity of the scene was shattered when a car careened into the driveway, spewing gravel and dust into the air. My attention was quickly diverted from the relaxed conversation I had just been involved in to an older gentleman exiting the car with a reddened face and obvious rage. A woman and two adolescent children, whom I assumed to be the family I sought, remained in the car. They watched helplessly as the man continued to move aggressively in my direction. He asserted his control of the situation and shouted, "Get off my (expletive deleted) property!" He further advised me, "I'm about to kick your ass."

As all of my social work training flooded my mind, I began backing toward my car. I gently but firmly explained, "Sir, I have every respect for you and your ownership of this property. I have not come here to harm anyone. I am here as an employee of the Department of Children and Family Services, and need to speak with your daughter about a report I have received." My plan was to continue with an explanation of how the Department's role is to ensure the safety of children, but also to assist families as needed.

Within seconds, it became obvious that the man was not processing this information. My first clue was when he continued with his aggressive stance, moved closer to me, and said, "Like I said, I'm gonna kick your ass! I know exactly who you are. You guys have been out here before. You sent some fag (expletive deleted) out here, and I ain't havin' no fag (expletive deleted) out here tellin' me or mine what I can do!"

At this point in the discourse, the man came at me with every intention of striking me. His wife stepped between us and calmly said, "Now, John, you are not going to hit this nice lady." I was thankful for the brief opportunity I had had to build some rapport with this woman, who now took on the much-appreciated role of bodyguard for me.

I was not confident of her ability to fill the position she had willingly chosen, as her husband assured her that his intention was indeed to "hit this nice lady." As they continued to argue over my fate, he was angrily making his way around the corner of the house, cussing at his wife and me as he made his dramatic exit. I said to the wife, "Please ask your husband to come back into my sight." Continuing to maintain her composure, she replied, "No, honey, you don't want that. If he comes back around here, I'm afraid he's going to hurt you."

My thoughts were racing as I wondered if this man had access to weapons, if he had a history of violence toward people, specifically women, more specifically social workers. I certainly was recalling my law enforcement friend's word, "He's a little odd," which took on a whole new meaning for me. I assured the woman standing with me that I would rather be able to see her husband, and she yelled at him, basically ordering him to go to the camper nearby and let her "deal with this."

The man's decision to obey his wife and go to the camper did not increase my comfort level considerably, so I continued to walk toward my car with the intention of contacting the police for assistance as soon as I was back in a place where my cell phone service was active. The mother of the involved children eventually exited her father's vehicle and came to my car. She apologized for her father's behavior and offered to bring the children to my office in town while her father stayed home to compose himself. This sounded like a great plan to me, so I was able to safely exit the situation, meet with the family in my office, and assess the safety of the children.

During this meeting, both children told me that this incident was not "nearly as bad as the time Grampa ran the neighbor off the property with a shotgun!" I later found out that this gentleman was alcoholic and prone to fits of rage. I contacted my deputy friend, and in a friendly manner, told him I would prefer that when someone might be violent, he use the words "violent" or "aggressive" rather than a "little odd." Of course, he assured me that he was not familiar with this side of the man and suggested that I might thank him since child welfare investigators, like police, always need a good story to tell.

The preceding incident is not a regular occurrence, yet it is not uncommon either. Many times a hotline report will provide a description of the condition of a home as being filthy or children being observed at school to be dirty and not well cared for. There have been many occasions when an investigator has been called to a home for a "dirty house," an allegation of environmental neglect, to find that the real problem is that the parents have been so incapacitated by their methamphetamine misuse that they are no longer cleaning the home or tending to daily household responsibilities. It is also possible that an investigator will stumble upon a clandestine meth lab. In such a situation, the protocol is that the worker immediately exits the situation and contacts local law enforcement.

It is always somewhat unnerving to walk up to a house for the first time to inform someone that their parenting ability has been called into question. When the parent is under the effects of a drug like methamphetamine, it is possible that the situation might quickly become life-threatening. It is important that workers be trained adequately to deal with such situations, because the assessment of children's safety almost never occurs within the confines of a safe office environment.

Gathering Information

Following the initiation of a child abuse/neglect investigation, in which the child's safety is paramount and decisions are made quickly without all available evidence, the process of gathering more complete information begins. Experience tells us that there are almost always underlying issues in cases of child abuse/neglect. Few parents set out to hurt their children. The effects of poverty, mental illness, domestic violence, and/or substance misuse are common in cases of child maltreatment, but these issues are not necessarily identifiable in the early stages of an investigation. Illinois child welfare rules and procedures require that each family be screened for such issues, but it is not reasonable to expect that families will be immediately forthcoming in regards to such personal information.

It almost goes without saying that a person involved in the manufacture and use of an illegal drug as stigmatized as methamphetamine will not sit down with a state worker and readily admit to the problem. It is often after a family has agreed to open a follow-up case, when a caseworker has been assigned to meet with the family monthly, that the underlying issues actually come to light and needed services are put into place.

Just as the alleged perpetrators—the parents or caregivers—are reluctant to share with the "helping professional" what is happening in the home, so too are the children. We know that families involved with addictions often are committed to a "conspiracy of silence," and certainly this "no talk rule" would apply when a stranger from the state comes asking questions.

On more than one occasion, I have met with a child at school for an interview to determine whether or not an incident of child abuse/neglect has occurred. It is typical that I meet with the child in a library or counselor's room in a small school where the staff is aware of who I am and has at least some idea of why I am talking to a particular child. Elementary-age children are often friendly and willing to respond to my prying questions. However, there are children who have been socialized by parents to not trust authority.

In fact, I recently had a 7-year-old child say to me during an investigation, "My mama says, 'What happens at home stays at home.'" This statement was made after the child had been taken into protective custody following a drug task force raid on her home, where crack cocaine was found lying on a coffee table in plain sight of her and her 1- and 10-year-old siblings.

It is so important that we be aware that children raised in families involved in substance misuse continue to love their parents even when circumstances might suggest to those of us on the outside that it is unwarranted. Children often remain loyal in spite of betrayal, neglect, and even abuse by parents or other primary caregivers.

As part of my work with this research project, I have had the privilege of providing intervention services for a 14-year-old child who was in foster care while his parents were serving an extended prison term for manufacturing methamphetamine. As I worked with this child, it became increasingly clear that the life he enjoyed with his parents was normal for him. This child never verbalized anger or mistrust of his parents. He described them as loving and caring. In fact, he happily shared stories with me about how he and his brother ate nothing but cereal for days when both parents were "crashed" from methamphetamine misuse.

As helping professionals, this type of story seems to be strong evidence of neglect to the involved children, and it is. However, we would be remiss not to recognize the family connections, values, and traditions. Family traditions do not always include family time around a supper table and holiday trips to the home of grandparents. It might be that a "tradition" for a substance-affected family is fixing cereal with your brother while Mom and Dad are sleeping.

This concept is easy for me to grasp since I grew up with an alcoholic mother and no other adults in the home. It was not unusual for my mom to warm up a can of green beans for supper or hand me a raw potato, telling me, "Put some salt on that and eat it! It's good for ya." This is not a painful memory for me, but rather, a fond memory of a mom who laughed easily and told exciting stories of her childhood escapades and current adventures. As was true of my young client in the preceding example, seemingly neglectful situations that occur consistently over time often become "normal," and may even become a part of a "euphoric" recall.

During an investigation, understanding how the child perceives his life is extremely important. It provides information to the investigator from the child's view.

Making a Finding

Although gathering information for an investigation is difficult, it is possible. Through collateral contacts and reports from law enforcement, schools, and community agencies, information does come forth that assists the worker in obtaining evidence that either supports or discounts an allegation. The worker then shares this evidence with a supervisor, who assists the worker in sorting inculpatory (evidence that supports the finding that an incident of child abuse/neglect did occur) from exculpatory evidence (information that an incident of child abuse/neglect did not occur) and thus making a decision as to whether or not the report will be "indicated" or "unfounded." When a report is *indicated*, it means that the evidence supports the allegation. *Unfounded* means there is insufficient evidence to corroborate the report. When the supervisor and the investigator have agreed upon a finding, the family is notified and, when warranted, offered services. If the situation is deemed to be dangerous to the child, and safety cannot be ensured through a formal plan with the family, it becomes of "urgent and immediate necessity" to remove the child, and he/she is taken into protective custody.

Protective Custody

As the pendulum of child welfare philosophy continues to swing from "child rescue" to "family preservation," "protective custody" takes on different meanings. Those who cling to the belief that parents who abuse and/or neglect their children are "evil" or lacking in some innate parenting ability, think of protective custody as the process whereby vulnerable children are "rescued" from their parents. The other extreme are the folks who are convinced that all caregivers would appropriately provide for their children if given the right programs and opportunities to correct the conditions in which the abuse/neglect occurred.

Protective custody is a controversial subject, and discussed philosophically in both academic and direct-service circles. However, in the case of a child abuse/neglect investigation wherein methamphetamine production is happening in the home, not many questions are asked prior to the children being taken into protective custody. The environmental dangers present during the cooking of methamphetamine often make the removal of children from the home of "urgent and immediate necessity," and any philosophical discussion is saved for another time, which is as it should be.

It is equally important to remember that taking children from their families, even when it is absolutely necessary for their safety, is a traumatic event. It is easy to keep in mind the disruption to the family, the trauma experienced by all members of the family, especially the children, and the extreme loss felt by everyone concerned, when one is looking into the faces of the family members involved in this process we professionals refer to as "best practice."

A Case of Parental Methamphetamine Misuse

I remember a time when I was sitting at my desk, overwhelmed with paper-work and pushing to meet deadlines. My supervisor appeared at my door-way with two sheets of paper in her hand. All investigators know that when the boss appears with paper in her hand, there is a new report. In the field of child welfare, a new report may mean going to a home that is alleged to have pet feces on the floor, interviewing a small child who has been sexually abused by her stepfather, or, in some rare instances, investigating the death of a child. One thing for certain is that a new report requires a prompt response.

On this occasion, I looked to the door and asked, "You got somethin' for me?" With an unmistakable urgency in her voice, my supervisor said, "There's been a meth bust in your county. The parents have already been ar-rested, and the police have taken custody of two young boys, ages 12 and 9."

Paperwork and deadlines were suddenly the last thing on my mind as I began to ready myself to leave the office and get on the road. I quickly grabbed a "protective custody" packet, which contains the documents needed to allow an investigator to obtain the necessary health exam and other re-quired services for the children after they have been removed from the home. My child protection team members were coming up to me periodically asking what they could do to assist.

"Will you need a car seat?"

Another asked, "Do you have medical cards?"

As would be expected, I had some of the needed items but looked to my colleagues to provide missing ones. There was a flurry of activity as we worked together to make sure I was on the road as quickly as possible. With all of the necessary items in my possession, I left the office on this hot, July afternoon and began the 45-minute trip to my destination.

As my colleagues and I were preparing for the protective custody pro-cess, none of us were aware of what had been happening throughout the day a mere 45 minutes away.

Two young boys, Billy and Justin, had risen early that morning, eager to spend a day enjoying the freedom of living in a small town in the Mid-west. The older child, Billy, was accustomed to caring for his younger brother, Justin, and had helped Justin to get his clothes out and prepare to leave the home. The boys had eaten a bowl of cold cereal and mounted their bicycles, planning to visit friends. As they innocently went about their day, they stopped by a friend's house, played at the local playground behind the school, and stopped at the local gas station to buy a soda pop. The day passed quickly because they were young, and the small town in which they lived was a safe and fun place to explore.

Around lunch time, Justin began to complain of hunger, so Billy took him home to get something to eat. They fully expected that their mom and dad would still be sleeping, but that really didn't matter. Billy had suggested they eat a bowl of Lucky Charms before returning to the community for more play. However, as they turned the corner toward their home, Billy immediately knew something was wrong. He saw police cars near his home, and his heart sank. Justin, although not as "street smart" as his older brother, remembered when his mom and dad had been arrested before, and the sight of the police car made him sick to his stomach.

By the time I arrived on the scene, Billy and Justin were standing under a tree with drug task force officers apparently engaged in small talk with the two children. I exited my vehicle and introduced myself.

"Hi, guys. My name is Linda, and I work for the Department of Children and Family Services. The police have called me to come help out."

Billy spoke up immediately, "So, are you the one who will take us to Gramma's house?"

In an attempt to shield the boys from the possible truth that they would not be going to Gramma's today, I skirted the issue somewhat and replied, "I will be working with my boss to make a decision about where you and Justin will be staying until we know for sure what is happening with your mom and dad".

Matt, the drug task force agent, asked, "Linda, could you come with me for a minute? Tom will stay here with the boys."

I complied, and we entered the family home. Matt said, "I just wanted you to see why we made these arrests and the conditions these kids have been living in."

What I observed was a home, not particularly unlike any other home. The only clue that this was not like any other home was the drug paraphernalia lying on the end tables in the living room, on the kitchen counter, and on the kitchen table, and the clutter throughout the home. At that time, we still entered homes where there had been recent methamphetamine production, unaware of the danger of such a situation. Not out of fear of the smell present in the home, but rather due to the stifling heat on this summer afternoon, I quickly made my way back outside to continue talking with Billy and Justin.

Per statewide protocol, a relative placement was our first choice for substitute care, so I asked, "Billy, that gramma you mentioned earlier. Do you happen to know her phone number?"

Billy immediately said, "Yeah, sure. I can give you her address too if you need it. She doesn't live far from here."

I took the number from Billy and dialed, hoping that Gramma would answer the phone and these two boys could be safely in the care of a relative by evening. Such was not the case. As the three of us, who had suddenly become partners in this crisis, waited expectantly, the phone rang and rang, but no one answered.

Billy said, "I have another gramma here in town. She is my mom's mom. Here's her number. We go visit her a lot. I know she'll take us."

I took the number and watched these two young, vulnerable children as they watched me attempting to get in contact with their grandmother. For a second time, the phone rang, but there was no response.

In an attempt to comfort the two children currently entrusted to my care, I said, "We will continue to try to contact your gramma, but for right now we need to get on the road because you need to go get a medical exam just to make sure you're okay."

Both boys were very polite and immediately got into my car. Then Billy said, "Oh, could I go back in the house a minute? There's something I need to get."

"You'll need to ask the police," I responded.

Billy obtained permission from Matt to reenter the home, so he ran inside and quickly returned to the car with a book in his hand. He said, "I had to get this book because it's due at the school library on Monday."

The thoughts burned into my memory during this incident are as clear today as they were the day after the experience. A 12-year-old boy with tussled, dark hair and engaging brown eyes was so responsible that, in the middle of possibly the most traumatic day of his young life, he remembered a library book that he needed to return to the school. Later, when speaking with the principal of Billy's school, I discovered that he was just as he seemed: extremely considerate and dependable, an excellent student. Unlikely as it may seem, these are not uncommon characteristics of children whose parents are drug addicted.

As we drove the 30 minutes to the local hospital, I talked with the boys while remaining acutely aware of the paradox of such a beautiful day in contrast to the ordeal this family was facing. All three of us were attempting to behave as if we were just "out for a drive" when each of us were, at the same time, lost in our own thoughts about the horror of the day.

Billy sat in the front with me and frantically wrote down contact numbers for different relatives who might "take us." "Okay, here's another number for Nanny." "Here's one for Aunt Betty. Her husband is a college professor. Their kids are grown up, and they have plenty of money. I know they'll take us."

Before saying anything in response, I thought, "take us." "TAKE US???" These two small words reflect a child's desperate cry for a relative, a familiar face to "take us" and prevent placement in the home of a total stranger. Although Billy and Justin had never been in foster care, it was obvious Billy had some idea of what this would mean for him and his brother. He was doing all that he could to ensure the well-being of his family, which had so rapidly been reduced to only two.

I said, "Okay, Billy. As soon as we get to the hospital, I'll make some more calls. So, do you guys understand what has happened today?"

Justin sat quietly in the back seat as Billy answered, "I know our mom and dad are in jail."

"That's right. Did you say this has happened before?"

Again, Billy responded to my question. "Yeah, a couple of times, but my gramma has always just come and picked us up. They never had to stay long before. They'll probably be out in a couple of days. Do you know why the cops didn't call our gramma?"

I said, "I'm not exactly sure, but I'm guessing it's because the police usually call us, DCFS, to make sure that the children are going to a safe place. What will happen now is that, when we get to the hospital, I will make some more calls to your gramma and aunt, but if I can't get in touch with them, we'll have to arrange for you to go to a foster home, at least for the rest of the weekend."

Billy asked, "If we go to the foster home tonight, can my gramma come pick us up tomorrow?"

"No, that won't be possible. If I can't get in touch with your gramma pretty quickly, you will be in what is called 'protective custody.' That means that DCFS will sort of be in charge of where you stay and who takes care of you. On Monday, we will go to court, and the judge will decide if you stay in foster care or if your gramma or another family member will take you home with them."

Billy looked at me with such confidence and then back at his little brother and said, "We won't be in foster care after that. I know someone from our family will take us. There's a bunch of people who love us, Justin. They won't let us stay in foster care."

We sat in the hospital for several hours, which is typical when awaiting a health works exam to make sure the children did not have any illnesses that the foster parent would need to know about. My supervisor contacted foster parents and eventually located a family in a small town within our service area. The boys, who were extremely connected to their community, their school, and their extended family, were going to be placed in a new community with a new "family," new school, and the daunting task of making new friends.

It is impossible to spend this amount of time with children like this and not develop some type of emotional bond and to gain respect for the often resilient spirit of a child. After Billy and Justin were given a clean bill of health and the foster mother came to pick them up, I faced the task of letting go. There were so many things I wanted to make sure the boys understood, to somehow instill hope in them that Billy was right. There *would* be relatives who loved them and would take them. I wanted them to know that foster care is tough, but, sadly, children do adjust. I wanted to hug them, but it seemed inappropriate. So, I muttered a few platitudes, which escape my memory now, and I watched them drive away, and I cried.

Protective custody almost always makes me cry. Even though it is clear that the removal of children occurs when there is "urgent and immediate necessity" for such action, I still empathize with the family. There is sadness that a family has been separated, sadness that children are facing traumatic circumstances which they did not cause and are unable to control, sadness that something like addiction is able to wreak such havoc on the lives of so many people.

It has been 4 years since Billy and Justin entered foster care. They have been in three separate placements, and relatives did not "take them" as Billy had so hoped. The home where Billy and Justin currently reside is excellent, and both boys have adjusted to their new community quite well. In fact, if anyone were to ask either boy if they would want to move back to their hometown (I have asked this question), they would quickly reply, "No way!" Their father is due to be released from prison within the next couple of years. Billy will be 18 years old by then, but Justin still talks about reuniting with his father, who plans to move to the new community and make his home so that Justin will be able to continue in his current school district. Billy has some emotional scars. It is uncertain yet the extent to which his trauma was the result of methamphetamine misuse by his parents or the "rescue" of the system.

Part Two

Methamphetamine-Involved Families

Recovering Mothers' Experiences and Perspectives

Upon our arrival at the rural field office this morning, Linda directed Teresa and me to the home of 25-year-old Margie. Although Margie had lost custody of her children due to methamphetamine misuse, she was actively engaged in a substance misuse treatment program and participating in regular visits. This morning, 8-year-old Belle was visiting her mother at her home, a camper parked on a relative's rural property. Belle and Margie were neatly dressed and waiting for us when we arrived. It was a beautiful morning, and Margie had placed a wooden crate and folding chairs outside on the grass. The crate was covered with a clean cloth and glasses of homemade lemonade. As Belle excitedly ran to catch her kitten to show us, Margie, quietly and intently, began to tell us about her struggles with methamphetamine addiction, its impact on her family, and her concerns for her children. Shortly, we were interrupted by Margie's paramour, a man in his mid forties who loudly declared that kicking methamphetamine was not a problem, and that he would tell us all we wanted to know, anytime. By then, Belle had captured her kitten and our attention turned to talking and playing with her. We promised to return later to talk with Margie about her experiences and concerns. (Adapted from a field note, May, 2004.)

Sadly, that was our last opportunity to talk with Margie. Our repeated attempts to contact her cell phone were unsuccessful and, soon after our visit, the rural child welfare office lost contact with her. Apparently, she and her paramour had moved to another county, and visits with her children

---

This chapter elaborates material originally published as Haight, W., Carter-Black, J. & Sheridan, K. (in press). Mothers' experience of methamphetamine addiction: A case-based analysis of rural, Midwestern women. *Children and Youth Services Review*. Permission was obtained to reproduce portions of this text.

Mothers identified their children as a primary motivation for recovery.
Photo by Carl Kingery.

were suspended. Our brief conversation that summer morning, however, was an important contribution to our increasing understanding of parental methamphetamine misuse.

Our conversation with Margie suggested to us that a good place to begin our study of the contexts in which children from methamphetamine-involved families are reared is with their mothers. In many ways, Margie fit the local stereotype of a methamphetamine addict: She was a young, impoverished, rural woman who had lost custody of her children and who was involved with an older man with a long history of substance misuse. In many other ways, she did not fit the stereotype: She was articulate, shared a loving relationship with her daughter, and was concerned for her children. Our contact with Margie motivated us to look more closely at the perspectives of mothers. How had they come to be involved with methamphetamine? How did they view their methamphetamine misuse as impacting them and their families?

This chapter considers the experiences of mothers who use drugs presented in previous research and case-based descriptions of four mothers from rural Illinois who talked with us about their methamphetamine addiction and its impact on them and their children.

Previous Research on Mothers Who Misuse Drugs

Engaging mothers who are at-risk for misuse or who are already misusing methamphetamine in social services and in research is extremely challenging.

Women who use drugs often are reluctant to engage in services for themselves or their children, for fear that their children will be taken from them or of how they might be treated by providers (Klee, 2002b). Substance misuse, in general, is highly stigmatized for women because it is strongly dissonant with cultural ideals of femininity and motherhood (Hans, 2004). In rural communities, parents who misuse methamphetamine can experience significant stigma (Haight, Jacobsen, Black, Kingery, Sheridan & Mulder, 2005). Media coverage of problem drug use, including methamphetamine misuse, and drug-related harm to children encourages punitive attitudes toward drug-using parents and pejorative labeling. For example, during the crack cocaine epidemic of the early 1990s, governmental bodies across the United States passed laws mandating loss of child custody and incarceration for women using drugs during pregnancy (Humphries, 1999). For no other mental illness have society's penalties to parents been so harsh (Hans, 2004). Rarely have mothers who misuse drugs spoken for themselves, and very little systematic research has considered their perspectives (Baker & Carson, 1999; Brown & Hohman, 2006; Klee, 1998; Klee, 2002c), including what first drew them to use drugs and how they view the drug use as impacting themselves and their families.

Existing research suggests that some women may be first drawn to methamphetamine as a "functional" drug. Brecht and colleagues (2004) interviewed 350 former clients from a large publicly funded treatment system in the United States. More women reported initiating use of methamphetamine because of a desire for energy—for example, to care for children and household chores—and to lose weight, whereas more men reported initiating methamphetamine use because of a desire for better sex and to work longer hours at paid jobs. Based on their interviews with 50 pregnant women and 240 parents who used illicit drugs in England, Klee (2002d) found that women initially perceived their amphetamine use as beneficial to their children because it gave them energy and enhanced their mood and behavior.

Women's functional use of methamphetamine also may include self-medication for unmet mental health needs, a perennial problem in isolated, rural areas. Those scholars and practitioners focused on substance misuse treatment for women have observed that addiction is rarely a single-dimension issue, but occurs in a larger context of risk factors, for example, a history of trauma (e.g., Covington, 2002). In general, drug use among women has been associated with a history of risk factors for mental health problems, including parental death or desertion, marital discord, divorce, substance misuse, and high rates of physical and sexual abuse in their families of origin (see Mayes & Truman, 2002). Women report that they use drugs when beset by personal problems, to deal with anger and tension, or to alleviate feelings of depression or worthlessness (Klee, 2002a).

Similarly, most of the 37 women interviewed by Joe (1996) in Honolulu who were moderate to heavy users of methamphetamine had experienced poverty, domestic violence, adult criminality, and parental drug misuse within their families of origin. Many were introduced to drugs in childhood or adolescence by family members or peers. They reported the misuse of methamphetamine as a means to cope with everyday life pressures, relieve stress, maintain emotional and physical well-being, and effectively care for their children.

Women who used methamphetamine prenatally also reported multiple psychosocial risks. Relative to mothers from similar urban environments who did not misuse methamphetamine, at 1 month postpartum, these women reported lower perceptions of quality of life and greater likelihood of substance misuse among family and friends. They also were at increased risk for legal difficulties and for developing a substance misuse disorder (Derauf et al., 2006).

For whatever reason it is used, methamphetamine use can rapidly spin out of control and into addiction. Derauf et al. (2006) found the addiction potential so high in their sample of mothers that they recommended that clinicians disregard the possibility of recreational methamphetamine use: They consider any use de facto dependency. The mothers interviewed by Joe (1996) continued to use crystal meth and experienced increasing isolation from others, including their children; irritability; anxiety; depression; hallucinations; paranoia; domestic violence; and inadequate nutrition. As their dependence on methamphetamine grew, they were unable to care for their children and began to rely heavily on extended family to rear them.

Some mothers who misuse illicit drugs recognize that their substance misuse presents risks to their children. They described how their lifestyle had negatively impacted their children when they were physically, financially, and emotionally unavailable and when they could not control their children's behavior (Baker & Carson, 1999). Other mothers described problems arising from inadequate monitoring and role reversal, as when children became caregivers for themselves, siblings, or parents (Klee, 2002a). Mothers also identified their depression and irritability resulting from drug use as a risk for their children. The majority of parents also recognized the dangers to their children when parents were inebriated or withdrawing (Klee, 2002a). Some parents interviewed by Brown and Hohman (2006) (N = 10) described that, as a result of their methamphetamine misuse, their children were exposed to violence, a chaotic lifestyle, and irritable, negligent parenting. They also attributed negative psychological effects on their children, including anger, distrust, and fear, to their methamphetamine misuse and related lifestyle.

Some mothers who misuse illicit drugs also attempt to protect their young children from risks associated with adult substance misuse, with varying degrees of success over time (Kearney, Murphy & Rosenbaum, 1994). In a qualitative study of 114 moderate to heavy methamphetamine users in San Francisco, San Diego, and Honolulu, mothers who were dealers expressed concern about protecting their home environment, especially dealers with small children (Morgan & Joe, 1996). Some mothers detailed practices to protect their young children from their harmful lifestyles and fulfill children's practical needs (Baker & Carson, 1999). Other mothers described a range of protective measures to remove or lessen the impact of their drug use on their young children, which included removing their children or themselves from the home when they were using drugs or withdrawing; using cannabis to ease depression, irritability, and aggression; eliminating drug parties in the home; following rules about not administering drugs in front of children; and keeping drugs in a secure place out of reach of children. Not all parents, however, recognized the situations in which such care was needed. Poor understanding of risk, poor insight into the child's capacities, and the psychoactive effects of the drugs themselves reduced some parents' sensitivity to the potential for damage (Klee, 1998).

Protecting school-aged children and adolescents from the risks of parent drug misuse may present additional challenges. It is much harder to hide drug use and the associated lifestyle from older children and adolescents. Indeed, a major concern of most parents across several populations of drug users is that their older children and adolescents would follow their own path into drug misuse (see Klee, 1998; Nurco, Blatchley, Hanlon, O'Grady & McCarren, 1998) and become enmeshed in lifestyles similar to their own. Mothers were concerned about children's exposure to those environmental factors that they themselves had been exposed to as children and that they viewed as shaping their own drug misuse (Woodhouse, 1992). Some parents realized that they had been poor role models in their families and reported seeing some of their own negative behaviors in their children, including aggressive behavior and stealing.

Despite desires to safeguard and nurture their children, the obstacles to adequate parenting are significant for drug-dependent parents. They may miscalculate dangers to their children, fail to recognize the potentially detrimental influence of other adults with whom they associate, or misidentify the degree and severity of their own problems (Klee, 2002a). With frequent use of amphetamine, strategies to protect children from adult drug misuse were not maintained (Klee, 1998). As their addictions progressed, the women interviewed by Woodhouse (1992) reported pushing or sending their children away, sometimes into dangerous environments. Similarly, some of the parents interviewed by Brown and Hohman (2006) reported that their strategies for protecting their young children from their methamphetamine misuse failed as their addiction and associated lifestyle progressed.

In summary, relatively few studies have focused on mothers who misuse methamphetamine, or explored the perspectives of mothers who misuse substances. Existing research does suggest a complex and varied picture of women struggling with addiction and parenting. The vast majority of studies of mothers who misuse illicit drugs focus on the prenatal period, infancy, and early childhood, with less attention given to the particular challenges of parenting school-aged children and adolescents while misusing substances.

Mothers from Rural Illinois Who Misuse Methamphetamine

The participants were four rural, white, single women in their 30s: Meryl, Amy, Mary, and Nora (all names used in this book are pseudonyms), all of whom identified methamphetamine as their drug of choice, and all of whom were in recovery from methamphetamine addiction. Recruited through community contacts with child welfare professionals and substance misuse counselors from different villages and small towns in the rural Midwest, they were the mothers of from three to five children each, ranging in age from 3 to 18 years. They were invited to share their experiences to help social workers and other professionals to better understand and more effectively intervene with families involved with methamphetamine. They received token thank-you gifts (e.g., perfumed soaps).

These women told their life stories to us during in-depth, face-to-face, individual interviews focusing on their illness and its immediate and long-term impact on them and their children. The women shared a number of characteristics with one another, other mothers who misuse illegal substances, and other individuals who misuse methamphetamine. All of the women reported use of other illicit substances prior to being introduced to methamphetamine. In addition, they described family and peer contexts that included the misuse of illegal substances. Amy, Nora, and Meryl grew up with parents who misused illicit drugs. Mary, Amy, and Meryl "fell in with the wrong crowd," a group of peers who abused drugs. Amy and Mary initially liked the energy provided by methamphetamine. Meryl and Nora emphasized the initial effectiveness of methamphetamine as a means of self-medication to help them to feel less depressed, lonely, and bored.

All of the women spoke of the power of their addiction to methamphetamine, and Meryl contrasted it with other drugs to which she had been addicted. They rapidly spun "out of control," and the drug became an "obsession." Amy, Nora, and Mary all described thought problems. They were "in a fog," unable to think rationally, and had lapses in judgment—for example, they misused methamphetamine around their children, were sexually promiscuous, or simply didn't "see the point of meeting [their] obligation[s]." Amy and Nora described psychiatric problems, including depression, suicidality, and paranoia. Mary and Meryl described physical illness, including extreme weight loss and significant skin and dental problems. As their addiction progressed, all women lost custody of their children. Three of the women had legal problems: Amy and Mary for producing methamphetamine, and Meryl for prostitution to support her habit.

All of the women were parenting during their active methamphetamine addiction. At the time of the interview, they acknowledged that their addiction negatively impacted their parenting. They expressed concerns about their children's exposure to neglect, physical danger, domestic violence, problematic family relationships, loss of significant relationships, and exposure to adult substance misuse and other antisocial behavior and beliefs, especially those associated with paranoia. They also were concerned about their children's parentification and risks for developing psychological disturbance and delinquency. Mothers also expressed love and concern for their children, and great pain at losing them. All of the mothers expressed fear that their children would begin to misuse substances. From their vantage point in recovery, mothers spontaneously voiced questions including, "What kind of mother was I?" "What kind of mother uses meth around her kids?" or "What was I thinking?"

The mothers described diverse pathways to recovery. Following her incarceration, Amy received treatment in prison. As Mary became increasingly dysfunctional, she relied on her grandmother's help to stop using methamphetamine, and her mother to care for her children. Meryl experienced multiple stays in various inpatient substance misuse treatment facilities, but, facing a prison sentence, she eventually found help through Narcotics Anonymous. After losing custody of her children, Nora also found support through Narcotics Anonymous.

Despite this diversity, all of the women characterized the process of recovery from methamphetamine addiction as very difficult, and Meryl and Mary discuss multiple relapses. All of the women emphasized reunification with their children as a primary motivator. Two women, Amy and Meryl, were also motivated by the realization that if they relapsed again, then they would be sent to prison.

All of the women described significant, lasting problems due to their methamphetamine addiction. They described broken or damaged relationships with their children and other family members. Three of the women described lasting physical effects, including nervous twitching, periodic feelings of being high without the use of methamphetamine, sleep disturbances, and cravings, as well as psychological effects including feelings of depression and paranoia.

Cases

The following case descriptions elaborate each mother's experiences and perspectives of methamphetamine addiction.

Amy: "When You Get Sober, You Get a Heart Again."

Amy is the mother of three children ranging in age from 5 to 18 years, of whom she no longer has custody. At the time of the interview, she had been drug-free for approximately 2 years. Amy did not go into detail about her family history, but some dysfunction is suggested by her reports of regular methamphetamine misuse with her mother and sister. She reported a diagnosis of bipolar disorder. At the time of the interview, Amy appeared to be relaxed and willing to discuss her life experiences. She was animated as she spoke and had good rapport with the interviewer.

Amy first used methamphetamine at a party. As her use progressed, Amy described the rapid deterioration of her parenting. ". . . one day, the drugs slipped up in front of me and . . . became more important than my children." She also experienced academic problems resulting in her withdrawal from college. Eventually, she and her husband lost their employment and began manufacturing methamphetamine at their home. Amy vividly described the experience of methamphetamine addiction as the drug "just took me over." She recounted her obsession with the drug that quickly became the center of her life, her inability to think clearly or rationally, and her deep depression and paranoia.

> It (methamphetamine) became an obsession for me, I was always looking for . . . different pipes, . . . I built my own bongs, you know, to smoke it out of. It was sick. . . . Ahhh, it got out of control—fast. . . . You're extremely paranoid when you're on meth, extremely paranoid. You live in a fog. You live in, it's like a fog. You don't think clearly. You don't think rationally. You don't think rationally about anything. You know, it's all about you. You, you, you. . . . "Them people aren't hurt by me. I ain't hurting them people. . . . how dare they try to take my children!" And there comes a point [in recovery] where your head just clears. You start thinking rationally again because it's just like you live in a fog. You don't see anything around you. All you see is what's straight in front of you. And that's your aim and that's what you're going for. You're going to do whatever it is you have to do to make yourself feel better and to hell with the rest of the world. You know, "They don't matter to me. If they cared about me, then they'd be in here doing drugs with me. If they were my friends, then they'd be helping me buy this dope. You know, if they were my family, they'd be

taking my kids so I could go get high." That's the way you think. . . . you're out of your mind. You're extremely out of your mind.

The drug messes with your chemical balances and endorphins, everything, you know. You can't get motivated unless you're high. If you're any kind of depressed before you start the drug, you're four, five times more. I mean, there's times that I have sat in my bedroom with a gun to my head thinking, "I just can't do this any more." Crying for hours. And . . . it had to be God telling me, "Amy you can't do this. You have a little boy sitting in there in front of the TV. He's 3 years old. This would be the last thing he ever remembers of his mother." But it just got to the point where you're so tired, you're so depressed. I mean, my husband would have to pick me up off the couch and say, "Amy you've got to go take a shower, come out of this." You just, you get tired. And even though you don't think clearly, there's a part of you that knows you're sick and you want help, but the addiction feeds on you, "You got to use me. You got to use me. I'm a drug. I'm the only thing that's going to be there for you. Everyone else has left you."

It's terrible. It's a terrible addiction. And . . . people don't just walk away from it. If I hadn't been taken away from it and put in prison for 9 months . . . I would have been right back on it . . . I was one of the lucky ones. I got forced to go to prison. And, right away, I got into drug rehab.

Amy characterized her parenting while actively using methamphetamine as deteriorating rather quickly. At the time of her active use and addiction, she had three children at home. As her addiction grew, she described her children's emotional neglect, social isolation, and lack of family structure; parentification; exposure to danger and adult criminality; problematic family relationships; getting her son high; and, eventually, loss of family. (In the following interview excerpt, "A" is Amy, and "I" is the interviewer.)

A: *And, I just, emotionally, it kept me happy . . . it would keep me up and happy all the time and energetic and going and I could get along with anybody. But when I would come down, I would be raging. I would be four times more depressed than I was before. I would scream and yell and throw things—just rage. I would get up in the morning, and the kids would have dishes in the sink or my husband because he's messy like that. And, cabinet doors open—he's always leaving those open. I'd go in the kitchen and slam the doors, and it was always first thing in the morning that it would hit me like that. When I would get up and I would throw dishes in the sink. "You guys can't pick nothing up." I'd just go nuts and I'd be like, "I just need to get high, you know, and not come out of this."*

And it got to the point where my husband would say, "You know, Amy, you're going to have to go to the doctor and find out what's wrong with you. The kids are diving behind the couch when you pull in the driveway. They don't want to hear you yelling and carrying on like an idiot."

And the kids, you know, . . . I kept thinking, I need to be out there playing with the kids, reading. I'd started reading the Adventures of Huckleberry Finn *every night before they went to bed. And then when I started using more, it was like, "Well, we'll read tomorrow night." "No, Mommy, you got to read another chapter to us."*

"Well, we'll read tomorrow night—it's getting late. You can go watch TV for a little bit or something. Mommy's got to go in the bedroom and clean." Crazy. Now that I look back on it, I know I was there for them physically, but not emotionally.

I: *For how long did that go on?*

A: *Probably about 6–9 months. The first 3 months or so wasn't that bad. We would be high and up and ready to go, "Come on kids, we're going to go to Terre Haute, go to Bogey's Family Fun Center. We're going to go see a movie." And then, eventually, it got to where Sundays were dragging. Well, we'll go next weekend. And then the money started running short. . . .*

I want to say they [the children] lived normally, but they were isolated as well as I was. I didn't take Rebecca—I didn't get her involved in Girl Scouts, I didn't take her to family reading night at school, I didn't let her play ball, you know. . . . It was just, they were pretty isolated as well. You know, we lived out in the country. . . .

Now, my oldest son did get stuck baby-sitting quite a bit. . . . and I even got him high once, that's how sick I was. I'll probably never forgive myself for that one. . . .

A lot of drug addicts don't have any structure in their life, whatsoever for their children, for their family. I can recall Christmas, the last Christmas before I got arrested, my husband and I got into it, I drank a fifth of whiskey and a can of coke while I was wrapping the kids' presents. Granted I just went and spent $1000 on presents for them, but the fact was I was hung over on Christmas morning, didn't want to get out of bed to watch them open them. You know. There was no structure in our family.

Amy spent 9 months in prison for methamphetamine manufacturing, and her husband remains incarcerated. She credited the 7.5 months she spent in the prison drug rehabilitation unit with saving her life. Although

Amy has some contact with her oldest son, now an 18-year-old father, she has minimal contact with her younger children, who reside with their respective fathers several hours from her current residence. She expressed deep concern that her children, particularly her oldest son, who smokes marijuana, will follow her pathway into addiction.

Mary: "This is a Whole Different World."

Mary is the single mother of five children ranging in age from 6 to 15 years, whom she is currently parenting. At the time of the interview, she had been drug-free for approximately 1 year. She described a middle-class, small-town childhood. She was not exposed to drugs or alcohol at home, but her two brothers currently do use drugs. Her parents divorced when she was 1 year old. She described a problematic relationship with her mother, who traveled frequently for her job, but a close, nurturing relationship with her stepfather. She began acting out in middle childhood after being sexually abused by her grandfather. She began drinking as an adolescent (age 16) on the weekends with friends. At the time of the interview, Mary appeared reserved, somewhat subdued, and hesitant about discussing the details of her experience.

Mary was introduced to methamphetamine at the age of 29 by her paramour. She reported a rapid decline in functioning once she began misusing methamphetamine. As an overwhelmed single parent of five young children, she stated that she initially was able to accomplish a lot while using methamphetamine. Within 6 months, however, she realized that she could not parent effectively while involved with methamphetamine and left her children, temporarily, with her mother. When her mother was later resistant to returning the children, Mary and her paramour began manufacturing methamphetamine to pay for the lawyer's fees in the custody case. After regaining custody of her children, Mary continued to misuse and manufacture methamphetamine. She described her lifestyle at this point in her illness:

> **I:** *What was your thought process in first deciding to manufacture?*
>
> **M:** *We just wanted to try it to see if we could do it. . . . We met a friend who had a friend who manufactured. We had the means, we had the place out in the country. . . . We had the money to get started because he was himself a business owner . . . I was a stay at home mom. So, I could basically cover for everybody when he left town. He went out of town on occasion to do his construction jobs. It was frequent for him to be gone overnight. And we did use, but we bought what we used. And then someone said,*

"Well, why don't you just start making it?" He said, "Okay, let's see what we need." And I went out, every now and then, and bought a little bit of everything we needed: jars, the home stuff that we needed, the pills, we would take trips to St. Louis. We would buy on the way up and buy on the way back. . . . Cause we were going to St. Louis and buying crack on the weekends anyway. Then, we got to leading a lifestyle down in St. Louis that was a swinger's lifestyle. And we thought that was just absolutely wonderful. We had friends everywhere now. We had friends in Wisconsin, we had friends—we could go anywhere in the United States and still have somewhere to go. Which was nice for about 3 years. We did that and manufactured. And, the last year him and I were together, I stopped using as much. Then I realized—I started opening my eyes more and more and seeing what I was doing. I went from a size 10 to a size 6. And, all my clothes were just—I was just nasty looking. . . . My eyes were sunken in my head. . . . My skin was picked . . . I had bad teeth. I had almost all my bottom teeth pulled except for my front ones. I'm having problems. . . .

I: *How aware were you of those things while you were using?*

M: *I wasn't . . . I thought it was just, my legs were shaking when I walked because I led a very active lifestyle. I was a lot more active, sexually active, when I used than at any other time. And it just wasn't with my boyfriend. It was with his friend because it was the thing. Everybody did that. Other females—it would be nothing—six, seven, eight people in one room.*

I: *You were using at the same time?*

M: *We were all using. We were all enjoying each other, and it was nothing. It was normal. It seemed normal. And it wasn't. It was not normal [sarcastic laughter]; far from normal.*

I: *How do you feel looking back on that?*

M: *Stupid, embarrassed. When I do talk about it, very embarrassed.*

After the methamphetamine-related arrest of her friends, Mary quit making the drug and, with the help of her grandmother, stopped using. She reported only one relapse a year ago. Mary currently lives with a new paramour and her five children. She stated that she rarely talks about this period of her life and tries to block out the past few years. She, too, is quite concerned that her children will misuse drugs.

Meryl: "Drugs Were More Powerful than the Love for My Kids."

Meryl is the mother of six children ranging in age from 4 to 15 years. At the time of the interview, she had been drug-free for 6 months and was facing prison time for prostitution if she were to relapse again. She had lost parental rights to all of her children, but still had contact with her two oldest. Meryl was raised as one of nine children. In childhood and adolescence, she experienced multiple losses and trauma, including the death of her father, sexual abuse by her stepfather, foster care, and exposure to adult substance misuse. After her stepfather first raped her at age 9, Meryl was introduced to marijuana by an older sister. She experimented with other drugs, and ran away from home on multiple occasions. With the exception of one brother, all of her siblings used illicit drugs regularly. Meryl was direct with her answers and open about her life experience. She maintained eye contact and had relaxed posture throughout the interview.

Meryl graduated to using methamphetamine last year, after a long history of misusing marijuana, crack cocaine, heroin, and alcohol. She was introduced to methamphetamine at a party. During the interview, she reflected on methamphetamine as a type of self-medication for feelings of shame, guilt, and other emotional pain, and expressed how the strength of the addiction and feelings of hopelessness kept her trapped.

> **M:** *I was a ho, . . . [I did] anything for drugs. You work on the streets for drugs. Give people sex for drugs. . . . I was worthless. . . . But I didn't care. I had the drug. And the drugs, when you do them, they make you forget about all that. It doesn't last very long, but it does make you forget all that. It makes you want to go get more.*
>
> **I:** *Forget what exactly?*
>
> **M:** *What drugs do to you, or what you're doing for drugs. All that. Or some of the shame or guilt you might be feeling, it takes it all away. That's why some people use drugs. To take the pain, the guilt, the shame—it takes that all away. And that's what keeps a lot of people using drugs, because they don't want to feel. . . . I had low self-esteem, and the thought that I would never get my kids back, I just gave up. I gave up hope, I gave up life. I didn't care. I just didn't care. Not having my kids made a big part of it. 'Cause I just gave up. 'Cause I want my kids, but drugs were more powerful than the love for my kids. And it shouldn't have been that way. Not that I don't love my kids, because I love my kids very much. It's just— drugs are powerful. They are really powerful, and they are hard to get off of. Especially meth and crack and heroin.*

Meryl's recovery is supported by an outpatient treatment center. She misused drugs during her pregnancies with her four youngest children and, over time, sought treatment with varying degrees of success. She has deep concerns that her children also will misuse drugs. The threat of a prison sentence and her desire to see her children are two key motivating factors supporting her present bid for recovery. She also found her current community, sponsor, support group, and renewed spirituality key to her recovery.

> *Once I stopped using drugs, the feelings and the hurts all started coming out, and that's when it gets real painful. And when I started using again, that's when you have to step up and talk to somebody about it. Then, when you talk about it with somebody, that's your healing process right there. It's when you talk to other people or your sponsor or whoever it might be. That's your healing process. Once you talk to them, you're giving it to them and they're helping you through this horrible time, and that's what heals you. That's what heals your heart from hurting and you don't hurt any more.*
>
> *Like with my kids, I was very shameful about using drugs with my kids and then to give my kids up. Because I was their mother. I was supposed to take care of them. And I didn't. So, I would talk to the other females that are in the same situations and talk to them, you know, "This is what I've done to my kids," and it's very emotional. So, the feelings would come out, the tears would come out. And the pain goes away. The pain will go away. If people just give it a chance. The only way for the pain to go away is to let it heal. And in order to do that, you have to stop using drugs, talk about it, cry, get the hurt out, and heal. That's the only way you're going to heal, is to get it out. And then you can move on with your life. . . .*

Nora: "You Still Had Your Responsibilities . . . Until Eventually . . . You Don't See the Point in it Anymore."

Nora is the single mother of five children ranging in age from 3 to 8 years. She lives in a homeless shelter; two of her children are in foster care. The other three live with their biological father and his current paramour. At the time of the interview, Nora had been drug-free for approximately 1 year. She had been immersed within a rural drug subculture since birth. She described both of her biological parents as alcoholics. She was raised primarily by her mother and stepfather, both of whom misused illicit drugs. Her stepfather also sold marijuana and methamphetamine. He eventually was imprisoned, and Nora attributed his early death to complications of methamphetamine misuse. Nora experienced physical abuse and neglect as a child. She also had been in a number of abusive relationships with men. Nora described no extended family for support in times of need because of the substance misuse problems in her family of origin. She expressed fears that her own children will misuse drugs.

After Nora began misusing methamphetamine, she lost custody of her children. At the time of the interview, she was in recovery and reported that she had not used in 12 months. Nora spoke with a clear and deliberate voice, and her eye contact was direct. She was coherent, logical, and often quite articulate as she described methamphetamine misuse as a "trap" into which she and her children were caught. Regaining custody of her children was a motivating factor for her to remain in recovery, but she described the process of recovery from methamphetamine addiction as a long and difficult process, involving a major lifestyle changes.

> *I quit using it . . . and I could not of if people kept coming around that I did not want myself involved with. You know? . . . I had to get rid of them. So I had to leave this area to go and get away from that lifestyle. Walking away from the drugs . . . was walking away from that lifestyle and changing my thinking and people to be around. . . . There's no other way to put it. They're using friends. They use you for whatever you got, and then they're gone. And I had to separate myself from them . . . to get my children. . . .*
>
> *I look down on myself 'cause I don't feel I am [a good mother]. But it's also my past . . . and realizing it didn't take me overnight to get myself in this position and . . . its . . . not going to take me overnight to get out of [it]. It's been a year. It's been more than enough time, but there's years and years and years ahead it's going to take to change everything and rethink everything. So, you know, I have that reassurance that it's going to be all right. I mean, I'm a lot better now, but I still have a long ways to go.*

Nora described the long-term effects of her methamphetamine addiction. These include physical effects such as a feeling of being high without having used any substances, nervous twitching, and sleep disturbances, as well as psychological problems such as a lasting paranoia.

> *I might use one day and be clean for three or four days, you know. I'd still be like, "What was that?" You know, constantly looking out the window because I'm thinking I'm hearing stuff. The paranoid feeling, I don't think it goes away. But now I still have problems sitting with my back to the door cause I'm afraid who is gonna walk in. It's more of a habitual thing. It really is. The habits you form during your use are the hardest things to break and get away from. It's the feeling of being high. . . . I'll be sitting*

there writing or doing something and my head will just feel all funny. It's still working its way out of my system. I feel like I've used. I'm like, "Whoa! I don't like this at all." It just happens. So that feeling of being high, I think honestly takes forever to go away. Because I don't even have to be thinking about it. My mind will be totally focused on what I'm doing and here comes that feeling again. And it's been over a year since I used.

That nervous twitch you get, and the way your body jerks from it affecting your nervous system. That still affects me. I still twitch and jerk in the middle of the night. It's crazy. Especially right after I go to sleep. My body wearing down. It's not just a little twitch. It's my whole body jerking and moving around and stuff, and I guess it's going to be normal either for the next few years or possibly the rest of my life. I don't know yet. It just depends on your use and how much you used and everything like that. The effects are there long-term, definitely.

Conclusion

Understanding mothers' experience of methamphetamine addiction can increase our awareness of this illness, reducing stigma and suggesting strategies for engaging them in intervention. An important contribution of the mothers who participated in this study were their first-hand accounts of the experience of methamphetamine addiction and parenting. Their narratives allow us a glimpse into the actual experience of methamphetamine addiction and recovery. Mothers vividly portrayed the rapid loss of control that can occur with methamphetamine misuse, as well as the power of the addiction. They became "obsessed" with the drug, and nothing was more important to them, not even the children whom they loved. Consistent with emerging research on the neurotoxic effects of methamphetamine (Kalechstein, Newton & Green, 2003; Newton et al., 2003), they lost the ability to think "rationally," experienced serious lapses in judgment, lost motivation, and lived for extended periods of time in a "fog." Women described recovery as possible only with significant external support, and they reported lasting physical, psychological, and social side effects of their illness.

In many respects, the narratives of mothers in this study were consistent with research on methamphetamine misuse and on women who misuse illegal substances. They suggest a combination of prior and current life experiences that may place women at risk of initiating methamphetamine misuse. As would be predicted by previous research, all but one woman reported that, when they were young, their own parents had misused substances (see Mayes & Truman, 2002; Joe, 1996), and all had misused other illegal drugs before they tried methamphetamine (Joe, 1996). These prior life experiences may have normalized drug use, thus lessening any initial resistance to using methamphetamine.

As would be predicted from existing research, the women who participated in this study all had histories of trauma and significant loss in early life (see Mayes & Truman, 2002; Otero, Boles, Young & Dennis, 2006), and all were experiencing significant psychological stress when they began using methamphetamine. Consistent with other research including women who abuse amphetamines (Klee, 2002a) and methamphetamine (Brecht et al., 2004; Joe, 1996), some women's descriptions of their initial use of methamphetamine could be characterized as functional; that is, it gave them increased energy to complete domestic, childrearing, and other work, and it alleviated feelings of depression, loneliness, and boredom.

Also consistent with previous research (Klee, 1998; Woodhouse, 1992), including women who misuse methamphetamine (Baker & Carson, 1999), women in this study expressed love and commitment to their children. From the vantage point of their recovery, they recognized that their drug misuse placed their children at risk. Some mothers attempted to protect their children from risks associated with their drug abuse (Kearney et al., 1994; Klee, 1998; Morgan & Joe, 1996), but these efforts eventually broke down, and all lost custody of their children.

Mothers also described their experiences recovering from methamphetamine addiction. Three of the mothers frankly admitted that, without very significant external pressure, prison, and the loss of their children, they would not have been able to recover. Amy was clear that without the 7.5 months of drug intervention she received in prison, she would, in all likelihood, be dead. All mothers characterized the process of recovery from methamphetamine as long and difficult. At the time of the interviews, several of the mothers reported continued cravings even after months of abstinence. Regaining involvement with their children and avoiding prison sentences were major motivators for recovery.

Mothers also described their perceptions of the lasting impact of their addiction to methamphetamine on themselves and their children. They described broken relationships with family and partners, as well as lasting physical and psychological effects. Similar to women who misuse other drugs (see Nurco et al., 1998; Woodhouse, 1992), all expressed a deep concern that their own children would become enmeshed in drug abuse.

Clearly, more research is needed into the experiences of mothers who misuse methamphetamine. Accessing parents who are actively misusing substances is difficult, and they are likely to be suspicious and apprehensive. The mothers in this study underscored their lasting paranoia, a characteristic of methamphetamine misuse that has been widely reported in the literature and which makes their engagement in research even more challenging. Increasing our knowledge of the experience of this illness, however, could help to reduce negative stereotyping among child welfare and other social service professionals, a potential treatment obstacle for mothers ill from methamphetamine misuse, as well as suggest strategies for effectively engaging them in services.

Chapter Six

Knowledgeable Adults' Experiences and Perspectives

This morning, Linda directed Teresa and me to a nearby village, where we were to interview the pastor of the local Baptist church who ran an intervention program for individuals addicted to methamphetamine. Joshua, an energetic man in his mid 40s, met us at the church and led us to the basement meeting room, where we began the interview. He described the methamphetamine problem in his community, the scarcity of local resources, and the substance misuse intervention program sponsored by his church. When, in passing conversation, Teresa asked about his family, Joshua proudly showed us a portrait of his children: three attractive teenagers and Lily, a healthy, smiling 3-year-old. Lily was Joshua's foster daughter. She also was his niece. As the story unfolded, we learned that Joshua's younger sister, addicted to methamphetamine, had called him in a panic from the hospital and begged him to take her newborn daughter. In a moment of clarity, Ann trusted Joshua and his family to love and care for the baby, and feared that Lily would otherwise be placed in foster care with strangers. With great trepidation, Joshua and his wife agreed. They and their children quickly fell in love with Lily. Joshua spoke of his anger at Ann who, high on methamphetamine, periodically approached him and accused him of stealing her baby. He also spoke of his fear that Lily, ill-prepared, would one day have to return to her mother, who cycled in and out of active drug misuse. Finally, Joshua wept as he spoke of the bright and funny younger sister he had grown up with and watched over. As he described her deteriorating

---

This chapter elaborates material originally published as Haight, W. L., Jacobsen, T., Black, J., Kingery, L., Sheridan, K., & Mulder, C. (2005). "In these bleak days": Parent methamphetamine abuse and child welfare in the rural Midwest. *Children and Youth Services Review, 27,* 949–971. Permission was obtained to reproduce portions of this text.

Collaboration between law enforcement and child welfare professionals is important in supporting children during their parents' arrests. Photo by Carl Kingery.

> *physical and mental condition, it was clear that Joshua desperately wanted Ann to get better, but feared she would die or be killed by her abusive boyfriend. He wanted Ann to be safe and live a normal life, but also feared that she would take Lily from his family and disappear. (Adapted from a field note, June, 2004.)*

For Joshua and his family, no simple responses to parental methamphetamine misuse exist. Like the mothers who shared their stories in Chapter 5, they see, up close, the devastation to their methamphetamine-involved neighbors and relatives, and their children. This chapter includes our observations from ethnographic field work and in-depth interviews with 35 knowledgeable adults like Joshua: rural professionals and foster parents, who live and work within communities affected by methamphetamine misuse. They discussed their jobs and their perspectives on local adults who misuse methamphetamine. They also described their observations of the contexts in which children from methamphetamine-involved families are reared, the impact of parent methamphetamine misuse on children, and possible protective factors for children. In addition, they offered advice regarding how to support children from methamphetamine-involved families.

Working in Rural Illinois

During our participant observations of rural professionals, we watched child welfare professionals perform their jobs as we shadowed them on visits to rural homes of methamphetamine-involved families and to rural schools to see children whose parents faced allegations of child maltreatment. Educators, teachers, and school counselors spoke with us about their roles in helping children from methamphetamine-involved families. We also visited rural foster homes, meetings of concerned citizens, courts, a rural hospital where approximately half of the inpatients on the psychiatry ward were suffering from methamphetamine-induced psychosis, and substance misuse and mental health treatment facilities.

As they performed their jobs, many of these knowledgeable adults demonstrated and emphasized their interdependency. For example, educators readily turned to their child welfare colleagues when a child was endangered by parental methamphetamine misuse. Likewise, child welfare professionals observed that educators may be the first people to recognize those signs of child neglect that may signal family involvement with methamphetamine, and they may provide critical support to children prior to and subsequent to children's placement in foster care. Some educators described keeping children after school to "help" the teachers, to delay sending them home to difficult situations. One school we visited had on stock basic toiletries, food, and clothing that counselors provided to children whose parents were suspected of misusing methamphetamine.

Another example of interdependence is the regular communication that occurred between child welfare professionals and law enforcement officers. Child welfare workers provided necessary support to police officers when children were discovered during methamphetamine laboratory seizures. Likewise, police departments and county law enforcement officers played a critical role in alerting child welfare investigators to potentially dangerous situations and provided necessary assistance, including accompanying them on investigations.

Adults also emphasized the importance of building good interpersonal relationships to support appropriate networking and communication among professionals and to facilitate work with other community members and clients. For example, in small communities, where clients often have relationships with one another, word spreads quickly as to a professional's ability to respect a client's individuality and humanity. The success of the rural field office in building relationships with community members is evident in a report from an in-depth federal review that found that community stakeholders consistently reported examples of their positive interaction with workers from the rural field office (State of Illinois, Department of Children and Family Services, 2004).

Adults' Perceptions of Methamphetamine Misuse in Their Communities

In the context of performing their jobs and describing their experiences, most adults also expressed their attitudes toward local adults who misuse methamphetamine: generally mixed or negative attitudes. Mixed attitudes included feelings of grief for the addicted parent, who may be a relative, neighbor, or former classmate or student, and anger and frustration at their failure to care for their children and at their creation of hazards within the community. One school counselor expressed her own mixed feelings:

> *Meth is just going to do you in. I've never known anything good to come of it. It tears up families, it destroys children's lives and . . . it destroys adults' lives, and that makes me really sad, but their job is to parent. And I go between hot and cold, hot and cold: It's tragic, I'm so mad I could spit, it's tragic [laughs] . . . I'm so mad I want to hit something. . . .*

Many adults also expressed fear of individuals who misuse methamphetamine. Some expressed fear of automobile accidents with adults under the influence of methamphetamine and driving on isolated, rural roads. Child welfare investigators were apprehensive about their own personal safety, for example, if they inadvertently walked into a methamphetamine lab during a routine investigation. Several rural educators described being confronted by angry, threatening parents because they had made reports to the child protection hotline. (Although hotline calls are "anonymous," in the context of a small school, it is not difficult for parents to deduce who has made the call.) One school principal described increased police surveillance of the school following threats from a parent involved with methamphetamine and his associates. During the period of our study, area police reported dramatic increases in crimes against educators, a situation that they attributed to increasing methamphetamine misuse.

Adults also expressed fear of clandestine methamphetamine laboratories. Some residents, for instance, expressed concern about contamination from clandestine meth labs of the groundwater used by their livestock and supplying their wells. Concern also was expressed about possible contamination of the food supply. For example, one sheriff of a local county testified to the Illinois legislative task force during harvest time that her officers had recently discovered a methamphetamine laboratory at the bottom of a (temporarily) empty grain bin. Had the farmer, who was unaware of the meth lab, dumped his harvest into the bin, then this food would be contaminated by toxic byproducts of the methamphetamine production. Fear also was expressed about accidents. During our study, a mobile methamphetamine laboratory in the back of a van exploded in an elementary school parking lot during a children's volleyball game (WANDTV & Lin Broadcasting, 2004). A survey of hazardous chemical events from 2000 to 2004 found that anhydrous ammonia thefts often resulted in injury to civilians, law enforcement professionals, and perpetrators (Arant, Henry, Clifford, Horton & Rossiter, 2005).

Adults' Perceptions of the Socialization Contexts of Children Whose Parents Misuse Methamphetamine

When asked to describe their experiences with families involved with methamphetamine, adults described characteristics of the contexts in which children are raised. Overall, adults described that children are brought by their parents into a rural drug subculture characterized by distinct antisocial values, beliefs, and practices. Children's experience of this culture is characterized by environmental danger, chaos, neglect, isolation, abuse, and loss. Children acquire the beliefs and practices of this subculture through direct teaching by their parents, and, indirectly, through observation of parents' antisocial behavior.

Environmental Danger, Chaos, Neglect, and Isolation

Adults characterized these children's living situations as dangerous, neglectful, isolated, and chaotic. Children may experience physical danger due to exposure to methamphetamine and its production. Addicts may leave drug paraphernalia within the reach of small children, and "Mom and Pop" cooks manufacture methamphetamine at home, thus exposing children to toxic chemicals, explosions, and fire.

Children also may experience chronic neglect and isolation, with their basic needs for food, sanitation, and medical and dental care unmet. Children may live in remote areas, in filthy homes with no electricity, running water, or phone service. As one adult observed, "The drug is so addictive, parents lose sight of everything else, including their children." In addition to being unsanitary, isolated, and possibly toxic, these children's living conditions were described as chaotic. According to one adult, on any given day, children may not know "when or if they will eat, where they will sleep, or what will happen from one hour to the next."

Adults also noted that many children whose parents misuse methamphetamine may be deprived of the typical, joyful activities of childhood such as play and recreation. In the words of one educator, "Children are deprived of a childhood." They "don't get to be children." They are "burdened with worry." Children may become caregivers for their incapacitated parents, younger siblings, and themselves. As one child welfare investigator described:

They [children] take care of themselves. Like, if there are several kids in the home, the oldest one will take the parent role, and they're all very protective of each other. I remember one [case], the oldest child was only 6, and she cooked, cleaned, gave her two little sisters baths every night. Yeah, 6 years old. . . . they [the children] were all very, very protective of each other. You know, just clung together.

A foster mother described the caregiving activities of her young foster daughter, including acting in times of danger:

She talks openly, from time to time, about her job as more or less the care-giver of Mom and how she'd have to go to the neighbor's and call 911 due to Dad holding a butcher knife to Mom's throat.

Abuse

Given children's living situations, it is not surprising that adults described them as experiencing a high level of physical and sexual abuse from parents and their associates. For example, children may be sexually abused by adult addicts who come to their homes to purchase and use methamphetamine, or physically abused by parents high on methamphetamine or experiencing extreme irritability or paranoia.

Loss

In a relatively short period of time, children may lose their parents, homes, families, and belongings, and find themselves in foster care. Since parents who are involved in producing methamphetamine typically get long prison sentences, it is likely that many children will not return home and will be raised by foster parents. Adults underscored that methamphetamine "destroys families" and "tears families apart."

Exposure to Antisocial Behavior

Adults described that some children are brought into a rural drug subculture through direct teaching by their parents and, indirectly, through example. For instance, children may be directly taught by their parents to lie to teachers, police officers, and child welfare workers to cover their parents' illegal activities. They may be socialized to be very guarded in their communications and interactions with teachers and others, so as not to incriminate the parents whom they love and to whom they often are loyal. Adults also report that some parents teach children to steal the precursors they need to manufacture the drug, and to use guns to protect the methamphetamine lab. In addition, parents may introduce children to gateway drugs, as well as methamphetamine, at an early age. Not surprisingly, adults also report that children may show a precocious awareness of substance use and misuse. For example, young children may know how to roll joints, mix various alcoholic drinks, and even help to make methamphetamine.

Adults also reported that children's induction into the methamphetamine subculture occurs more indirectly, through observation of parents' antisocial behavior. Children may observe frequent domestic violence, other out-of-control and violent adult behavior, substance misuse, and their parents' arrests. Given the context of children's lives, it is not surprising that adults report children's early substance misuse. Some children may begin using gateway drugs, such as alcohol and tobacco, routinely at 8 and 9 years of age, and methamphetamine in early adolescence. As a local substance misuse counselor described:

Kids are taught . . . the paranoid lifestyle, where somebody's always coming after you or somebody's always coming to get you. . . . [The kids are not] free to play in the yard without having to step across a couple meth bottles and getting burnt. It's just a totally different environment . . . if you're in the meth household, you're learning the drug lifestyle, whether you want to or not. The kid, at the time, may not even realize it. . . .

Adults' Perceptions of the Effects of Parental Methamphetamine Misuse on Children

When asked to describe the effects of parental methamphetamine misuse on children, adults described disturbed psychological, social, and educational development. Descriptions of psychological disturbance included psychological pain and trauma; for example, staring into space, disturbed sleep, nightmares, flat affect, intense worry about parents, fear of police, fear about what will happen to them (where they will live, who will take care of them), fear of adults, grief, and hopelessness. Children also may experience shame, especially living in small towns, where they feel that everyone knows and gossips about their parents. Adults also described externalizing behavior such as lying, disrespectful behavior toward adults, delinquency, truancy, and general out-of-control behavior. Some children also were described as emotionally unstable, having problems with expressing emotion appropriately and regulating strong emotion. In addition, adults described behaviors suggestive of more serious psychopathology such as hoarding, self-mutilation, and suicide attempts.

Not surprisingly, adults observed that many children from methamphetamine-involved families experience disturbances in social development. Children were described as having an unusually hard time following rules; fitting into "normal" social contexts of family, school, and community; and understanding the consequences of their own decisions. Some were described as "lost" children, alone and isolated; as indiscriminately friendly; or as vicious to other children. In the words of one foster mother of two children:

These two [children] that I have now, . . . they're emotionally dead. . . . the little girl, she laughs, but it's such a fake laugh. Like the past few days, my grandson, he giggles all the time. So she tries to copy him, but what happens is, it's very inappropriate when she does it. You know, like the other child's not acting silly or they're not rough-housing, like maybe we'll be listening to a serious movie, and she'll giggle. You know, or she plays in softball, and maybe they're losing and she'll giggle. And tears only appear when something's going to benefit her. . . . she is very manipulative, and she is a compulsive liar. She lies about whether she's drunk her juice, and the juice is sitting there visible to anyone. And she'll say, "Yeah, I did it." When they first came, they would take it [food] to their bedroom. She hides everything. She hoards everything . . . from food to stuffed animals to whatever. . . . Like it's shoes, it doesn't matter if they're three sizes too big. She'll take 'em. . . . the little girl is very uncaring, but the little boy is vicious. In fact, 3 weeks ago, he took his ball bat and whacked her [because] she did not do what he told her to do. . . . Not only were they damaged at birth from mom's use, then they were damaged every month of their life until a year and a half ago when they were removed. Then you're putting them out here in this big strange world, that you know you have to chew your food, you don't have BMs just wherever you want to have BMs. You have to use toilet tissue, you have to use Kleenexes, you know, you have to bathe once in a great while. . . . I don't know how much you can attribute to drug use, except for, like I said, the emotional deadness I see in both of them.

Despite descriptions of disturbed psychological and social development, adults reported that, within these rural communities, children's access to quality mental health services is extremely limited. For example, the two children described in the above excerpt had not had a psychiatric evaluation. They each were receiving 1 hour of mental health service per week by a young counselor with only a few years of experience.

Adults also described some children's normal development and education as stunted. The "burdens they face" interfere with learning and normal development. In the words of an elementary school principal, children are "robbed of opportunity."

In discussing the effects of parental methamphetamine misuse on children, many adults qualified their responses in recognition of what they viewed to be substantial individual variation across children. In addition to describing children with apparent, serious mental health issues, they also described a few children who appeared to be developing well in spite of their parents' methamphetamine misuse. These observations of individual variation are consistent with children's responses on developmental and mental health measures (to be presented in Chapter 8). Individual variation in children's functioning led us to probe factors adults perceived to be responsible for relatively better outcomes for some children.

Protective Factors

In discussing cases in which children have done relatively better, adults discussed length and intensity of exposure to parental methamphetamine misuse. Children who had experienced briefer periods of parent substance misuse, or periods of relative stability in early life more conducive to optimal development, and/or who were not directly exposed to their parents' substance misuse were viewed as faring better. Adults also identified a variety of potential individual, interpersonal, family, and community protective factors.

Children who appear relatively resilient were described as inherently intelligent and sociable, with easy-going temperaments, coping even as their siblings struggled. In the words of one elementary school counselor:

I had one family, two of the girls get along and fit in. And I think it probably has a lot to do with their personality. Because they're just as dirty and smelly as the other two kids. . . . the one girl just has an easygoing, pleasant temperament. The other two children, one's very sensitive, it's a boy and he's the youngest one, and it's really damaging him. He doesn't roll with the punches, he's embarrassed, he feels humiliated. And the middle girl, she's the one who's strong enough to think, "This isn't right. This is not the way I'm supposed to be living— stinking and having DCFS involved in my life every minute." Two are actually friendly and outgoing, it's just like it's washing off of them. It's like they're not hardly affected. And the other two are just like sponges. Every bad thing that comes along, they just sop it up.

Adults also discussed characteristics of the child's interpersonal context. They emphasized the importance of the child having an adult to talk with about what had happened who will emphasize that it is not the child's fault and that their parents are "not demons." One foster mother reported that she explained to her foster children: "They [parents] don't want to take drugs, but their bodies are telling them that they have to have it." A child welfare caseworker emphasized:

> I think it's really important just to reiterate to all age children that it's not their fault, it's not anything they did or didn't do, or should have done. . . . That Mommy or Daddy are sick or—I'm not beyond saying—"have used bad drugs." And that makes it not safe. I reiterate that the parents do care for the children because I would say in 99% of the cases, they do. And that we're going to help Mommy and Daddy do whatever we can to help make that home safer. But in the meantime, we need to keep them [the children] safe. I just think it's really important that they understand that it's not their fault. You know, to maintain the relationship, to make sure they're able to visit. I also encourage, if the children are old enough and I know the parents well enough to help facilitate it, to have the children ask the parents questions, where they need to answer as honestly as they can.

Family also was viewed as an important protective factor. Support from extended family members, especially relationships with relatives who are stable, educated, and understand substance misuse, was viewed as ideal. In describing two relatively well-functioning brothers, a foster mother noted:

> I just feel that these boys are very fortunate because they've had a good family upbringing from their extended relatives. . . . They have one grandma that, basically, the mom and dad lived with grandma, and the grandma made sure the oldest one got to school everyday and that he had his homework done. And she bought him a skateboard pass at the YMCA, she just made sure she took care of him, but she's an elderly lady and . . . now her health has deteriorated.

Adults consistently discussed school as an important protective factor. Children were viewed as receiving a great deal of support from teachers and principals. For example, teachers with whom children had built trusting relationships were viewed as having an enormous impact on those children's lives. As one elementary school principal noted:

> Oh this [school] is their haven. This is where they receive the positive reinforcement . . . I think this is a safe harbor for a lot of [children]. . . . When they come into the building . . . they're told . . . "You're fine here, you're safe here. We will help you." They eat here, they get food here. If they don't

have a jacket and its cold outside, we find them something to put on. . . .
A lot of nurturing . . . we came out of a faculty meeting one evening . . .,
and here on the bench outside this teacher's door was this little girl, and
she was sitting on a little bench and she had just fallen asleep, and she
said, "Oh, I was just waiting for my teacher." And she's one that's involved
in one of these [methamphetamine-involved] families. But here it was
4:30, quarter to five in the afternoon. Now, wouldn't you be looking for
your child? But she had probably walked out one door and hung out a lit-
tle while and then came back in. We were all involved, didn't see her. She
was just kind of taking a nap. Yeah, "Just waiting for my teacher."

Advice From Knowledgeable Adults

When asked what they would do to better support children if they were "in charge and had unlimited resources," adults made many suggestions such as implementing effective substance misuse treatment programs for parents, supporting child welfare, and facilitating access to other services (viewed as a substantial barrier in rural communities). Adults advised of the urgency to meet children's physical and developmental needs, provide them with effective mental health services, and then ensure that they do have a positive environment for future development through education.

Adults recognized children's need for food, clothing, shelter, safety, medical care, and the basic socialization experiences necessary to function in school and other social settings. Children not in foster care also were seen as particularly vulnerable during school holidays and summer vacation, when they no longer had the support of school programs (e.g., breakfast and lunch programs), and monitoring by educators. Children also were seen as needing the basic developmental experiences that many adequately functioning families take for granted. One child protective caseworker emphasized:

I guess offering them experiences in life . . . swimming lessons and team
sports and trips to the library and culture, museums, our kids have not
had the luxury of exposure to.

Adults emphasized the importance of providing effective mental health services to manage posttraumatic stress disorder and other mental health problems, and to deal with neglect and abuse. Children were viewed as needing help in interpreting their experiences and in building hope for a better life. Some adults also mentioned the possible role of support groups like Ala-Teen (an offshoot of Alcoholics Anonymous for adolescents affected by others' substance misuse), in which children could learn that they are not the only ones whose parents misuse methamphetamine and that parental addiction is not their fault. Unfortunately, many children in foster care do not experience high-quality mental health services, as noted by a foster mother:

> First of all, I would make it clearer-cut that we did not have to take second-rate doctors and second-rate mental health [care]. I have dealt with foster children now for twenty-some years. . . . I have yet to run into a mental health facility that didn't slap a Band-Aid on my child's arm for sexual abuse and drug abuse. You know, whatever it is. "Come back next Monday and we'll talk for 45 minutes." You know, I think that's a big downfall of the state of Illinois. We take these children to help them, and then when we take them, we make them second-class citizens automatically because you can't see the good doctors. You can't go to the good psychiatrists. . . . So you know, I think that's a big downfall. I think if these children [her two foster children] could have been given quality counseling when they were placed a year ago, therapeutic-level counseling, you know, I think they'd have had a chance, maybe.

Adults also emphasized the importance of education. Succeeding in school is especially important for children from methamphetamine-involved families, as a way out of poverty and despair. In addition, substance misuse prevention education and family life education is important in showing children alternatives to violence, substance misuse, and other antisocial behavior. Substance misuse prevention education for all children was seen as important in discouraging children from ever experimenting with methamphetamine and possibly becoming addicted themselves.

Continuing education also was seen as essential for foster parents, teachers, and other adults who care for children. For example, adults emphasized the importance of compassionate, quality foster care to children's well-being and development. Understanding the contexts in which children have developed may better prepare adults to handle constructively certain predictable challenges (e.g., following rules and schedules for a child who has experienced neither) and to avoid negative attributions about the child's lasting personal qualities (e.g., that he is irresponsible, just like his addicted father). In the words of a counselor from a private social service agency:

> They're not children. They don't know how to play. Usually, the older child—if there's several siblings—you may have a 5-year-old that's been cooking dinner and changing diapers. So, [foster] parents need to go into

*the experience knowing that they're not going to change these kids over-
night. They can't get into power struggles over I'm the parent and you're
not. That's generally one of the biggest issues that we see with stability, having placement stability problems. Is that the caregiver and that 5-year-old
get into a power struggle about who's the parent. . . . And we have children
that have a large vocabulary of profanities, and being more tolerant of
that. That it's not going to—these kids are not going to be fixed overnight
just because you have a loving, nice house. It's not going to fix 5, 6, 7 years
of damage that's been done.*

Conclusion

The perspectives of knowledgeable adults interviewed for this chapter had
much in common with the mothers interviewed in Chapter 5. They described that many children from methamphetamine-involved families are
brought by their parents into a rural drug subculture characterized by exposure to toxic environments, neglect, abuse, isolation, loss, and antisocial behavior. They emphasized that this rural drug subculture places children at
risk for physical and mental health problems. The adults interviewed for
this chapter were somewhat more concerned than the mothers in Chapter 5
about the risks of child abuse and developmental or educational disturbances. Not surprisingly, mothers may have expressed somewhat more sensitivity than other knowledgeable adults to the potential impact of domestic
violence, family problems, and loss on their children's well-being.

Consistent with research on parental substance misuse (e.g., Hans,
2004), adults also reported that not all children exposed to parental methamphetamine misuse will develop mental health or substance misuse disorders. They suggested that individual-, family-, and community- level protective factors exist. For example, some children are more adaptable than others,
have relationships with well-functioning relatives or educators, or live in
communities that offer positive socialization experiences, such as sports
teams, 4-H clubs, and church-sponsored youth groups. Sources of individual variation in children's responses to parental methamphetamine misuse
should be examined in subsequent empirical research.

We would like to underscore that the adults' discussions reflect their
beliefs and perspectives on the impact of parental methamphetamine misuse
on children and protective factors. They are not necessarily accurate—for
example, they may overemphasize the relative risk of sexual abuse given a
few salient cases. Nonetheless, these beliefs, correct or incorrect, presumably
provide a frame of reference from which adults make decisions about children.
In addition, the convergent perspectives of diverse adults occupying various

social vantage points, as well as ethnographic field work, do suggest a number of possible strategies for enhancing the development of school-aged children whose parents misuse methamphetamine.

Enhance Substance Misuse Education in Schools and Communities

Adults emphasized that substance misuse education is critical for children, educators, foster parents, and the community at large. Any substance misuse education interventions must address the social stigma of methamphetamine misuse. As suggested by our ethnographic data, the strong, negative views of adults who misuse methamphetamine held by community members may be problematic for children. Most adults viewed children as loyal and loving to their parents, despite parents' neglect and abuse. Given children's tendency to identify with their parents, most adults cautioned against negativity toward parents. Yet, they also recognized that, in many cases, parents who are misusing methamphetamine put their children in very difficult positions of mixed loyalty toward educators and child welfare workers who represent a very different lifestyle, one that rejects substance misuse. Children do need clear messages that methamphetamine misuse destroys lives and that alternatives exist, but such messages must be expressed in the context of a compassionate understanding of their parents' illness.

Enhance Timely, Child Welfare Involvement

Adults emphasized the need to provide for children's basic physical, social and emotional needs. These needs can be addressed through timely, high-quality child welfare interventions, such as foster care. Early identification of children, however, can be problematic given the isolated, rural drug subculture in which many children from methamphetamine-involved families develop. In this context, many children learn to fear outsiders, such as teachers, and to keep secret their parents' methamphetamine misuse. They may even lie to protect their parents and families from legal consequences. Denial or fear of revealing their experiences to adults such as teachers and child welfare workers can impede the early identification of at-risk children. Continuing education is needed to alert community professionals about the effects of methamphetamine misuse on children and to facilitate timely identification of at-risk children.

Provide Access to Quality Mental Health Services

Adults consistently advised that urgent attention be turned to providing quality and timely mental health services that specifically address the needs of children from methamphetamine-involved families. Consistent with existing reports of parental substance misuse (The National Center on Addiction and Substance misuse at Columbia University [CASA], 1999) and childhood trauma (e.g., Sroufe, Dougal, Weinfeld & Carlson, 2000), adults emphasized that many children whose parents misuse methamphetamine have experienced significant trauma and, as a result, display psychological disturbances. In addition, they described that many children have developed within a rural drug subculture in which they have learned beliefs and behaviors antithetical to successful functioning in mainstream society.

The adequate assessment of children's mental health and developmental needs is a prerequisite to any successful intervention. As adults described, and we have observed (see Chapters 7 and 8), there is considerable individual variation in the functioning of children whose parents misuse methamphetamine. Such individual variation in children's functioning is likely related to length, context, and intensity of exposure to parental substance misuse, as well as to individual, family, and community factors. Mental health services must target children's unique areas of risk and address children with the most urgent needs. The importance of comprehensive, individual assessment is reflected in an Integrated Assessment Program implemented throughout Illinois by June 2005. This program provides for comprehensive medical, developmental, and mental health assessments to all children entering into protective custody (State of Illinois, Department of Children and Family Services, 2004).

Effective mental health interventions with children whose parents misuse methamphetamine will likely address trauma symptoms and socialization issues. Since children may remain in long-term foster care due to the extended prison sentences given to their parents, they may also need to address the loss of primary caregivers. These needs, identified by adults, are consistent with children's developmental and mental health data (see Chapter 8).

At the same time when their needs are greatest, many children in foster care in Illinois have little access to quality and timely mental health services. Poertner (2002) examined children in out-of-home care in Illinois who were receiving Medicaid-billed mental health services. In fiscal years 1995–1998, only 17%–20% of foster children received mental health services of any kind or quality within their first 2 years of care. The problem of inadequate access to mental health care is likely to be even more serious in rural areas where fewer mental health professionals specialize in child development and mental health, children are relatively isolated, and transportation is limited. Indeed, adults consistently reported that mental health services to children in foster care is inadequate. In the service area of the rural field office, mental health services, when available, are typically provided through weekly, hour-long sessions with counselors having varying levels of expertise and for no more than 6 months. Psychiatric care is extremely limited, and there are no child psychiatrists in the service area. No child in our study had seen a psychiatrist. The widespread urgency of addressing the problem of inadequate mental health care for children is recognized by the Children's Mental Health Partnership, a 35-member interdisciplinary committee that is crafting a plan for a statewide system of services in Illinois, including prevention, early intervention, and treatment for children from birth to age 18 (Governor's Office News, 2004).

In this chapter, we have emphasized the common ground on which diverse adults stand in relation to methamphetamine misuse by parents. It is important to recognize, however, that conflicting opinions were identified around a number of issues. For example, some difference of opinion existed within the community regarding the wisdom of family preservation efforts, especially in the absence of effective substance misuse treatment programs for parents. Many adults saw legal intervention, such as police and child welfare investigations, as tools for gaining leverage and cooperation with parents. Others questioned the wisdom of imposing stiffer prison sentences and other legal sanctions when resources are urgently needed to implement effective substance misuse treatment interventions. Recognizing tensions within communities is critical, since they can impede effective cooperation or result in different parties working at cross-purposes to implement interventions.

It also is important to underscore that we interviewed adults from seven counties in rural Illinois. Although findings from adults in this region may be relevant to and contain lessons for other rural settings, this is an open empirical question. Clearly, there are no easy answers to this difficult problem of parental methamphetamine misuse. Effective interventions for children will require complex, integrated, and sustained child welfare, educational, and mental health services, as well as the development of effective substance misuse treatment programs for their parents.

Chapter Seven

Children's Experiences and Perspectives

Twelve-year-old Jess lived with her parents and younger brother in a trailer on the property of her great aunt. Jess's parents, who have misused substances since adolescence, were arrested and sent to prison shortly after they began producing methamphetamine in a Mom and Pop lab. Jess and her younger brother spent little time at the family's trailer. They enjoyed a Huck Finn–like childhood, spending long days riding their bicycles around their small town, playing with friends, sometimes eating cold cereal for every meal, and participating in sports and church activities. Bright and attractive, the children were well liked in the community and participated in the gifted program at their local school. In addition, they enjoyed a close and loving relationship with their great aunt, often spending the night with her. She made sure that they had school supplies in the fall, warm coats in the winter, and passes to the community swimming pool during the summer. Unfortunately, when the children were taken into protective custody, their great aunt was too ill to assume guardianship, and they entered foster care in another small town. The children's new foster mother soon became frustrated by what she viewed as Jess's stubborn unwillingness to follow the family's many rules and routines, and her insistence on "parenting" her younger brother. She responded with punishment and the withdrawal of positive attention. When Jess became depressed and began failing in school, her caseworker successfully advocated for her placement along with her brother in another foster home. Here, they are receiving more supportive care and appear happier. They continue regular visits with their parents in prison and

---

This chapter elaborates material originally published as Haight, W., Ostler, T., Black, J., Sheridan, K. & Kingery, L. (2006). A child's eye view of parent methamphetamine abuse: Implications for helping foster families to succeed. *Children and Youth Services Review*, 29(1), 1–15. Permission was obtained to reproduce portions of this text.

In many methamphetamine-involved families, older children become the primary caregivers of themselves and their younger siblings. Photo by Carl Kingery.

their great aunt. Prison has allowed both parents to gain sobriety for the first time in decades. They have contact with their children's foster parents and, during visits, encourage their children to "be good" at home and do well in school. Jess views substance misuse as "stupid" and aspires to study math in college. She also continues to struggle with following rules at her foster home and school, and recently stole a popular iPod music player. She longs to return home to her parents. (Adapted from field notes, 2006.)

As Jess's case suggests, children's perspectives of their methamphetamine-involved families often vary somewhat from those of the adult professionals who serve them. Child protective services professionals found evidence of child maltreatment sufficient to take Jess and her brother into state care, but from Jess's perspective, the life she led with her family, including her parents' substance misuse, was "just normal." Despite their illness, Jess knew her parents loved her and her younger brother. Intelligent, adaptable children, they were able to find support in their small town from extended family and community members. From Jess's perspective, the "saddest, scariest" time of her life did not involve directly her parents' substance misuse, but being up-rooted to an unloving foster home in another community.

In this chapter, we present the perspectives of 29 children on their families of origin, including parental methamphetamine misuse, based on in-depth, individual, face-to-face interviews. Care was taken with these interviews because children can find discussions of family experiences upsetting or even retraumatizing. As described in Chapter 3, child interviews were embedded in a variety of activities and standardized assessments. Each child was interviewed by a social worker, developmental psychologist, child clinical psychologist, or psychiatrist, all of whom had experience with children. We spent several hours with each child. Prior to the interviews, we visited children's homes, admired their pets, sports teams, and the like, and talked with their caregivers. Our interview questions were embedded in expressive activities of the child's choice, including doll-house play, puppet play, drawing, or just talking. The interview was conversation-like and proceeded at the child's pace, and no child was pressured to answer sensitive questions. Following the interview, we spent time with the child "winding down," for example, playing a board game or with dolls. Although it proved unnecessary, we were prepared to spend additional time with the child, or to provide an immediate clinical referral if the child became distressed.

All of the children in our study had experienced major life disruptions because of parental methamphetamine misuse. We begin by considering how children experience their families of origin. Children's perceptions of their parents' methamphetamine misuse likely overlap somewhat with those of the adults perspectives presented in Chapters 5 and 6. They have lived in the physical and social contexts that knowledgeable adults and recovering mothers describe as a rural drug subculture characterized by environmental danger, violence, adult criminality, misuse of methamphetamine and other substances, and child neglect and abuse. On the other hand, children like Jess and her younger brother know and love those individuals others may stigmatize as "meth heads" as "Mom and Dad," and feelings about these relationships surely color their experience of parental substance misuse. Children's perceptions of their parents' methamphetamine misuse also may be affected by their limited life experiences, for example, of families not involved with substance misuse, and by their limited knowledge, for example, of methamphetamine misuse.

In this chapter, we also describe what the children know and believe about methamphetamine. We consider the accuracy and completeness of children's information, including any distortions that may result from immaturity and lack of experience. Lack of information, or inaccurate or distorted information, may leave a child vulnerable, for example, to self-blame for family problems or social stigma of individuals who misuse methamphetamine. Information on children's understanding of methamphetamine is basic to the design of any successful substance misuse prevention program and mental health intervention.

Children's Experiences Within Their Families of Origin

Exposure to Adults' Misuse of Methamphetamine and Other Substances

Consistent with the reports of adults presented in Chapters 5 and 6, adults' substance misuse was a major theme in children's discussions of their experiences within their families. Thirteen children (45%) reported observing their parents misuse methamphetamine, and four of these children, along with two additional children, reported being present when other, non-kin adults misused methamphetamine. In the words of 9-year-old Amy, "It was not very pleasant . . . I felt bad, scared. It was miserable." When asked to describe a sad or scary time, 14-year-old Andy noted, "I'd have to say when my mom started doing drugs . . . that is the most horrible, sadness and stuff that was scary in my whole entire life. . . ." Five children (17%) reported exposure to their parents' drugs, drug paraphernalia, or drug-seeking behavior: for example, 11-year-old Jerry was frightened when he accompanied his mother to purchase methamphetamine in the parking lot of a local grocery store. Nine children (31%) also reported observing their parents misuse other substances, primarily alcohol and marijuana; six of these children, and two others, also reported observing non-kin adults misuse other substances. Nine-year-old Carl commented, very simply, on his parents' parties, "I was scared. They were doing drugs."

Three children (10%) reported that they were forced to ingest substances: alcohol, marijuana, and tobacco. Nine-year-old Amy was troubled by an incident that occurred when she was in kindergarten, "My mom got me high one time. . . . She and a man were smoking dope under a blanket, and they put me under there and got me high."

Exposure to Adult Criminality and Other Antisocial Activities

Consistent with the observations of adults presented in Chapters 5 and 6, most children reported a range of adult criminal or other antisocial behavior in their families of origin. When invited to talk about sad or scary times in their families, 25 children (86%) spontaneously described exposure to adults' illegal or other antisocial behavior. Twenty-four children reported observing their parents' illegal or other antisocial behavior, and 14 of these children also reported exposure to the illegal or other antisocial behavior of other, non-kin adults. Thirteen-year-old Karen described a lifestyle in which:

> *You just grow up, and you don't know anything better. You just know your family does drugs. And there's, like, nothing you can do about it . . . you're*

so used to hollering and screaming. . . . You're used to everything that you grew up around. . . . All the people I knew were drug addicts.

Exposure to the illegal or other antisocial behavior of non-kin adults left some children feeling particularly vulnerable. For example, in response to the question involving a "sad or scary" time in his family, 14-year-old Andy described, "All these people [methamphetamine addicts] started moving into the house," and some "broke into the house to steal." He was afraid because his father, who slept deeply for days after a methamphetamine binge, could not always wake up when these other adults, some of whom Andy knew to be violent, came into the house.

A total of 17 children (59%) discussed their parents' imprisonment because of methamphetamine misuse, and three children discussed the imprisonment of other adults (family friends) for methamphetamine misuse. When asked about a sad or scary time in his family, 13-year-old Tony recalled:

Just here lately whenever my mom went to jail. . . . She was supposed to come and get me that day. . . . It was . . . we were out of school [crying]. She didn't come and get me . . . 'cuz that night she went to jail.

Five of the children (17%) described drug busts in their homes. According to 14-year-old Tim:

I watched all the other kids before. And then the cops came and searched our house. They found some drugs. And then we got took away to our grand-pa's, who does it [uses methamphetamine] with them [his parents]!

Exposure to Adult Violence

Also consistent with adult reports, violence was a major theme to emerge from children's responses to interview probes regarding "sad or scary times" within their families. Eleven children (38%) described violence between adults at home, primarily between their parents or a parent and paramour, but including other adults as well. Ten-year-old May recalled:

My dad beating up my mom. . . . All the time. I would hit my dad because he wouldn't get off of her. He would stand her up against the wall and started choking her. I kept on hitting him and I kicked him. . . . [One time] my mom pulled out a hammer and hit my dad in the head. And then she took it out and hit herself in the head. . . . And then my dad went

The experience of many children from methamphetamine-involved families included substandard housing, where basic needs for food and shelter were not adequately met. Photo by Sheriff Michael Miller.

outside, and we locked all the doors and windows, and he busted the back window out when I was there. I got a piece of glass stuck in my eye . . . my dad took me out the window. . . . And I had to get in his girlfriend's car. And my mom went out there and took a hammer and busted her windshield. . . . And my mom tried to grab me, but she [the girlfriend] had pulled out with my dad. . . . And, so, we went back to their house, and I didn't want to so I started hitting her [the girlfriend], and I started cussing at her because I was so mad because my mom said if anybody tries to take you, you just beat them. And, so I beat on her because I was so mad at her. 'Cuz she almost ran over my mom. . . .

Participation in Antisocial Activities

Six children (21%) reported that they were actively involved in adult antisocial behavior. Five children reported that parents had involved them actively in antisocial activities. These included abuse of alcohol ($n = 2$) or illegal drugs ($n = 2$), exposure to sexual activities ($n = 1$), and stealing precursors for methamphetamine production ($n = 1$). Thirteen-year-old Karen was troubled by lying to school officials, and other adults.

And one day, when we lived in [town] and I was real little . . . everyday for the past week, I would come to school with real red eyes because I was crying because of my dad every morning . . . and these workers or whatever, they were there with the police . . . I think they was DCFS people. They were there, and they were asking me questions, and my dad didn't tell me . . . not to tell the truth, so I told them about all the bad stuff. And then when they called my [older] brother in next, he told them a whole different story. And when I went home that day, my dad yelled at me . . . because I told the truth and didn't lie. . . . And then like ever since, when I talk to people like that, he told me to lie.

Two of the oldest children in the study, boys from families with long histories of substance misuse and parental involvement with law enforcement, reported initiating antisocial behavior. Fourteen-year-old Andy, whose mother began giving him alcohol from about the age of 11, also reported abusing alcohol and marijuana. Fourteen-year-old Tim reported smoking cigarettes from the age of 11, as well as drinking, stealing, and behavior problems in school.

Divergence from Adult Perspectives

In many respects, children's reports converged with those of the knowledgeable adults presented in Chapter 6. Children, however, placed relatively less emphasis on chaotic living situations, neglect, and environmental danger. Like their mothers, they placed relatively less emphasis than other knowledgeable adults on maltreatment. Only a few children reported that the violence in their families extended to them. A total of four children (14%) reported physical abuse by their parents, and one of these children and two other children also reported physical or sexual abuse by another adult. Parents' abusive behavior typically was attributed by the children to their substance misuse. As 14-year-old Andy explained, "I don't think she [mother] expected to hit us that hard because she didn't know what she was doing, but sometimes, you know, it got out of hand. . . ."

Despite widespread evidence of neglect from child welfare investigations, only five children (17%) reported neglect, either lack of supervision ($n = 2$), or inadequate food and shelter ($n = 3$). As 14-year-old Tim described, his family moved around a lot, and he "never knew where we would end up sleeping." During his parents' methamphetamine binges, the children would get very hungry. Tim described hoarding junk food for these occasions:

At one time I was scared. They wouldn't let us come down the stairs or nothing. . . . I usually just took some of my mom or dad's money and went to the store. I bought soda for whenever they kept us upstairs.

Note that children's failure to report maltreatment does not mean that it did not occur. For example, they may have lacked reference to more normative family lifestyles, attempted to protect their parents, or found other issues such as the loss of a parent more salient.

Similar to the recovering mothers in Chapter 5, and in contrast to many knowledgeable adults in Chapter 6, children emphasized loss and separation from parents. When asked to describe a time when they felt scared or unhappy, 17 children (59%) reported the loss of a parent. Eight of the 25 children in foster care (32%) discussed being taken into protective custody because of their parents' methamphetamine misuse. Eleven-year-old Jerry described the "saddest, scariest" time in his life as, "The night when we got taken away." He was at his grandmother's house when his parents were arrested. He described to the interviewer (I):

> **J:** *They just came in and took us.*
> **I:** *Who came in, do you remember who it was?*
> **J:** *The cops.*
> **I:** *The cops.*
> **J:** *My grandma knew they were going to take us because they called my grandma's house and told her, and I heard what she said.*
> **I:** *What did she say?*
> **J:** *She told my cousin, quietly, that they're going to take us, and I knew that. I was in the room hiding because I didn't want them to come get us.*
> **I:** *Right. Well, that must have been very frightening for you.*
> **J:** *My dad said they're not taking us, either.*
> **I:** *But then they did.*
> **J:** *[quietly] yeah.*

A number of children went on to comment on foster care. For example, 11-year-old Kim noted that the "saddest" thing was being "put away from your mom. Separated." Thirteen-year-old Sam described his worry about his parents' safety. His 9-year-old brother, Steve, described his feeling upon entering foster care: "I didn't like it. I felt like I wasn't gonna get feeded. I would be starving back there." In contrast, their 11-year-old sister, Mary, looked forward to living in a mansion with the "rich people."

Children's Active Role in Socialization

It is important to underscore that children took a variety of stances toward their parents' antisocial behavior. Some children appeared to embrace their parents' beliefs, values, and lifestyle, and expressed strong attachment, love, and loyalty for their parents. Some actively resisted child welfare or law enforcement interventions. In contrast, 14-year-old Andy adamantly rejected his mother. He was very clear that after his mother began misusing methamphetamine she no longer "acted like a mom should. . . . She was letting us kids do drugs and us getting drunk and . . . letting us have sex and everything and, you know, it was just horrible." Andy eventually reported his mother to the police officer presenting the Drug Abuse Resistance Education (DARE) program at school. "I didn't want to do it but I knew I had to or somebody was going to die. . . . " Andy attributes his courage to God,

I was in church, and I just got baptized, and I prayed a lot, and stuff like that and I just felt God saying inside of me, you need to tell him [the DARE officer], you need to tell somebody. And I just felt like I was OK. And I think God gave me the strength and courage just to go up there and say, "Hey, this and this is happening."

Turning to religion provided Andy with a new identity, support system, positive adult role models, faith, and hope for the future. His abrupt conversion, however, may make it very difficult to eventually reconcile his early experiences and love for his mother with his current life. Indeed, he expressed no desire to be reunited or even visit with his mother. "She's lost trust with me. . . ."

Children's Understanding of Methamphetamine

Children's development following exposure to their parents' methamphetamine misuse may be facilitated by an understanding of the illness that so disrupted their lives. We began our exploration of children's understanding of methamphetamine misuse by considering the extent and accuracy of their basic information about methamphetamine. In response to our probe, "What is methamphetamine" (or "meth" or other slang term used by the child), 18 children (62%) accurately described some characteristics of methamphetamine, the consequences of misuse, and/or motivation for use. Fourteen children (48%) provided partial definitions. More specifically, nine children described it as "a drug," and five qualified it as a "bad" drug. Two 13-year-olds further classified methamphetamine as similar to crack cocaine, but more intense, in the words of one, a "super stimulant." Three children (10%) commented on its delivery via smoking, and one via sniffing. Four children (14%) described its physical characteristics (e.g., "it smells bad," "it's a white powdery stuff," and it "usually is in crystal form"). Four children described production, "It's a drug that people make."

Fifteen children (52%) discussed the consequences of methamphetamine misuse. Fourteen children (48%) described negative psychological or behavioral consequences to the user. Seven children (24%) described aggressive behavior. Users became "mean," "aggravated," "fought a lot," "hit kids," and just wanted to "hit somebody." Six children (21%) described changes in energy level. Users "stay up for a really long time," "never sleep," and are "all hyper." Six children (21%) described unusual behavior. Users "went wacko," and were "weird." 14-year-old Andy provided a narrative account illustrating his mother's methamphetamine-induced psychosis:

> *She would see stuff that wasn't there. I had this gator golf toy . . . I'd bring it out, I'd play with it. She'd say, "Put it away, it's a real gator." Or she'd say, "You should throw it outside," thinking it's some animal. And I'd have all these [stuffed] animals, and she's thinking they're alive and attacking her and everything.*

In contrast, 13-year-old Brad, also a child of parents with long-term histories of substance misuse, insisted that his parents and other people at his house just "acted normal."

Four children (14%) expressed concerns about the physical consequences of methamphetamine misuse to their parents including rotten teeth, cancer, and death. Three children explicitly discussed social consequences. Methamphetamine can get users "into trouble," and has implications for their children. Children's lives are "destroyed," or they "get taken away. It's hard on children."

Six children (21%) spontaneously speculated on why people misuse methamphetamine. Three children (10%) discussed social pressure. Their parents were introduced to methamphetamine by an intimate partner (spouse or paramour), or they did it to "fit in" with a group. Two young girls, aged 9 and 10, speculated that their parents "picked meth" over them because they "cared more" about the drug. One astute 13-year-old girl explained that her father is involved with methamphetamine to "get some pain relief . . . the pain he feels inside," and also to "make money."

Variation in Children's Knowledge and Responses to Probes about Methamphetamine

This analysis of children's knowledge and beliefs about methamphetamine suggests individual variation and large gaps in the knowledge base of most children. Of this group of children, all of whose families had experienced major disruptions because of parental methamphetamine misuse, 11 (38%) articulated no information about methamphetamine, and less than half could provide any definition. A number of children claimed not to know anything about methamphetamine. Some of these claims are credible. For example, Ted was relatively young, and prior to his placement in foster care, Don had spent much time with relatives. Both children disclosed that their parents did "drugs," and related some memories of troubling adult behavior, but could provide no information about methamphetamine per se.

Many children expressed some accurate information about methamphetamine, but that information was incomplete, or the child also expressed inaccurate information. For example, some children knew methamphetamine is a "bad drug," but did not connect that knowledge to their parents' problematic behavior. The knowledge base of other children contained obvious inaccuracies. For example, 13-year-old Tom had some accurate information about methamphetamine, but believed that his family was the only family so affected. Other children told very fragmented narratives. The following interview excerpts are from 7-year-old Bradley. Bradley scored well within the normal range on the Peabody Picture Vocabulary Test (PPVT), a standardized assessment of children's expressive language, and yet his story has some significant gaps. ("I" is the interviewer, and "B" is Bradley).

I: *Sometimes parents use meth. Has that been something you've ever seen or known about?*
B: *My dad. He did have drugs.*
I: *OK, I see. When did that happen?*
B: *A while ago.*
I: *A while ago. Where is your dad now?*
B: *In prison.*
I: *In prison?*
B: *For two more years . . .*
I: *Well, when your dad took meth, how did he act?*
B: *I forgot.*
I: *Did your brothers know that he was on drugs?*
B: *Jacob didn't, but Jared did.*
I: *OK. And you knew too? And did he take them often or not so often?*
B: *It was on the table.*
I: *It was. What did it look like?*
B: *I don't know, I didn't look at it.*
I: *You didn't look at it, but it was on the table. And what about your mom?*
B: *She saw it on the table.*
I: *And what did she say, and what did she do?*
B: *She yelled at him . . . angry. . . .*
I: *And what did your dad do when your mom yelled at him?*
B: *I just forgot.*

I: *Did he get mad?*

B: *He hit something. It was glass.*

I: *That must have been sort of scary, I bet. . . . When he broke the glass, what did you do?*

B: *I did nothing. . . . I heard something break, but I didn't go look. . . .*

I: *Did your mom cry at all?*

B: *She cried.*

I: *That was what I was wondering. Was that pretty scary?*

B: *No.*

I: *Did you and your brother ever talk about it?*

B: *No.*

I: *Did your mom ever tell you what was going on?*

B: *No.*

I: *OK. . . .*

Knowledge expressed by Bradley and other children seems to have resulted from direct exposure to substance misuse, for example, isolated observations about the physical characteristics of methamphetamine, mode of delivery, or addicts' behavior, rather than explanations by adults.

The knowledge base of other children was impossible to assess. Some apparently followed the lead of their parents in resisting any communication about methamphetamine misuse and its consequences with outsiders. Nine-year-old Jay and his 7-year-old brother, Terry, refused to answer any direct questions about methamphetamine. Their mother refused treatment and, according to case notes, instructed them not to cooperate with child protective services.

Other children, who did provide information about methamphetamine misuse, vehemently denied that their parents used methamphetamine despite much evidence to the contrary. For example, three children from a family with a long history of substance misuse, including methamphetamine misuse, whose father suffered from paranoia, independently told interviewers that their parents were framed by the government. In the words of 8-year-old Steve, "Mom and Dad has to do a drug test and then go to counseling. Why should they have to do all that when they was set up? I hate it. I don't *think* they was set up. I *know* they was set up." His 13-year-old brother, Tim, who asked the interviewer to confirm that she was not "with the government," provided further elaboration:

> He [father] told me everything. Because he knew I'd pretty much be the only one that could comprehend it. And even then I had problems. Like

for some reason I couldn't understand why the government wanted to be bothered with us instead of all the 500 million people out there . . . targeted. . . . And then I'm sitting there in court and she's [caseworker] lying, both the cop and her . . . are lying on the stand. And I can't do a thing about it. . . . And a cop . . . came to check our house and she's the one that lied on the stand . . . the cop went downstairs and my dad really loves chocolate because he has low blood sugar. And, the cop emptied our trash can and just dumped it on the floor. . . . He was talking about foils and you know Hershey bars come in foil packages, and besides, if you smoke a foil its going to melt away anyway. . . .*

Thirteen-year-old Tim and his siblings appeared to believe a family story of government persecution told to them by their beloved, but paranoid, father. If the father's story were true, then there was hope that the parents would be exonerated, and the family would be reunited. Even in this case, however, Tim did find room to actively wonder "why the government wanted to be bothered with us instead of all the other 500 million people out there." Although accepting their father's story kept hope alive for these children, it also resulted in their turning away from their foster parents or other adults currently in their lives who might otherwise have been able to provide help and support.

The defiant positions of some children, and the paranoid and antigovernment stances of some others, raise the issue of children's active socialization into a rural drug subculture by their parents; that is, the extent to which children are groomed by their parents for antisocial behavior. Understanding this subculture and socialization processes is critical to the construction of effective interventions for children from methamphetamine-involved families.

Conclusion

As children enter and remain in the foster care system due to their parents' misuse and production of methamphetamine, careful consideration needs to be given to supporting their successful development. Understanding the contexts in which children from methamphetamine-involved families have

---

* One method of smoking crystal meth is to use aluminum foil "boats" to heat the product for inhalation. The foils can litter drug houses like crack pipes in other regions. Alternatively, this child may have been referring to the discarded foil blister-packs of cold medicine tablets used in cooking methamphetamine.

been reared, as well as children's interpretation of those experiences and basic knowledge base regarding methamphetamine, is a necessary first step toward improving interventions for these vulnerable children. Although much more research clearly is necessary, these results do have some implications for helping children to succeed.

First, foster parents need information about the contexts in which children have been reared, and children's understanding and perceptions of those contexts, in order to interpret and respond to challenges that may emerge. In a number of respects, the reports of children in this study parallel those of knowledgeable adults within their communities and suggest that methamphetamine misuse can fundamentally disrupt adults' abilities to successfully parent their children. Children in this study reported extensive exposure to adult criminal and other antisocial behavior within their families. Children described not only that their parents misused methamphetamine, but that they engaged in a constellation of activities related to drug misuse or drug seeking. Parents misused other substances such as alcohol and marijuana, produced methamphetamine, and engaged in a variety of illegal activities as a result of, or to sustain, their substance misuse. In various families, these activities led to children's exposure to domestic violence, disrupted family relations, and homelessness, as well as their involvement in substance misuse and related criminal activities, and experiences of abuse and neglect. Furthermore, the defiant positions of Jay and Terry; the paranoid and antigovernment stances of Steve, Sam, and Mary; and the active involvement of Amy, Andy, and Tim by their parents in substance misuse suggest that some children are actively socialized into a rural drug subculture by their parents.

Given children's experiences, foster parents might anticipate that regular mealtimes and bedtimes, adult supervision of children, and other activities of family life that pass unnoticed by them may result in "culture shock" for their foster children from methamphetamine-involved families. They can anticipate that their foster children may require a relatively extended period of adjustment, support, and teaching. Furthermore, children who have been socialized by parents to distrust, fear, and lie to outsiders may require persistent and sustained relationship-building before they respond to foster parents with respect or affection. If foster parents fully understand the commitments they need to make to successfully nurture a child emerging from a rural drug subculture, the placement may be less likely to be disrupted.

Second, substance misuse education is likely to be essential to children from methamphetamine-involved families. Children reared by parents who misuse drugs are at risk to misuse substances themselves (e.g., Cretzmeyer, Sarrazin, Huber, Block & Hall, 2003; The National Center on Addiction and Substance Misuse at Columbia University, 1999). Despite the fact that their lives had been disrupted by parental methamphetamine misuse, the children interviewed had relatively little information and understanding of methamphetamine addiction. The knowledge base of most children contained major gaps and misinformation. Few reported learning about methamphetamine through direct discussion with adults. Most of their information seemed to emerge from their observations. Without accurate information, children are vulnerable to drawing conclusions about family disruptions that do not facilitate their continued development and well-being, for example, that they are responsible for the family problems or that their parents are "bad." Some children with faulty knowledge may be tempted to use drugs as a way of connecting with parents or addressing their own emotional pain. School-based prevention programs may be a good start, but children whose family lives have been fundamentally shaped by parents' misuse of drugs such as methamphetamine may require more emotional support, and more and different information than children whose lives have not been so affected.

Finally, professionals and foster parents must recognize that law enforcement and child welfare interventions may be distressing to children even months later. In a number of respects, the reports of children in this study were distinct from those of knowledgeable adults. Most child welfare professionals, law enforcement professionals, substance misuse counselors, educators, and foster parents focused on the profound neglect of children by parents who misuse methamphetamine. Despite the inadequacies of their families, relatively few children mentioned maltreatment. In contrast, many children described involvement with law enforcement and child welfare as the "saddest, scariest" time in their families. Far from embracing their placement in safe and stable families, many children mourned the loss of their parents and family, even after months in foster care, and expressed distress at their parents' arrests and imprisonment.

Chapter Eight

Children's Psychological Functioning

*Thirteen-year-old Sally lived with her parents and four younger
siblings in rural Illinois. The family home was isolated, run-down,
and unsanitary. There was little food in the house, and the children often
missed school. Their primary social contact outside of their immediate
family was their parents' "friends," who frequented the family home in
search of drugs. Sally experienced sexual abuse at the hands of one such
adult when her parents were crashed after binging on methamphetamine.
Her father, who had a long history of methamphetamine misuse, espoused
many unusual and paranoid beliefs, for example, that the generator* used
to produce methamphetamine "blew" into the backyard, and the family
was "set-up" by the government. Sally, who perhaps desired nothing more
than her father's approval, readily adopted her father's beliefs as her own.
She angrily declared to us that the child welfare worker was lying during
her parents' trial. Sally was not only failing in school, she scored in the
clinical range on standardized assessments of trauma, and showed other
emotional and behavioral problems as well. (Adapted from case notes, 2006.)*

Sally and her siblings were reared in a methamphetamine-involved family
with multiple generations of substance misuse, poverty, and isolation. When
taken into foster care, they displayed many mental health needs likely emerging from a combination of trauma, socialization and, possibly, genetic vulnerability. In the absence of intensive and sustained intervention, Sally and

Chapter 8 elaborates material originally published as Ostler, T., Haight, W., Black, J., Choi,
G., Kingery, L., & Sheridan, K. (2007). Case series: Mental health needs and perspectives
of rural children reared by parents who abuse methamphetamine. *Journal of the American
Academy of Child and Adolescent Psychiatry,* 46(4), 500–507. Permission was obtained to
reproduce portions of this text.
* Hydrochloric acid (HCl) generators produce the HCl used in the Birch methamphetamine
manufacturing process. They can be industrial units or home-made, but are among the most
dangerous items in the methamphetamine lab.

Involvement in church was identified by some young adolescents as a source of support. Photo by Camilla Black.

her siblings are at high risk to follow their parents, grandparents, and other extended family members into substance misuse and mental illness.

This chapter explores the complex mental health needs of rural children affected by parental methamphetamine misuse. To date, studies on the mental health outcomes of children whose parents misuse substances have focused predominately on alcohol abuse (e.g., Johnson & Leff, 1999). These studies report that children reared by parents who misuse alcohol show elevated symptom levels for both externalizing and internalizing behavior (e.g., Fals-Stewart, Kelley, Fincham, Golden & Logsdon, 2004). As discussed in Chapter 1, research on children whose parents misuse illegal drugs also underscores increased emotional problems and an increased incidence of psychiatric disorders (e.g., Luthar, Cushing, Merikangas & Rounsaville, 1998).

Current research has not examined the impact of parental methamphetamine misuse on children's mental health. The bulk of the research in this area has focused on the effects of methamphetamine on children's physical health or on the hazardous conditions that children are exposed to, including fires and explosions resulting from methamphetamine production in their homes (Cretzmeyer, Sarrazin, Huber, Block & Hall, 2003; Grant, 2007; Hohman, Oliver & Wright, 2004; Smith, Chang, Yonekura, Grob, Osborn & Ernst et al., 2001).

There has been some suggestion by child welfare professionals that recruiting and retaining foster parents for children from methamphetamine-involved families is difficult because they often have serious behavior problems (Zernicke, 2005). In rural areas, these problems can be compounded by the large distances these families must travel to reach specialized services to support children's recovery.

The research reported in this chapter employs a mixed-methods design (Cresswell, Fetters & Ivankova, 2004; Tashakkori & Teddlie, 2003), utilizing case records, child interviews, and child and caregiver standardized assessments. By combining qualitative and quantitative methods, we aim to provide a more complete account of children's perceptions and functioning. Children who have been reared by parents who misuse methamphetamine may display patterns of denial and poor communication that characterize families who misuse other substances (e.g., Black, 2001; Kroll, 2004), especially given the illegal nature of methamphetamine. By drawing upon both standardized assessments completed by foster mothers and children, and semi-structured interviews with children, we provide multiple opportunities for children to communicate, and for the triangulation of child and caregiver reports.

In this chapter, we address two issues pertaining to children's psychological functioning. First, what are children's emotional and social experiences in their families? We pay particular attention to how children characterize their family experiences, the emotions they express, the social support they identify, and the strategies they describe for coping with challenges they faced within their families. Second, we consider children's mental health, including any clinical or subclinical scores on standardized assessments that indicate trauma and behavioral problems.

Children's Emotional and Social Experiences

We first examined children's psychological functioning through their responses to the in-depth, individual interviews (see Chapters 3 and 7). Similar to children's discussions of methamphetamine and experiences related to their parents' methamphetamine misuse in Chapter 7, children's discussions of their social and emotional experiences in their families varied. During interviews, 17 of the 29 children (59%) expressed clear emotional pain when describing their experiences within their families. Some children spontaneously reported feelings of "tension," "fear," and "misery." Others expressed feelings of intense anger or sadness. Some children discussed nightmares and wanting to cut themselves, as well as recurrent fears. One child, for instance, noted that she woke up often at night thinking "that somebody's going to shoot me or somebody's after me. Every time I look out the widow, I think I see somebody." Three children reported suicidal ideation or behavior. One older child who tried drugs came close to serious harm. As this girl stated, "I had myself a knife, and I was high, and I was drunk, and everything else, and I about cut myself here." Another child told the interviewer that she feels intense sadness when reminded of the times when her mother wasn't there. She summed up her feelings by stating that she has "a lot of history that really hurts." In contrast, 12 children (41%) reported more neutral or positive emotional experiences in their families of origin. One child, for instance, talked about the "freedom" he enjoyed at home. He enjoyed visiting with friends and neighbors and staying out late at night.

Many children reported difficult family relationships. Eighteen children (62%) reported ambivalent or negative relationships with their parents. Some children described having lost a parent, feeling a lack of trust in the parent (e.g., parents lied or broke promises), or lack of care from a parent (e.g., feeling that parents cared more about "meth" than about them). As one child said, "I just liked getting away from the house. . . . There was too much arguing, too much stress." One child continued to worry about his parents' well-being; another stated that she felt abandoned by her mother, but noted, "when I was with my mom, I always had someone to go to if I was scared or anything." One child described her parents "always lying" and underscored that "they didn't care what I did." In contrast, five children (17%) described relationships with their parents as primarily positive, even though these adults were not consistently available to them physically and emotionally.

Twenty-one children (72%) talked about relationships with siblings at home. For 10 children (35%), the descriptions were positive or neutral. Five children (17%) described negative experiences. One child, for instance, described physical assaults by his older brothers when they abused substances. Five children (17%) described parentified behavior (e.g., feeding younger siblings, holding a younger sibling who was crying during parental fights). Three children (10%) felt they had lost a sibling relationship. (Note that these categories are not mutually exclusive. Some children, for example, described both a lost sibling relationship and current positive relationships with other siblings.)

Many children reported relatively few social resources for coping with emotional pain at home. Fifteen children (52%) reported that they felt isolated from adults in their families of origin and received little scaffolding from them to understand what was happening at home. To deal with family problems, 10 children (35%) reported that they used avoidance or passive strategies. While adults were using drugs, these children described staying away from home, getting out of the way, waiting until adults were no longer intoxicated, going to their rooms, ignoring or daydreaming, or listening to music through headphones. As one child noted, "I don't talk to anybody. I just listen to my CD player." Four children (14%) joined in the violence to protect their mothers or siblings from an intoxicated adult male.

Other children were able to identify social resources they had used to cope with emotional pain and difficult family relationships. Six children

(21%) reported talking to a grandparent, two (7%) to a parent, two to the Drug Abuse Resistance Education (DARE) officer providing substance misuse prevention education at school, two to another adult, and two to a close child friend. (Note again that these categories are not mutually exclusive.) Some children reported positive coping strategies. Three adolescents (10%), for instance, turned to religion. One found a safe haven in talking to her preacher, who "won't say anything." Another reported that "putting God first" and going to church and praying regularly protected and guided him, giving him strength. One child drew on internal resources through writing down her experiences in a journal.

Fourteen children (48%) perceived that talking about their parent's methamphetamine misuse was taboo. Three children explicitly said, "we don't tell no one." Ten reported that they could not discuss experiences they had with other adults or siblings. As reasons for the silence, several children noted a fear of adults. As a 9-year-old girl explained, "I was always afraid to go over to my neighbors because I thought that if I did, [mother's paramour] was going to hunt me down and come get me." Other reasons included not wanting to get parents in trouble, fear of being taken away from parents, adults not wanting to know or be involved, or a lack of emotional or geographical closeness to relatives. One child reported teasing as a reason for not talking. He told how a child taunted him at school by repeatedly whispering to him, "meth daddy." Although this child ignored the taunts, he noted afterward, "I'd just want to bash his head in."

We also considered how children talked about their family experiences. Children responded to the invitation to talk about their families in a variety of ways. Eleven children (38%) had marked difficulties in the semi-structured interview in openly discussing their experiences at home. Five children (17%) explicitly denied any parent involvement with methamphetamine. In some cases, this denial contained inconsistencies, or it was contradicted by other sources. One child, for instance, stated that she had never seen adults use methamphetamine, but later provided a detailed account of a methamphetamine user's "hyper" and "wacko" behavior. Two children refused to talk about parent substance misuse, pointedly ignoring the interviewer's questions. Another seemed to want to cooperate, but became so choked up emotionally that he was unable to articulate any narrative of parental methamphetamine misuse. Three other children cast themselves in the unlikely role of a rescuer, providing heroic tales of how they handled situations. One young child, for instance, provided an unlikely account of bursting into a shed where adults were using, knocking the "meth" off the table, and castigating her parents, who then discontinued their drug misuse.

Fourteen of the children (48%) provided a straightforward, factual report of parental methamphetamine misuse. Many of these accounts focused on concrete events: For example, "I heard the window break," or the reactions of others, "Mom was crying," and were markedly impoverished with respect to the child's own feelings, for example, of fear or horror.

Children's Mental Health

We also considered children's psychological functioning through their responses to standardized mental health assessments: The Childhood Behavior Checklist (CBCL) and the Trauma Symptom Checklist for Children (TSCC). Although some individual variation occurred, most children did display some mental health problems. As indicated by Table 8.1, 15 children (52%) scored in the clinically significant ($n = 12$) or borderline clinically significant ($n = 3$) range on the CBCL total score. Fourteen children (48%) scored in the clinical or borderline range for externalizing, and 12 (41%) for internalizing problems. Seventeen children (59%) scored in the clinical or borderline range on two or more narrow-band scales. The most common narrow-band

Table 8.1 Children's mental health functioning according to the CBCL

CBCL Sub-Scale	Mean (T-score)	SD	# of children scoring in clinically significant or borderline range (CS/BC)
Withdrawn/Depressed	58.79	9.90	3/5
Somatic Complaints	54	5.0	0/1
Anxious/Depressed	57.03	8.85	3/5
Social Problems	55.76	12.61	3/2
Thought Problems	62.24	9.18	7/6
Rule-breaking Behavior	59.48	9.57	8/1
Aggressive Behavior	61.14	11.70	4/8
Attention Problems	61.24	9.31	4/6
Internalizing	54.24	12.59	8/4
Externalizing	58.17	13.65	12/2
Total Score	58.21	13.44	12/3

CS/BC: The first number refers to how many children scored in the "clinically significant" or CS range; the second number refers to how many children scored in the "borderline clinical" or BC range. Note: Children can have scores on multiple scales.

clinical or subclinical scores were on thought problems (45% of children), aggressive behavior (41%), attention problems (35%), rule breaking (31%), and withdrawn/depressed (38%) and anxious/depressed (28%). Only one children scored in the subclinical range on somatic complaints. Children's scores were not related to age, gender, or other demographic variables.

Children's mean score on the CBCL dissociation/posttraumatic scale was 5.7 (SD = 3.8, range = 0–12). Sixteen children (55%) received a score of 6 or higher on this scale, suggesting significant dissociative symptoms. Dissociation scores were not linked age, gender, or other demographic variables.

Eight children (28%) had invalid TSCC protocols due to clinically significant scores on the underreporting scale (n = 7), or hyper-reporting scale (n = 1). Of the 21 children with valid TSCC protocols, 18 (86%) scored in the clinically significant (n = 4) or borderline (n = 14) range on one (n = 6) or more (n = 12) of the TSCC subscales. As shown in Table 8.2, the most frequently indicated scales were anger (one clinical, nine subclinical = 48% of children), posttraumatic stress disorder (nine children, borderline range = 43%), dissociative (one clinical, eight borderline range = 43%), depression (one clinical, seven borderline = 38%), and anxiety (one clinical, seven borderline = 28%). The TSCC scores were not linked to gender or to any demographic variables.

Both the CBCL and the TSCC were instruments that had limitations. The validity of some CBCL scores was called into question; for example,

Table 8.2 Children's trauma symptoms according to the TSCC

Subscale	Mean (T-score)	SD	# children scoring in clinically significant or borderline range (CS/BC)
Under-response	58.41	13.76	7/3
Hyper-response	50.31	12.33	1/0
Anxiety	45.59	10.21	1/7
Depression	45.07	10.40	1/7
Anger	47.21	13.26	1/9
PTSD	45.55	8.93	0/9
Dissociation	46.03	8.74	1/8

CS/BC: The first number refers to how many children scored in the "clinically significant" or CS range; the second number refers to how many children scored in the "borderline clinical" or BC range. Note: Children can have scores on multiple scales. N = 21 children with valid scores.

some new foster parents had relatively little knowledge of the child in their care at the time of the data collection. As discussed earlier, a number of TSCC scores were invalid primarily because of under-reporting. Therefore, we attempted to gain perspective by merging these two instruments. Summarizing across standardized assessments, of the children with valid TSCC protocols and CBCL protocols ($n = 21$), 17 (81%) received scores indicating they had significant or borderline posttraumatic or dissociative symptoms. Of these children, six received borderline or clinically significant scores on both measures, five received elevated or clinically significant scores on the TSCC only; six scored on or above our clinical cutoff (score of 6 or higher) on the CBCL dissociative/posttraumatic scale.

Conclusion

With increasing numbers of children entering foster care because of parental methamphetamine misuse, an urgent need exists to understand the psychological well-being and mental health functioning of involved children. Yet, to our knowledge, this is the first study to describe the mental health needs and perspectives of children in foster care because of parental methamphetamine misuse.

Most children described difficult family relationships at home, including losing trust in the parent, worrying about the parent's well-being, and feeling abandoned and neglected by the parent. A number of children, however, reported supportive relationships with extended family members, grandparents, aunts, and uncles, who may be tapped as resources for children during their recovery from parental methamphetamine misuse. A number of children also reported positive or at least neutral relationships with siblings, and these, too, can be tapped as continuing sources of comfort and support for children.

In general, children reported few social resources for coping with emotional pain or understanding what was happening at home. Many described passive or avoidant coping strategies. Many children found open discussion of their experiences difficult, and required support and scaffolding from the evaluators. Children's perceived lack of social scaffolding or support to talk about feelings at home, socialization not to talk about their families and their homes to outsiders, and passive or avoidant coping strategies, all could have contributed to their denying problems or suppressing their intensity (Bowlby, 1988), as reflected by their relatively high levels of under-reporting on the TSCC.

Use of standardized assessments allows some preliminary comparisons with other samples. Consistent with findings on children of parents who misuse alcohol (Fals-Stewart et al., 2004) and other substances (Luthar et al., 1998), the study documented a high level of mental health needs. Many of the children displayed significant emotional or behavior problems on the CBCL and posttraumatic or dissociative symptoms on the CBCL or TSCC.

Other studies using the CBCL estimate that between 34% and 50% of children in foster care may exhibit significant behavioral or emotional problems (Clausen, Landsverk, Ganger, Chadwick & Litrownik, 1998; Halfon, Mendonca & Berkowitz, 1995, McIntyre & Keesler, 1986). The prevalence of problems in this sample, then, is at the higher end of rates for children in foster care. Children's reluctance to speak openly, and their tendency to under-report symptoms, may have contributed, however, to an underestimation of the extent of their mental health symptoms. If untreated or under-treated, these problems could jeopardize their future well-being and mental health. Although more research clearly is necessary, our data do have several implications for social workers and other social and health services providers.

Social workers and other service providers should be aware of the complexities in assessing the mental health needs of children exposed to parental methamphetamine misuse. Multiple sources and informants will be needed to assess children's mental health. Several children reported that their parents told them not to talk to outsiders about family problems, reported that it was a taboo topic or source of social stigma, and/or reported punishment following disclosure to outsider adults. In addition, many children found discussing their families of origin emotionally painful. Not surprisingly, a number of children obtained invalid TSCC protocols because of an under-reporting of symptoms. In addition, foster parents had varying levels of knowledge about their foster children and the conditions under which they had been reared. For example, several children who scored high on the TSCC, but not on the CBCL, were new to their foster homes. For children in relative care, we found some caregivers reluctant to admit to any problems in their charges.

In addition, children from methamphetamine-involved families may require mental health services for trauma symptoms as well as other significant emotional and behavioral problems. Such interventions will be most effective if children establish trusting and continuous relationships with a therapist (Bowlby, 1988). In this relationship, it will be essential to reassure children that they are safe. Helping children to overcome taboos or fears of talking about their families will be an important component of the intervention. For children who show dissociation, the role of the therapist will be to provide the conditions (a sense of support, safety) under which children can begin to explore and make sense of their feelings and experiences.

For children who have passive and avoidant coping skills, clinicians may need to help them to contain painful feelings and experiences (Symington & Symington, 1999), to understand the limits of their options as children, and to correct distortions that they may have caused, encouraged, or been to blame for what has occurred in their families (Bowlby, 1988). Helping foster parents to support a child's recovery and to understand the complexity of each child's experience, without condemnation, are other essential therapeutic components.

Chapter Nine

Narrative of a Midwestern Psychiatrist

Our research collaboration included a number of individuals with extensive experience in practice and research. These practitioner-scholars brought a broad perspective to our research program. In this chapter, we once again depart from our traditional academic discussion to present the narrative of a professional practicing in rural Illinois. James Black, MD, PhD, a professor of psychiatry at Southern Illinois University and practicing psychiatrist, has over 12 years of postresidency clinical experience in rural mental health centers, inpatient psychiatric units, and prisons in Illinois during the methamphetamine crisis.

My medical experience in Illinois began in the 1980s, when I enrolled in medical school at the University of Illinois at Urbana-Champaign. During that time, we heard very little about methamphetamine misuse. The Veteran's Administration (VA) Hospital, where some of our training occurred, was in Danville, a small city outside of Urbana-Champaign, which at the time employed many citizens in a General Motors auto plant, a steel plant, a cannery, and the VA Hospital. In subsequent years, Danville experienced significant financial stress after the auto plant, steel plant, and cannery all closed, and the VA Hospital downsized. Poverty, despair, and a perceived lack of opportunity may have contributed to Danville becoming a hotspot of crystal methamphetamine misuse.

When the problems of methamphetamine misuse were just beginning in Illinois, however, I was in Salt Lake City, Utah, completing my psychiatry residency at the University of Utah from 1991 to 1995. During that period in Utah, crack cocaine was a bigger problem than methamphetamine, still largely controlled by outlaw motorcycle gangs. My residency training in addiction medicine focused primarily on alcohol, marijuana, and cocaine, with prescription drug abuse and heroin as other common problems. In Utah, as in Illinois, however, this situation was to change rapidly. In 1997, there were 1992 admissions for substance misuse treatment for methamphetamine addiction and 2238 for cocaine addiction in Utah. By 2001, there were

Rural Illinois in winter. Photo by Carl Kingery.

3785 treatment admissions for methamphetamine and 1620 admissions for cocaine. Heroin admissions were relatively steady at 1524 and 1567, respectively. To fight the growing drug problem, the Utah State Legislature appropriated about $1.6 million annually from tobacco settlement money to fund drug courts, with 2300 citizens participating in 2005. At that time, methamphetamine was the primary substance of misuse for 40% of drug court participants (Utah Division of Substance misuse and Mental Health, 2005).

Following my residency training, I returned to Illinois, where I have worked in both rural counties and medium-sized cities. My consistent observation is that on the inpatient psychiatry units in the medium-sized cities of Peoria, Springfield, and Urbana-Champaign, the primary stimulant that is misused is cocaine, with crystal methamphetamine accounting for less than 5% of stimulant misuse. My colleagues in rural communities such as Olney and Mattoon, however, find that crystal methamphetamine is the primary problem, with up to half of their inpatient psychiatry beds occupied by patients suffering from crystal methamphetamine complications like suicidality or psychosis. Given that this is a recent change, and these small communities have relatively few psychiatric beds or doctors, and the patients typically do not have insurance, methamphetamine misuse has been a problem not only for those afflicted, but for rural hospitals and other medical service providers.

My clinical experiences working in Illinois during the methamphetamine crisis echo many of the themes elaborated by recovering mothers, knowledgeable adults, and children in Part 2 of this book. Their accounts are strikingly similar to those of my patients, including their motivations to begin using methamphetamine, the power of the addiction, the impact of the addiction on them and their families, and the difficulties of recovery. The following case descriptions (all of which have been disguised), illustrate some of the issues encountered by rural health and mental health care providers during the methamphetamine crisis of the 1990s and 2000s.

Given the dangers of methamphetamine misuse, understanding why individuals begin to misuse this drug is important to prevention efforts. Some of the patients I've seen began using methamphetamine for functional reasons, such as to stay awake or work longer hours. One of my patients, for example, was a truck driver who began using crystal methamphetamine to stay awake while driving. He was admitted to the hospital after becoming depressed and suicidal. He was in the "tweaking" stage, having a great deal of difficulty thinking clearly, but was willing to stay in the hospital and take medication. At one point in his stay, he became irritable for no apparent reason and, without warning, slammed his fist through a security-glass window, requiring stitches and a cast. He was later observed on camera to be standing on his bedside table preparing, as he explained later, to kill himself by jumping out of the fifth-floor window. Although he could walk, talk, and was fully oriented, he was unable to participate in groups or interviews due to cognitive impairment from methamphetamine misuse. He improved slowly with high-dose antipsychotics over a week, and was discharged on medication. He refused drug rehabilitation, stating that he could quit methamphetamine on his own as he had done many times before. His current status is unknown.

Other patients apparently begin using methamphetamine as part of a long history of substance misuse and other untreated mental illnesses. One of my patients, for example, was a homeless alcoholic man in his 50s who had been sober for some years and was admitted to the psychiatric unit for acute psychotic symptoms. He was working as a house painter and began using methamphetamine for energy to do the work. He enjoyed the methamphetamine, and didn't see any problem with using it. About 10 years earlier, he had convinced a doctor to prescribe Ritalin for attention deficit/hyperactivity disorder (ADHD), but instead of using it therapeutically, he had similarly used it for extra energy. He didn't see any relationship between the two events. He also complained of a bad back, and his current physician was prescribing large amounts of OxyContin, which he also was apparently misusing with no insight about substance misuse. His crystal methamphetamine problem caused hallucinations and delusions that he was infested with bugs, resulting in his scratching at imaginary bugs in and on his arms. The infestation was so bothersome that he developed deep lacerations and abscesses requiring intravenous antibiotics and a psychiatric admission. He accepted the antibiotics as treatment for the "bugs." He did not see himself as mentally ill, and refused psychiatric medications, but eventually accepted our antipsychotics because they helped him to sleep. During his hospital stay, he never acknowledged that the bugs were not real or that he had had any psychotic symptoms. However, within a few days of treatment, his symptoms receded and he was ready to be discharged. He refused rehab, but agreed to take psychiatric medications prescribed by his primary care doctor in his home town. We also wrote a letter to his primary care doctor about his psychosis and abuse of medications. His current status is unknown.

Some of my patients began using methamphetamine socially. In Peoria, for example, I treated a young, white, single man who was a "raver." He was unhappy with what he considered to be the dull party scene in Peoria, and sought out the parties in Chicago. He described himself as a connoisseur of methamphetamine. He had been using heavily and had started tweaking, becoming depressed, irritable, and suicidal. He felt he knew more about methamphetamine than the staff did, and told us how to manage his symptoms. He felt that, with a couple of days support and rest, he would be ready to leave. He explained that he used only the best quality crystal and was fond of a brand imported from Siberia via Alaska and favored at raves. We discharged him 2 days later, but he refused rehab or any follow-up care. His current status is unknown.

Regardless of their pathways into methamphetamine misuse, many of my patients have experienced the power of the addiction. For example, an inmate I saw in a prison located in rural Illinois suffered from posttraumatic stress disorder (PTSD). He had been a methamphetamine "cook," and was badly injured when his clandestine methamphetamine laboratory exploded and burned off his corneas. He received government medical assistance for cornea transplants and regained his vision. However, his methamphetamine addiction remained dangerously active. He continued to use, and soon was manufacturing again in order to obtain more drugs. He soon had another explosive accident that burned his corneas off again. He regained his vision from yet another corneal transplant, but this time his prison sentence is extended, hopefully long enough for him to fully recover from his addiction.

Another of my patients had been out of prison a few hours when he got into trouble with crystal meth. At a party with his friends, they gave him a special present of a large pile of white powder, which he immediately dunked his face in to inhale. The result was cardiac arrest, delirium, paranoia, and a brief stay on the intensive care unit. He transferred to inpatient psychiatry for further stabilization with powerful antipsychotics. He left after a few days, no longer psychotic but uninterested in further treatment. Given his status as drug addicted, the State of Illinois program to cover hospital care for uninsured patients did not pay for his ICU/psychiatry stay.

When rural hospitals and doctors see significant numbers of such patients, they can experience financial burdens.

Clearly, methamphetamine can have many serious effects on the user. As a psychiatrist, I am perhaps most aware of the cognitive and psychiatric effects. For example, in Peoria, I treated a young white woman in her 20s from an adjacent, rural county. She came into the hospital with a florid psychosis, having not slept for 5 days during a methamphetamine binge. Her children were in the care of their grandmother. She needed inpatient hospitalization because she was severely confused. The psychosis cleared quickly, but the confusion did not. We did brain imaging and other testing to make sure that she had not had a stroke or other illness. As best we could determine, she had minimal brain atrophy due to chronic methamphetamine misuse. After several weeks, she was discharged to a residential rehabilitation program and then outpatient follow-up in her home county. A few months later, she was readmitted to the psychiatry unit with similar symptoms after another methamphetamine binge. She again recovered slowly, and was once again referred to residential rehabilitation. We understand that she had several more relapses until she was sentenced to prison and her children placed in foster care. A major contributor to her relapse was her inability to think clearly due to methamphetamine-related brain damage. Her cognitive difficulty with tasks of ordinary living, such as holding a job, maintaining a family or relationship, or resisting urges to use, made it difficult to remain clean and sober.

At the peak of the methamphetamine crisis, some of my colleagues in rural hospitals reported that patients suffering from methamphetamine-induced psychosis comprised up to half of their patient populations. Patients with methamphetamine-induced psychosis also presented to hospitals in the small cities in which I practiced. For example, in Peoria, I treated a young white woman, aged 25, who had been misusing methamphetamine in one of the adjoining rural counties. She was admitted for severe psychosis and agitation. As is often the case with methamphetamine- induced psychosis, her symptoms did not respond quickly to antipsychotics. Her behavior was dangerous enough that she needed an involuntary inpatient stay. One of her delusions was that she was to participate in a music video in Florida. She believed that she could obtain the airline ticket, the doctor's discharge order, and record contract by simply wishing it so. During her whole hospital stay, she made no mention of her family, including three young children. Her psychosis eventually cleared, and she was returned to her family and outpatient rehabilitation.

Some of the psychiatric symptoms we see may not only be the result of methamphetamine-related damage to the brain per se, but also to experiences associated with methamphetamine misuse, especially exposure to violence.

One of the most psychiatrically-disabled patients I worked with at a rural prison was a young man who had been heavily involved in using and dealing methamphetamine. While on a "speed run," one of his friends became violently paranoid toward the patient's girlfriend and murdered her while they were driving around in the car. He then threatened to kill the patient, put the murdered girlfriend in the backseat with the patient, and drove around for a day. The combined experience of being high on methamphetamine, being threatened, and riding in the backseat with his dead girlfriend was sufficient to render the patient severely ill with PTSD and dissociative symptoms.

In my practice, I also glimpse the devastating impact methamphetamine can have on families. One of the inmates I saw for depression at a rural Illinois state prison was struggling with child custody issues. He and his wife were arrested for producing methamphetamine and sentenced to prison. They struck a plea bargain, so that the wife could be released earlier and regain custody of the couple's children from the Department of Children and Family Services (DCFS). She had been released as planned, and was taking care of the children. When I saw the father, however, he believed that his wife was refusing to let their children visit him in prison. Like many men in prison, he was worried that she was going to leave him and take custody of the children. He felt helpless and vulnerable to being exploited by his wife and DCFS. He was especially angry at DCFS because he viewed their treatment of fathers as unfair, a complaint echoed by other of my patients.

As we have elaborated in this book, the effects of parental methamphetamine misuse on children can be devastating. I recently interviewed a child who had been admitted to the children's psychiatric inpatient unit for disruptive behavior at school and a severe depression. We initially had some concerns about whether he was exaggerating about the amount of violence in his life, or whether he might even be quietly psychotic, because he described having been close to four adults who had hanged themselves recently. His family, however, corroborated his account. His small community had been hit hard by crystal methamphetamine, with a resulting cluster of suicides among his extended family. Part of this child's treatment would include psychotherapy to address his grieving.

Although many of the family members, friends, and neighbors of my patients addicted to methamphetamine become discouraged, recovery is possible. One of my recent patients, a white man in his 50s with long gray hair and numerous tattoos, has been clean from methamphetamine for decades. He openly discussed his IV methamphetamine misuse, and was proud of his sobriety. He had kicked his habit in the Arizona state prison, which he described as one of the toughest prisons in the United States, and had held a blue-collar job for years to support his family. He was happily married with two children. He presented to us for chronic pain and associated depression. His recovery from methamphetamine addiction seemed stable and was not a focus of our treatment.

Recovery, however, can be extremely difficult, especially without adequate treatment. One of my patients was a woman in her 30s with one young child. She presented for psychiatric care after release from an Illinois state prison. She had developed bipolar disorder after becoming addicted to crystal methamphetamine that she used to treat pain and fatigue due to a severe medical problem. She quickly advanced from using methamphetamine to producing methamphetamine in the home. Her child was placed in foster care, and she was sentenced to prison. Even though she had gotten clean in prison, her mood swings wouldn't go away, and she felt that she was on the edge of losing her sanity. With great effort, she had managed to stay clean outside of prison for a year. We prescribed a mood stabilizer to help her become less impulsive and more emotionally stable. The psychiatric medications were quite helpful for further recovery, but one of her strongest motivations was to stay healthy and get her child back from DCFS.

Conclusion

In this chapter, I have described a few of my experiences as a psychiatrist working in central Illinois. My patients include those who have become ill and disabled through misuse of methamphetamine. They are not necessarily representative of people who misuse methamphetamine, or even of psychiatric patients addicted to methamphetamine. Their stories, however, echo the accounts of the mothers, children, and knowledgeable adults described in Chapters 5–8. They also provide a flavor of psychiatric practice in Illinois during the methamphetamine crisis of the 1990s and 2000s.

Part Three

Meeting the Mental Health Needs of Rural Children in Foster Families

Chapter Ten

Conceptual and Empirical Bases of Life Story Intervention for Rural Foster Children

As we visited communities and towns in East Central Illinois to gather ethnographic data on parental methamphetamine misuse, teachers, principals, child welfare workers, and other local professionals often asked us about what could be done to help affected children and families. At that time, regional child welfare offices were flooded with investigations of parents suspected of misusing and producing methamphetamine. Educational systems also were becoming increasingly overwhelmed with the multiple needs of affected children in rural areas. Articles appeared daily in local newspapers describing new police raids on Mom and Pop meth labs, or individuals caught at a pharmacy purchasing precursors for methamphetamine production, and many articles noted the presence of children. Given that we came from a large land-grant university whose charter underscored the need to address relevant needs of the region, some community appeals for information and support were directed to us.

As professionals who work with children both clinically and in research, we began to discuss how we might help. Often these discussions took place during "windshield time," a term coined by Linda Kingery to describe the thinking that goes on as rural child welfare workers drive from one family to another, sometimes covering distances of more than 100 miles per day. Windshield time also encompassed many hours on the road during our own field work and participant observations in rural Illinois. It was during these drives by barns, corn and soy fields, through small towns, and down lanes "3 miles from the last barn," that we first began serious discussion of an appropriate intervention to help rural children affected by parental methamphetamine misuse.

Rural Illinois in summer Photo by Carl Kingery.

We designed Life Story Intervention for use with individual rural children (aged 7–17) affected by parental methamphetamine misuse. The overarching goal is to help rural foster children who are struggling psychologically onto healthier developmental trajectories; that is, to enhance their mental health and overall well-being. In Life Story Intervention, this enhancement occurs through personal storytelling, a culturally familiar and widespread practice. Through co-constructing stories with a supportive adult, children can begin to consider and express their memories, feelings, and thoughts about their lives through a "gentler tone, slower pace, a different use of the mind" (Coles, 1989, p. 14). During storytelling, children are encouraged to take an active role in making sense of their experiences and, in so doing, create a sense of continuity in their lives (Holmes, 2001). Through narrative, children can gain perspective on difficulties and see the trauma they experienced as only one part of their lives. Such perspective-taking can help children to disentangle themselves from dysfunctional ways of thinking and find healthy ways to promote development.

A central feature of Life Story Intervention is the relationship children develop with an adult skilled at supporting children's mental health. Few of the communities in which the rural children in our study lived, however, had specialized mental health services for tramatized children from which to recruit such adults. Their communities did, however, have rural professionals used to assuming multiple roles in support of children. For example, we met a teacher who routinely put food in the backpacks of children from substance-involved families, a child welfare professional affectionately greeted as "Ms. DCFS" by children from her client families residing in a rural trailer park, and an elementary school principal who allowed a little girl whose mother was involved with methamphetamine to stay after school to "help" her plant spring flowers. We recruited "community clinicians": master's-level social workers, counselors, educators, and child welfare workers who work with children professionally. They each implemented Life Story Intervention with one or two children, and we provided them with weekly, ongoing training and supervision. Life Story Intervention thus involved considerable collaboration between university-based researchers and locally based professionals.

Life Story Intervention was designed by a transdisciplinary team, including a child clinical psychologist, counselor, teacher, psychiatrist, developmental psychologist, child welfare professional, and social worker. Life Story Intervention is evidence-informed (Gambrill, 2000, 2003). It draws upon our descriptive, ethnographic research on parental methamphetamine misuse and children's psychological functioning described in Part 2; empirical research on the treatment of trauma in children who have experienced family violence (e.g., Lieberman, Compton, Van Horn & Ghosh-Ippen, 2003); the American Association of Child and Adolescent Psychiatry (AACAP) guidelines for intervention with children who have experienced trauma (American Academy of Child and Adolescent Psychiatry, 1998); clinical discussions of children from substance-involved families (e.g., Black, 2001; Freeman, 1993; Kroll, 2004); and the considerable clinical experience of team members who have assessed and treated traumatized children in foster care who are affected by parental substance misuse and mental illness.

The overarching conceptual framework of Life Story Intervention is sociocultural. From this perspective, effective interventions necessarily are transdisciplinary and address biological, psychological, and social components of development as they interact and are shaped within a particular sociocultural-historical context. In considering "context," we draw on Bronfenbrenner's (1979; Bronfenbrenner & Morris, 2006) interacting levels of social ecology critical to human development, including the microsystem, mesosystem, ecosystem, and macrosystem. To these levels, Dolores Norton (n.d.) added the focal system: the analytic vantage point of the ecological analysis and perspective from which related systems are viewed, which, in Life Story Intervention, is the child. In later formulations of his ecological model (e.g., see Bronfenbrenner & Morris, 2006), Bronfenbrenner discussed the chronological system—in other words, the historical context in which development is embedded and shaped. We underscore here that our understanding of parental methamphetamine misuse and intervention for children is based in the rapidly changing policy context and drug misuse patterns of the early twenty-first century.

In this chapter, we provide an overview of the conceptual and empirical bases of Life Story Intervention. We begin by highlighting how understanding of the macrosystem of rural Illinois shaped our choice of intervention strategy. Then, we discuss how specific biological, psychological, and social aspects of children's development are addressed in the context of micro-, meso-, and exosystems. In Chapter 11, we detail the clinical implementation of Life Story Intervention.

Addressing Children's Development in Sociocultural Context Through the Macrosystem

According to Bronfenbrenner (1979), "The macrosystem refers to the consistency observed within a given culture or subculture in the form and content of its constituent micro-, meso-, and exosystems, as well as any belief systems or ideology underlying such consistencies" (p. 258). From our sociocultural perspective, careful examination of the macrosystem as it permeates all other levels of the social ecology is a prerequisite to the design of a culturally appropriate intervention. The cultural patterns of the rural Midwestern community (see Part 2) were a primary consideration in the design of Life Story Intervention.

Although much progress has been made in the development and implementation of mental health interventions for children, limitations remain regarding the cultural sensitivity and appropriateness of many interventions. For example, much progress has been made in substance misuse prevention research over the past two decades (e.g., Dishion, 1996; Etz, Robertson & Ashery, 1998; Kumpfer, Olds, Alexander, Zucker & Gary, 1996), but challenges remain regarding the implementation of effective interventions for culturally diverse families (see Spoth, Kavanagh & Dishion, 2002). The limited research with culturally adapted prevention programs suggests these adaptations can enhance effectiveness with non mainstream families (Kumpfer et al., 2002). Existing cultural adaptations, however, have been criticized as superficial—for example, changing photos to depict the targeted group. Researchers have argued that a deeper understanding of cultural context will lead to stronger outcomes (e.g., Spoth et al., 2002; Kumpfer et al., 1996). Therefore, several features of Life Story Intervention are designed to enhance its cultural appropriateness.

Life Story Intervention Involves Collaboration with Local Professionals

Life Story Intervention builds on existing psychotherapeutic interventions for children (e.g., Holmes, 2001; Lieberman et al., 2003, 2005), adapted to the cultural context of the rural Midwest through collaboration with local professionals. How adults support children and help them to understand and respond to their experiences, including parental methamphetamine misuse, reflects their culturally constituted socialization beliefs. Groups differ in their folk theories about the nature of children and development, in the practices used to encourage development, and in the principles that organize interaction (Shweder et al., 2006). For example, the pattern of sustained, dyadic conversation and mutual negotiation of meaning between adults and children familiar to middle-class European Americans is but one variant among many. Evidence from North American families suggests that normative socialization strategies for helping children through adverse life events, including the perceived appropriateness of direct discussion, vary across communities in relation to culturally specific belief systems (Burger & Miller, 1999; Cho & Miller, 2004). By collaborating with local professionals, we enhance the possibility that the intervention, by design and in its implementation, will reflect local socialization beliefs—in other words, that it will "make sense" to the child and the child's family. We also increase the likelihood that the intervention will be sustainable, as the clinicians may utilize it with other children in similar circumstances in their communities.

Life Story Intervention Brings the Treatment to the Child

The cultural appropriateness of Life Story Intervention also is enhanced by providing the intervention to children within a community context in and around their homes. For some foster parents in rural communities, a trip to yet another "provider" leads to resistance to participation or missed visits. Bringing the intervention to the home also can facilitate the participation of children. When the clinician travels to see them individually and on their own turf, children can feel valued and cared for, a rare experience for some foster children.

Providing an intervention to children within a context familiar and emotionally meaningful to them has other benefits as well. The community context is rich in cues for children to talk about their life experiences. For example, one child began discussing his father for the first time after he saw a truck like the one his father drove. Another child told a narrative of when he was taken into foster care while visiting his former school, and of his previous experiences in foster care while driving past his various foster homes. Going to the home setting and having regular contact with foster parents also provides invaluable information about the child's relationships with family and community members. It also provides an opportunity to learn from foster parents' observations, and to exchange information, for example, about the goals of Life Story Intervention.

Life Story Intervention is Narrative-based

Life Story Intervention employs narratives of personal experience as a central component of a culturally appropriate intervention. "Narrative is a cultural universal, and one of the most powerful interpretive tools that human beings possess for organizing experience in time and for interpreting and valuing human action" (Shweder et al., 2006, p. 744). Oral narratives are basic to socializing children into the meaning systems of their cultures (e.g., Bruner, 1986; 1990; Fivush, 1993; Miller, Wiley, Fung & Liang, 1997; Nelson, 1988; Sperry & Sperry, 1995) including in rural (Sperry & Sperry, 1996) and working-class families (Miller & Moore, 1989). Children from a wide range of cultural communities within and beyond the United States participate in storytelling during routine conversations with adults, beginning very early in development (e.g., Fivush, 1993; Heath, 1996; Hodge, Pasqua, Marquez & Geishirt-Cantrell, 2002; Shweder et al., 2006; Wiley, Rose, Burger & Miller, 1998), and they also overhear emotionally and socially significant stories told around them by others (Shweder et al., 2006). Each story provides an opportunity for the child to hear which events are significant and how they are experienced and assessed.

Although storytelling appears to be a cultural universal, stories do vary systematically within and across cultures along many dimensions (Shweder et al., 2006) that may or may not be consciously accessible or articulated by community members. Sociocultural contexts vary in the types of events that are acceptable or preferred topics for narratives. Such preferences may even shape children's developmental trajectories. For example, developmental analyses of everyday talk revealed that young boys and their rural, working-class, African-American caregivers preferred producing narratives about the self involving fictional events rather than literal past events (Sperry & Sperry, 1996), as were preferred, for example, by young girls and their white, urban, working-class mothers (Miller & Moore, 1989). In this community, where both children and their caregivers frequently enjoyed telling thrilling fantasy stories (Sperry & Sperry, 1996), young boys' participation in fantasy stories preceded, developmentally, stories of actual personal experience. By collaborating with those adults from within the rural community who have professional experience working with children, we enhance the likelihood that they will adhere to implicit cultural conventions for storytelling, thus facilitating children's abilities to tell their stories.

Of the various genres, stories involving the actual experiences of the narrator emerge early in development, and these occur habitually in the language of children and adults from a wide variety of cultural communities, including white, working-class communities (Shweder et al., 2006; Miller & Moore, 1989). The process of retelling and revising stories of personal experience is basic to the socialization process and is assumed to be transformative in a wide variety of developmental theories (Shweder et al., 2006). These small, mundane stories that reflect values and culturally patterned meanings, are viewed by many as integral to the development of concepts of self (e.g., Bruner, 1986, 1990; Fivush, 1993; Wiley et al., 1998). Through stories of personal experience, people create, interpret, and publicly project images of the self. Within the context of the family, adults and children together routinely apply culture-specific interpretations to their past experiences, allowing children to construct a sense of self in conjunction with significant others (e.g., Miller et al., 1997; Wiley et al., 1998).

Storytelling in various forms also has been used clinically with children in foster care. Since the 1950s, child welfare professionals have used "life books" with children in foster care or preparing for adoption (Glickman, 1957). Co-created by the child and child welfare worker, the books encompass important life events and the child's feelings about those events to support a sense of continuity for children whose lives and primary relationships have been disrupted. Wenger (1982) used a "suitcase" story to help children in foster care acknowledge their feelings of abandonment, to express their anger, and to talk about their longings for permanence. In this technique, a foster child is helped through the prop of a suitcase that has been many places and "talks" about its experiences and feelings.

Not surprisingly, narratives of personal experience also have comprised a central component of a wide range of therapies. Therapists working within a narrative framework have emphasized the importance of creating stories as a way to help children make sense of and gain a feeling of control in their lives, rethink views of themselves and others, and alter problematic beliefs (e.g., Hanney & Kozlowska, 2002). Stories of personal experience are central to most "talking therapies," especially those based in attachment and psychodynamic theories (e.g., Holmes, 2001). In psychotherapy, as in everyday life, stories reflect how individuals view themselves, others, and the world. Such stories are repeated and reinterpreted in a dynamic and social process.

Supporting Children's Biological and Psychosocial Development: Focal and Microsystems

The analytic vantage point of an ecological analysis may be an individual, family, institution, community, nation, or other entity. In Life Story Intervention, our vantage point is the child. It is from the child's perspective that we view all other levels of the social ecology. At the focal system level, we attend to the child's unique biological and psychosocial characteristics. We also attend to the microsystem that includes those settings in which the child has face-to-face, sustained, and significant relationships with others, for example, families and schools. A primary focus of Life Story Intervention is supporting children's social and emotional development through the formation of a microsystem involving a relationship with a community clinician.

Addressing Children's Biological Development Through Attention to Medical Needs

As discussed in Chapter 1, children whose parents misuse methamphetamine may be at risk for a variety of medical conditions. Existing evidence is not extensive. It suggests that the neurotoxic effects of pre- or postnatal exposure to methamphetamine or methamphetamine production on children's developing central nervous systems may result in adverse neurobehavioral outcomes, such as lags in academic and physical development (Cernerud, Erikkson, Jonsson, Steneroth & ZetterStorm, 1996; Wouldes, LaGasse, Sheridan & Lester, 2004). Furthermore, individuals who misuse methamphetamine often misuse other substances, such as alcohol, known to have toxic prenatal effects on children's developing central nervous systems (Garcia-Bournissen, Rokach, Karaskov & Koren, 2007). In addition, children whose parents have been preoccupied with methamphetamine misuse may not have received routine medical and dental care.

Routine physicals that children receive when taken by child welfare professionals into protective custody partly address children's medical needs. More subtle medical issues, however, may become apparent only later and may adversely affect children's functioning, including their participation in Life Story Intervention. These medical needs are interpreted by foster parents, child welfare workers, community clinicians, and other community members, and interact in complex ways with Life Story Intervention. For example, a child participating in Life Story Intervention was having difficulty remembering the content of sessions from week to week. Having observed similar behaviors, his foster mother viewed him as noncompliant, his teacher was concerned that he might suffer from attention deficit disorder, and psychologically oriented Life Story Intervention team members were concerned about dissociation due to past trauma. All of these factors may or may not have impacted the child's functioning. In addition, the psychiatrist on our team, suspecting a seizure disorder, referred the child to a pediatric neurologist who confirmed the diagnosis. Following the initiation of medication, the child's participation in his foster home, school, and Life Story Intervention, while still problematic, was notably improved. The point we wish to underscore is that all of the interpretations of the child's behavior by the foster parent, teacher, therapist, and psychiatrist, regardless of their accuracy, reflected adults' culturally based beliefs and impacted their responses to the child. Attention to medical needs played an important role in facilitating this child's ability to participate at home and school, and in Life Story Intervention.

Addressing Children's Psychosocial Development Through Prevention Education

As discussed in Part 2, many children whose parents misuse methamphetamine may be at psychological risk both because of any violence and neglect that they may have experienced and because of inadequate socialization, including a lack of support in making sense of their experiences and feelings. Substance misuse is a primary strategy for dealing with everyday life stress or mental health issues observed by many children whose parents misuse methamphetamine. Such socialization experiences, especially in conjunction with trauma, place children at risk to begin misusing substances when they are under stress or experiencing emotional pain.

A necessary component of any intervention for children affected by parental substance misuse is explicit education about substance misuse. As part of the intervention, we drew on existing preventive research and clinical techniques, including books and other information (e.g., Black, 1989), to discuss the negative behavior that can result from substance misuse and the prevention of addiction. One of our goals was to help children to differentiate between their parents and the illness of addiction, so that they did not see their parent as being inherently bad, something many had heard from others.

Given the emotionally sensitive nature of this topic, as well as the socialization messages children may have received regarding the discussion of such information with family outsiders, our approach to substance misuse education is flexibly adapted to the individual child's tolerance and developmental level, and is embedded within the co-construction of personal narratives. For example, a 7-year-old girl struggled with memories of maltreatment from a mother whom she loved and who was serving time in prison. The child also had been strictly taught by her mother not to talk about the mother's substance misuse. As the child became more comfortable with her community clinician and began offering more details of her story, the adult communicated a simple but fundamental message: "Yes, your mom did some bad things. She was using drugs. Drug addiction is an illness that is very hard to overcome." They then went on to discuss ways in which the little girl could take care of herself to prevent the illness of addiction.

Addressing Children's Development Through Psychotherapeutic Intervention for Trauma

Life Story Intervention addresses the psychological aspects of children's development through intervention for trauma. Children who have been exposed to trauma may develop significant psychological symptoms including posttraumatic stress disorder (PTSD) and other anxiety disorders, depression, and a variety of behavioral problems (AACAP, 1998; Pine & Cohen, 2002) which, if left untreated, may become chronic and persist into adulthood (Cohen, Mannarino, Berliner & Deblinger, 2000). Indeed, as discussed in Chapter 8, the majority of the children we observed were experiencing significant posttraumatic or dissociative symptoms, as well as other emotional and behavioral problems, including problems with anger and attention. Like many other children who enter foster care, they had not received sufficient emotional and intellectual support for understanding difficult or traumatic life experiences. Like many other children from substance-involved families, they told us that talking about their feelings or experiences was not done, or that it was taboo. Children were separated from their parents, who might have had knowledge of any traumatic events in their children's lives. Foster parents may have been unaware of details of the child's history. In fact, most foster parents had, at best, a very limited knowledge of children's previous lives. A few viewed the children's biological parents in a negative, moralistic light or believed that the children would follow in their footsteps. Child welfare professionals focused on pressing issues of physical health and safety, whereas teachers focused on children's equally pressing educational needs. Peers lacked the perspective to adequately interpret children's experiences.

A variety of approaches to therapeutic intervention are possible with children who have experienced trauma. Cognitive behavioral therapies (Cohen, 1998) and psychodynamically based therapies (Lieberman et al., 2003) deal with the psychological sequelae of trauma and family violence in various ways. Although there is considerable debate within the field, there also is some convergence across diverse perspectives (see Hanney & Kozlowska, 2002). Life Story Intervention incorporates as key components three such basic elements to design an effective intervention for traumatized, rural foster children: (a) attention to children's understanding of events, (b) their emotional reactions to trauma, and (c) establishment of a trusting relationship with a supportive adult with mental health expertise.

Children's Understanding of Events

Strong empirical support exists for cognitive interventions in the treatment of PTSD, depression, and other symptoms in traumatized children.

Cognitive therapies for traumatized children emphasize the modification of negative or maladaptive belief systems (e.g., Cohen, 1998; Cohen, Deblinger, Mannarino & Steer, 2004). Cognitive distortions may occur as children attempt to understand or explain a traumatic event. To regain a sense of control over their lives, children may look for something that they did or did not do to cause the traumatic events, with the hope that they might prevent such events from happening in the future. Alternatively, to protect themselves from the pain they experienced during the traumatic events, they may "prepare" themselves for future traumatic events by believing that the world is generally unfair and dangerous, therefore developing an expectation that bad things are going to happen. Other distortions include a negative view of the self and others (Cohen et al., 2000). According to cognitive theory, such distorted cognitions lead to negative emotions and behaviors including depression, anxiety, and PTSD symptoms, and self-destructive or aggressive acts (Beck, 1976). The goal of cognitive therapy is to explicitly challenge negative beliefs about self, other, and the world, thereby correcting destructive beliefs and enhancing cognitive coping strategies. This also is a goal of Life Story Intervention.

In Life Story Intervention, cognitive distortions are brought to light and challenged primarily through discussion with the child over time and in the context of a supportive and reciprocal relationship with an adult. A variety of strategies used in some cognitive therapies, however, are *not* part of Life Story Intervention. Desensitization techniques or techniques in which children are exposed in a systematic way to reminders of past traumatic experiences are not used in our intervention. Flooding, or interventions in which the child is encouraged to immerse himself in past traumatic experiences, also are not part of our approach. Similarly, using aversive stimuli to change behavior and internal representations is seen as counterproductive to our efforts to help children interpret past traumatic experiences. We do not use these techniques, in part, because they place the adult in control of what happens. In our view, this does not foster the establishment of a safe, reciprocal, and trusting relationship between child and adult, which is the cornerstone of our approach to addressing children's emotional responses to trauma (see Lieberman & Van Horn, 2005).

Children's Emotions and Relationships

Life Story Intervention is relationship based. The focus of the psychotherapeutic component of Life Story Intervention is to facilitate children's social and emotional development through a supportive relationship with a caring adult professional. As described in Part 2, many children from methamphetamine-involved families experience emotional pain, especially in relation to their parents. We have found attachment theory (Bowlby, 1988; Holmes, 2001; Lieberman & Van Horn, 2005) and some related psychodynamic approaches to therapy (Fonagy, 2001; Fraiberg, 1980) to be useful in designing the psychotherapeutic component of Life Story Intervention.

A key premise of attachment theory is that children's experiences with their caregivers during infancy, childhood, and adolescence play a central organizing role influencing their development and mental health (Bowlby, 1988). In early childhood, children first construct internal working models of attachment; that is, of close, loving, and enduring relationships, based on their everyday experiences with their caregivers (Bowlby, 1988). These models affect how children view themselves and others; for example, their expectations for how other adults such as teachers will respond to them, trust in foster parents, and self-confidence. If children's experiences with others remain constant, internal working models can remain stable, exerting a continuing influence on how they engage in other relationships. From this perspective, the experiences of many children from methamphetamine-involved families of neglect and other maltreatment can seriously undermine their sense of trust, safety, and self-worth, as well as their expectations of their foster parents, teachers, and other adults.

It is important to underscore, however, that working models are not fixed; they may be modified if children experience different types of relationships. The modification of maladaptive working models may begin through the development of a secure relationship with a community clinician, an important goal of Life Story Intervention.

A second premise of attachment theory is that children's experience with their attachment figures is a main organizer of how they respond to safety and danger (Ainsworth, Blehar, Waters & Wall, 1978; Bowlby, 1982). When children experience violence in their families, their sense of trust may become undermined, resulting in anger, hypervigilance, and fear (Lieberman & Van Horn, 2005). Moreover, children may use aggression and anger as a way to cope with stress in other close relationships. Children of families involved with methamphetamine may experience their parents' failures in their role as protectors. Parents may act in dangerous or frightening ways, or allow others to harm the child. Such experiences typically overwhelm children. They may be left with frightening images and memories that are hard to understand, as well as apprehension, uncertainty, confusion, anger, and a shattered sense of safety. Life Story Intervention helps children to understand and modulate negative feelings and to express them in ways that are socially acceptable.

Another key premise of attachment theory is that working models of attachment vary in how painful feelings and thoughts are kept from awareness (Bowlby, 1988). In insecure models, children's abilities to deal with painful memories, feelings, and thoughts has been compromised. For example, parents may forbid children from talking or fail to help children to talk about feelings and experiences, or overwhelm the child with their own attachment needs. Children may respond in a variety of ways. They may discount personal stories as unimportant, not be able to tell their stories because they have forgotten them, or they may normalize traumatic experiences and their impact on them. Alternatively, children may be angry or fearful about traumatic attachment-related experiences—caught up in the details of the experiences without strategies for making sense of them. They may recall vivid images, but be unable to pull together a coherent sequence of events in a verbal, narrative form. Their working models of self may be infused with shame, and they may feel rejected and unworthy of attachment.

The dynamic of denial, distortion, and secrecy that is a central organizing principle in many families where parents misuse substances may make it difficult for children to talk openly about their experiences and feelings (Black, 2001). Instead, children may learn "not to tell," in a shared "conspiracy of silence" (Kroll, 2004). The longer this pattern of secrecy and denial persists, the harder it is for mental health professionals to penetrate. As Kroll (2004) underscored, "the process of denial, where the adult has an emotional attachment to either drugs or alcohol . . . makes acknowledging . . . (problems) very difficult" (p. 132). Children may become mistrustful of others and suspicious of offers of help. They also may mistrust their own senses and judgment, since what they have felt and observed has been denied or distorted. At the same time, they must cope with numerous losses— loss of a parent who was not available, loss of a feeling of being loved and cared for, loss of a normal family life and childhood, loss of confidence and self-esteem, loss of a parent who has been imprisoned due to methamphetamine misuse. Life Story Intervention allows the child to engage in a dialogue with a community clinician to develop a coherent, shared narrative of important life events.

Another premise of attachment-based interventions is that telling a story about painful attachment experiences and feelings helps children to make sense of what has happened, and reflect upon and learn from these experiences. Traumatic memories may be stored in a "raw, sensory form" (Holmes, 2001), making it difficult for clinicians to elicit a coherent verbal account (Van de Kolk & Fisler, 1996). The integration of memories with the thoughts and feelings that they evoke is difficult, because children may become overwhelmed, fearful, or panicky as the memories emerge and are addressed. Memories may also trigger painful flashbacks and a reliving of chaotic and frightening experiences and feelings. Through the co-construction of a narrative with a safe and trusted clinician, children can begin to integrate experiences and feelings, thereby better regulating the overwhelming feelings they evoke. Over time, the child comes to internalize the clinician's words and ways of soothing distress and making sense of experience.

A related and central premise of attachment-based interventions is that a safe and reciprocal relationship with a clinician is a prerequisite for traumatized children to begin telling and making sense of their stories. Holmes (2001) has underscored that many individuals who seek therapy because of trauma are torn between the need for a secure attachment and a fear of such intimacy. A primary and overarching therapeutic goal of Life Story Intervention is to help children to form a trusting, reciprocal relationship with a clinician, a secure base from which they can explore their feelings and memories. Bowlby (1988) underscored the importance of this task, noting that it is "difficult or perhaps impossible to think about and reconsider without a trusted companion to provide support, encouragement, sympathy, and, on occasion, guidance" (p. 138).

Establishing a healthy, trusting, and reciprocal relationship with a child who has been traumatized and who has grown up with familial patterns of denial and secrecy is likely to require a lengthy period of time. If a child has experienced different foster placements, his trust in others may have been chronically undermined. In our experience, most children who have experienced parental methamphetamine misuse can develop a trusting relationship with an adult and have meaningful discussions about their lives, but much individual variation occurs. Some traumatized children may require an extended time period to feel comfortable in sharing experiences, thoughts, and feelings freely with another person.

The clinician helps children to establish a safe and reciprocal relationship in which conversations go two ways and in which their needs for safety and support are respected. Many children who grow up with violence have experienced relationships only in a one-way manner, with the adult imposing her wishes, anger, and needs on the child. Clinicians listen; tailor the intervention to children's unique personalities; respect children's individuality; focus on their natural strengths and resiliency; encourage them to explore their thoughts, feelings, and wishes; and focus on future goals and activities.

Once a relationship with the community clinician has been established, the adult may address several other primary therapeutic goals.

Contain Children's Intense Emotion.   Containment is a clinical concept introduced by Wilfred Bion (1962). It is an apt metaphor for a socialization process whereby parents provide support to children experiencing intense emotions. A parent who is able to contain a child's emotion tolerates and considers the child's intense feelings. The parent then reflects the feelings in a manageable form back to the child, thereby helping the child to understand, regulate, and accept his feelings.

Children who have experienced trauma may have difficulties in coping with overwhelming feelings of anger, blame, loss, shame, and guilt. Moreover, they may have learned that it is taboo to talk about such feelings. When children begin to discuss past traumatic events, they typically experience intense emotion. The role of the community clinician, like that of the parent, is to contain the child's intense feelings. By providing emotional support and guidance, the community clinician helps the child to tolerate intense emotion, access memories, and reflect upon attachment experiences. It is through repeated experiences with successfully negotiated containment that the child slowly comes to construct a more integrated life story and a better way of dealing with distress.

It is important to underscore that children are not passive in this socialization process, but actively negotiate an interpretation of their lives and feelings. In fact, it is through actively negotiating, understanding, containing, and renegotiating that the child's feelings, memories, and thoughts emerge and develop. In co-constructing the narrative, children may respond to any given adult contribution in a variety of ways, for example, by ignoring, rejecting, elaborating, modifying, or embracing the interpretation.

Help Children to Gain Insight into the Impact of Trauma on Their Well-being and to Place Such Experiences in the Larger Context of their Lives and Futures. Life Story Intervention helps children to consider what they experienced, and how they thought and felt about what happened to themselves and others. The role of the community clinician is to consider the child's narrative and make sense of it with the child (Symington & Symington, 1999), including helping children to connect their feelings to the events and experiences that triggered them and to integrate both feeling and memory into concepts of self (Bowlby, 1988). By talking with children about their life stories, adults help them to place traumatic experiences within the larger context of their lives, so that trauma does not fully define them, but is seen as one part of a larger life trajectory.

Help Children to Create New and Healthy Life Experiences. According to Lieberman and Van Horn (2005, p. 16), an important goal of therapy for children affected by trauma is to provide support and encouragement for "developmentally appropriate achievements and for daring to try new and adaptive ways of functioning." Many children who have experienced trauma have difficulties in appraising danger, especially in adults they encounter. They may minimize actual cues of danger or, alternately, may exaggerate the danger in relatively benign situations. Life Story Intervention helps children to realistically appraise relationships with adults who can help them onto healthier developmental pathways. It supports children in establishing healthy relationships with safe adults in their communities. More specifically, Life Story Intervention helps the child to identify and approach a "natural mentor"; that is, a trustworthy and supportive adult in the child's own social network who may serve as a long-term, ongoing source of support for the child after the intervention is concluded. By providing children with an opportunity to develop a supportive relationship with a reliable and trustworthy adult, the gains made by the intervention are consolidated and maintained over time. In the context of this new relationship, the child can continue to express, interpret, and contextualize memories, thoughts, and feelings.

Support of Children's Psychosocial Development: Exo- and Mesosystems

Although not the focus, Life Story Intervention does consider meso- and exosystems. The mesosystem encompasses the interrelationships between two or more of the person's microsystems. Life Story Intervention facilitates the formation of mesosystems through interactions between the community clinician, foster parents, and child welfare workers. The exosystem encompasses one or more settings that do not involve the person as an active participant, but in which events occur that do affect the person. Life Story Intervention impacts exosystems through communications with professionals from a range of organizations, to develop procedures to best support children from methamphetamine-involved families.

As described in Part 2, children from methamphetamine-involved families often have multiple risks to their social development. They may have lived in isolation and have few sources of social support. Our focus at the mesosystem level is on the creation of a mesosystem between Life Story Intervention and the foster home. In the foster parent component of our intervention, we develop relationships to support and provide assistance to children's current caregivers. Interventions with children are more effective when they include parents as well (Cohen & Mannarino, 1996; Lieberman & Van Horn, 2005). For example, caretakers may benefit from understanding the normalcy of children's posttraumatic reactions (Shelby, 2000), and the community clinicians benefit from caregivers' knowledge of children's functioning in diverse contexts. At least once a month, the community clinician meets with foster parents to listen to and discuss their concerns and observations, check in regarding how the child is functioning at school and home, share information with the foster parent about how they can support the child emotionally, and obtain valuable information on the child's daily social and emotional functioning.

At the mesosystem level, we also attend to communication among the various professionals involved in the care of children, for example, any mental health professional seeing the child. Creating a mesosystem between Life Story Intervention and the child welfare office is necessary to referrals of children who may benefit from the intervention. We also provide child welfare workers with information on methamphetamine and its effects on children and families. They provide us with feedback and share their perspectives. Such relationship are invaluable to supporting children. For example, a young girl was placed in a foster home in which she experienced considerable conflict with her foster mother. As the foster mother's punishments escalated to abuse, the community clinician implementing the Life Story Intervention—who had established a relationship with relevant professionals at the local child welfare office—discussed her concerns with the child's case worker. Following a child welfare investigation, the child was moved to another foster home. The community clinician spent extra sessions with the child, to help her through this transition. In another instance, a child struggled academically in school. His community clinician facilitated the creation of a mesosystem comprised of the foster home and school by helping his foster mother to initiate an assessment with the school for a possible learning disorder. Following an assessment, the child was provided with additional educational resources at school.

At the ecosystem level, we partnered with a range of professionals within rural communities. Children whose parents misuse methamphetamine may have a broad range of needs spanning multiple community resources, from medical to educational to mental health to child protection. Adults in our study emphasized the importance of interagency collaboration in meeting the needs of children whose parents misuse methamphetamine. Interagency collaboration may result in practices that enhance attention to children's social and emotional needs, for example, when child welfare professionals are present during police raids of clandestine methamphetamine laboratories (Altshuler, 2005).

Conclusion

This chapter has described the conceptual and empirical bases of Life Story Intervention. This intervention emerged from a sociocultural tradition to help address the mental health needs of rural children affected by parental methamphetamine misuse. We integrated sociocultural theory with key premises from attachment and psychodynamic theories to address children's trauma symptoms in a culturally appropriate manner. We collaborated closely with community professionals as we designed and implemented Life Story

Intervention, utilizing local traditions of storytelling. In approaching the children, we used a holistic approach to address the biological, psychological, and social components of development as they emerged and interacted within a particular sociocultural context. Helping children to form a supportive relationship with a community clinician through whom they may contain intense emotion and co-construct and reflect upon a story (or stories) of their lives are viewed as key mechanisms of change.

Although Life Story Intervention was designed to address the dynamics of rural methamphetamine use, certain of these dynamics also may apply to other groups and settings. The transferability of Life Story Intervention to rural children primarily affected by parental misuse of alcohol and other illegal drugs, or to foster children experiencing trauma in other contexts is an important issue for future study. In Chapter 11, we discuss the implementation of Life Story Intervention.

Chapter Eleven

Implementing Life Story Intervention

Margaret participated as a community clinician in Life Story Intervention. Having grown up on a farm in East Central Illinois, she brought an understanding of many common socialization practices and rituals in this region to her work with 15-year-old Alex. She noted, for instance, that whenever she arrived at Alex's foster home, he was underneath his foster father's car, working to change the oil or to repair a faulty part. Margaret recalled the centrality of cars to the lives of rural adolescents, separated by many miles from friends, school, paid work, and public recreation, and the receipt of the first driver's license as an eagerly awaited rite of passage. As a young girl, Margaret observed a ritual involving her older brothers and parents in which her parents would buy model cars for their sons similar to the ones they would soon be learning to drive. Margaret's brothers would then build the model with their parents. As the car was being built, their parents talked about their own history of driving and other stories about the dangers of the open road. In searching for ways to connect with 15-year-old Alex, Margaret brought him a model car to build. Although Alex was clearly delighted, Margaret had questions about his ability to concentrate on the many small steps necessary to successfully assemble the kit. With some support from his foster parents, Alex worked the next weekend to assemble the car and proudly showed Margaret the product the following week.

Many rural children, like Alex, entering foster care from families involved with methamphetamine have multiple, complex needs that will require many years to resolve. Forming relationships with supportive adults such as Margaret, and taking initial forays into personal storytelling are only a beginning. Life Story Intervention may be thought of as a bridge from the time children enter into foster care until they obtain longer-term mental health care. It prepares children to form relationships and begin talking about

During Life Story Intervention, several children lost parents to methamphetamine-related illness. Photo by Camilla Black.

their experiences. This chapter provides a more detailed description of Life Story Intervention and an overview of implementation issues. We focus on challenges we've encountered and the strategies we've used to address them. This chapter is intended as a flexible guide. Intervention strategies must be tailored to address each child's unique needs, developmental level, and circumstances.

Child Eligibility

We have relied on colleagues from child protection services to identify children who may benefit from Life Story Intervention. Although we took all referrals for the purposes of our pilot study, we recommend that child welfare professionals be asked to refer those children from methamphetamine-involved families who have had exposure to traumatic events and appear to be experiencing some level of depression, anxiety, or behavioral disorder. Our experience also suggests that a number of situations require a level of involvement beyond the scope of Life Story Intervention. We do *not* recommend Life Story Intervention if:

- The child has significant linguistic or cognitive delays that would interfere with understanding and constructing meaningful verbal narratives. To benefit from the intervention, children must be capable of discussing and reflecting upon their experiences.

- The child has significant neurological or other medical disorders that could interfere with regular, sustained participation in the intervention. Exploring and understanding children's feelings and perspectives occurs over a period of many months. Children experiencing significant memory problems, or other neurological or medical conditions that would disrupt continuity in the intervention, may benefit less from this approach.

- The child is not in a safe living situation. Children can freely discuss and reflect upon their experiences only if they feel safe. Furthermore, a child who is living in an abusive or otherwise dangerous situation could be placed at increased risk if she inadvertently discussed feelings or thoughts with caregivers that threatened family patterns of secrecy or denial.

- The child is not in a stable living situation. Continuity is necessary to the development of a supportive relationship with a community clinician. If a child is in transition between foster homes or in the process of being removed from her home, it is better to initiate the intervention when the child is in a stable setting.

- The child is placed with foster parents who are not supportive of the intervention. Foster parents must trust the community clinician and be supportive of children's participation. Children benefit from the encouragement of their foster parents. In addition, children's regular and sustained participation may require some flexibility on the part of foster parents, for example, with scheduling. Finally, the intervention may bring up disturbing feelings for children, who may experience a temporary worsening of behavior requiring support and patience from foster parents.

- The child is likely to experience interference from biological family members. Assessing early on how supportive biological family members are of the child's participation in the intervention can be essential. If children have regular visits with parents or other significant family members, such as grandparents, it is important to gain the trust and support of these individuals. Biological relatives who are not willing to make time for the intervention, make disparaging comments about it, demand that the child disclose information told to the clinician in confidence, or instruct the child not to participate could undermine the intervention.

Eligibility of Participating Community Clinicians

We recruited clinicians from within the community and university who work professionally with children. They were child welfare professionals, social workers, educators, and counselors. We identified community clinicians primarily on the basis of referrals from community contacts in child welfare. Some individuals learned about the program and self-referred. We also used several social work PhD students with master's degrees in social work and practice experience. Community adults must meet several basic criteria to participate as clinicians in Life Story Intervention:

- The adult must work in a professional capacity with children. Many rural clinicians have experience working with traumatized children and families and, especially when given continuing education and support, can effectively intervene to support their positive development.

- All adults working with wards of the state must undergo fingerprinting. Such individuals also have undergone police background checks to eliminate adults who might prey on vulnerable children.

- The adult must be willing and able to participate in weekly supervision. Participating clinicians are supervised on a weekly basis by clinicians who are licensed and have expertise in child trauma and substance misuse. The supervising team is transdisciplinary and includes mental health and child welfare professionals, as well as social work professors. Weekly supervision is important for maintaining the integrity and quality of Life Story Intervention. Supervisors are available for phone consultation, and the team must have a plan in place for crisis intervention.

- The adult must be reflective. Many children from methamphetamine-involved families who have experienced inadequate socialization and multiple traumas can be very challenging. Relationship-building may proceed slowly, children may have some negative behaviors, and they may avoid important topics. Clinicians must be able to step back and reflect, for example, upon why, after several weeks of positive exchanges, the child behaved in a rejecting way, or why particular topics are difficult for the child. Such nondefensive reflection is the first step toward developing new strategies, for example, to reengage the child in the relationship, to understand why the child is responding as she is, or to better support the telling of particular stories.

- The adult must be skilled at forming and sustaining positive, supportive relationships with children, including those who are distrustful or even negative toward adults. In addition, the empirical research on other relationship-based interventions, such as mentoring, indicates that the formation of a sustained, trusting, and reciprocal relationship is prerequisite to children's positive developmental outcomes. Relationships that are not positive or that terminate early can be detrimental to children, especially those who have problematic relationship histories with adults. (e.g., Rhodes, 2002).

- The adult must be respectful of children and attentive to their strengths as well as their vulnerabilities. Many foster children from methamphetamine-involved families have experienced significant neglect and abuse. They are not, however, only victims. Many show remarkable intelligence, adaptability, and maturity during difficult times. These strengths deserve respect, and can be drawn on in supporting children and addressing any trauma they have experienced.

- The adult must be capable of maintaining boundaries. Placing children in foster care rarely is a panacea. Many children in foster care continue to face significant, heart-wrenching life problems, and the clinician may be tempted to assume other roles within the child's life, for example, friend or surrogate parent. Assuming these roles is problematic for a number of reasons, including that they may create unrealistic expectations in the child that ultimately are disappointed and may lead to "burn-out" of the community clinician.

Challenges and Strategies

A challenge that we encountered early on regarded dual roles. Community clinicians also may encounter children and their families in their jobs as counselors, child welfare workers, and the like. For example, three of the adults who joined our team were working as caseworkers in the local child welfare office. Dual roles can be problematic for a number of related reasons. First, they can be confusing for children and families regarding expectations of the role community clinicians will play in Life Story Intervention; for example, talking about the child's experiences or advising on child welfare cases. Second, the adult's ability to respond as a clinician could be compromised by demands resulting from his job; for example, removal of children from their parents' custody. Finally, dual roles can undermine what children and families reveal in Life Story Intervention; for example, if they are suspicious of a child welfare worker.

To address this issue, we tried to assign children to community clinicians who were not involved directly with them in another capacity. In addition, clinicians explained their professional roles to the child and foster family, clarifying that during work hours they are, for example, involved with the Department of Child and Family Services (DCFS), but during Life Story Intervention, they are only clinicians. In all circumstances, the clinicians were careful that children and families understood the Health Insurance and Portability Accountability Act (HIPAA) rules, confidentiality, and its limits.

The Intervention Setting

Life Story Intervention is designed for use in home and community settings. For many families in rural areas, transportation is a barrier to intervention. Mental health clinics are few and far between, requiring families to travel long distances to obtain needed help for children. In Life Story Intervention, clinicians go to the child, and the intervention takes place in the child's foster home or at churches, schools, child welfare offices, community centers, and libraries in the child's community. In good weather, we also have used parks and forest preserves. We also have found that many important conversations occur while driving around or sitting in cars. Community clinicians have commented that while traveling, children relax. They feel safe and contained and often open up more than they do in an office setting.

The following criteria guide the selection of sites for the intervention:

- The location must afford privacy and some sense of containment. Confidential conversations should not be overheard by third parties.
- The location should be regularly available. Children who have been traumatized benefit from continuity. Providing the intervention in the same setting each week can be important.
- The location must be within reasonable distance of the child's home or school. Foster parents often feel overwhelmed by their foster child's many needs. If the intervention can be conducted in a location near

to the home, it will support foster parent participation and ensure regular sessions.

- The site must be comfortable for the child. Children who participate in Life Story Intervention may not feel comfortable in some settings. For example, they may associate the child welfare office with unpleasant and difficult experiences.
- It is important to check malpractice coverage or insurance policies. Note that DCFS has a mechanism for obtaining permission to transport children and work with them in the community.

Challenges and Strategies

Finding a suitable location can present a variety of challenges. In public settings such as the library or park, the children's friends or familiar adults may approach them. The clinician and child may prepare a nonstigmatizing (for the child) way of introducing the clinician and a comfortable strategy for disengaging, for example, with a child friend who wants to play. Another challenge may be in dealing with the distractions of public settings. For example, a child may divert the conversation by engaging in an activity that is antithetical to talking, for example, playing on a swing or a slide. The clinician can negotiate with the child in advance how long and when they will engage in such activities.

Note that doing clinical work in community settings provides unique opportunities for children, but also may introduce challenges not encountered in the more controlled office setting. Although it is rare, children who have experienced trauma may decompensate when dealing with difficult material. Community clinicians may find themselves dealing with aggression while driving or dissociation while sitting on a park bench, or they may be required to do crisis management in the library.

Assessing Children

Assessments of the child's strengths and vulnerabilities are the basis for implementing meaningful, effective interventions (Gambrill, 2005; Jordan & Franklin, 2003). Prior to initiating Life Story Intervention, we conduct an assessment of the child's psychological functioning that includes data from different individuals, measures, and points in time. Our focus is on children's stories and on their mental health symptoms, particularly symptoms of trauma. We synthesize these various types of information to identify children's strengths and vulnerabilities and track their progress over the course of the intervention.

Record Review

Access to children's child welfare records can provide invaluable historical information. In reviewing records, we gather information regarding the number, length, and type (kinship or traditional) of foster home placements; reasons for placement in foster care; diagnosed medical or mental health conditions (including addictions) in the child or the child's parents; and any parental involvement with the legal system.

Foster Parents' Report of Children's Emotional and Behavioral Issues

Foster parents provide information on children's behavioral functioning by completing the Child Behavior Checklist (CBCL) (Achenbach & Rescorla, 2001) (see Chapter 4). Care must be taken in interpreting the results. For example, if the child is new to the foster home, the foster parents may not have adequate information for a valid response. We supplement the CBCL with several open-ended questions regarding the foster parents' perceptions of the impact of parental methamphetamine misuse on their specific foster child's adjustment to foster care and general functioning.

Children's Assessment

The primary assessment of children's functioning is obtained from the children directly. We typically use the following format in assessing children:

Rapport Building and Informed Consent. Before beginning the assessments, it is helpful to have a casual conversation with the child, for example, the adult might ask about the child's pets, admire the child's bedroom, or ask about the child's family. For example, "I'd like to get to know you better. Tell me about who's in your foster family? Who's in your family?" These questions provide a "buffer" around more emotionally difficult discussions. In this phase, adults clearly describe why they are there and what they will be doing, and they obtain the child's assent to proceed. This should be done as directly and clearly as possible. As part of this process, adults let children know that they do not need to answer questions. Most children are eager to participate, and providing a clear overview of what they can expect from the assessment can help to put them at ease.

Language Assessment. To participate in Life Story Intervention, children need to be able to use language to make sense of their experiences and feelings. As a baseline of their language skills, we use the Peabody Picture Vocabulary

Test-III (PPVT-3) (Dunn & Dunn, 1997) (see Chapter 3). Most children enjoy this test, so it is often a good ice breaker for introductory sessions. (Note that a variety of standardized assessments of children's language or intelligence would be adequate substitutions.)

Trauma Assessment. We use the Trauma Symptom Checklist for Children (TSCC) (Briere, 1996) to obtain information on the extent to which children are experiencing trauma symptoms (see Chapter 3). For some children, items on the TSCC stimulate rich narratives, especially if the adult reads the questions to the child and leaves room for inquiry into items that the child denies or strongly endorses. If children report, for example, feeling scared, then the adult can ask about a specific time when this occurred. Other possible probes include: "Tell me more about that. . . . Where were you? What happened?" Adults should, however, avoid "grilling" the child. As a general rule of thumb, one or two probes of an item is sufficient. In addition, adults should only add probes to at most five or six of the many items in the TSCC. In deciding which items to probe, consider probing those items that represent diverse feelings or topics, items that represent extreme feelings as reported by the child, or items that represent feelings that possibly are being denied. For example, during one of our interviews, a child denied ever feeling frightened. The clinician responded, "Well, the reason I ask is that a lot of us feel scared at one time or another." At that point, the child was able to acknowledge that he had often felt frightened. He then went on to elaborate an incident when he was very frightened at home. Assessors should keep in mind that some children prefer to answer the questionnaire on their own. After completing the TSCC, they may, however, be open to discussing their answers further.

Assessment of Other Behavioral or Emotional Issues

As discussed earlier, foster parents completed the CBCL (Achenbach & Rescorla, 2001) to obtain information about any other behavioral or emotional issues in addition to trauma that the child may be experiencing.

Perspectives and Experiences. Semi-structured interviews can provide rich information on children's perceptions of self and other, and on important experiences in their lives. We typically begin with more general questions and then focus in on areas that the child is capable of talking about in more detail. The following are the main general probes that we use in talking with children: "Tell me about a happy time in your family," "Tell me about a sad or scary time in your family," and "Tell me about a fun time in your family" (see Chapter 3).

Children vary in their responses to the interview. Most are able to elaborate on positive experiences, but struggle with more difficult or frightening experiences. Taking time to proceed at the child's pace, with consideration to how much the child may tolerate, is essential. It is important to provide comfortable conditions, so that the child can elaborate not only on events, but on memories of past relationships and feelings. For instance, the adult might ask, "When you were alone that time and riding your bike and your parents were gone? What did it feel like for you? Can you remember another time when you felt that way?" Important areas to obtain information on include who the child feels understands him or her best; who the child turns to (or turned to) when ill, distressed, or tired; and how the child was comforted (Holmes, 2001).

Debriefing. It is important to spend time with the child after the assessments, especially if a child still seems to be pondering what was said. Many children will have disclosed very painful or even traumatic memories. It can be helpful to acknowledge, for example, "We've talked about some difficult topics today. You are really brave, and I appreciate your talking so openly with me." Asking children how they experienced the assessment can be helpful. Assessors also may wish to play a brief game or talk about other more positive or neutral topics such as pets, swimming, sports, and the like.

Challenges and Strategies

Many mental health measures inquire directly into past traumatic events and trauma symptoms. These questions can be upsetting to children. The challenge is to obtain information to inform the intervention without further traumatizing the child. Some general guidelines are:

- Listen "deeply" to the child. We convey attentiveness through intonation, pacing and nonverbal feedback (e.g., empathetic smiling, nodding). Interest and understanding also can be conveyed nonverbally through quiet attentiveness and emotional presence, and through verbal comments such as, "I'm listening," "That's very difficult," "You're brave to share that with me."

- Invite elaboration if a child appears willing to share more, but do not "grill" the child. We may begin with open-ended probes, such as,

"Can you tell me more about that?" To provide a scaffold for the child's narrative, we may move to one or two more specific descriptive questions (involving, for example, questions of what, when, and where), and then, occasionally, to more difficult interpretive questions (involving, for example, questions of why). We avoid yes/no-type questions or leading questions that assume an understanding of the child's experience. As a general rule of thumb, we encourage children to tell us their perspectives and feelings.

- Attend to pacing. If a child becomes distressed at particular memories, it is essential to slow down or stop all together. Helping a child to focus on one small part rather than dealing with the whole may be critical. If a child cannot go on, then we move to a comfortable topic and remain with the child until he or she has calmed down and regained self-composure. As much as possible, the assessment should be conducted as a conversation that is serious, yet interesting, respectful and not burdensome. If a child does not want to talk about particular feelings or events, then this should be respected.

- Attend to context. The adult should be sensitive to the situational context in which the assessments are administered. A variety of factors, such as missed or disturbing visits with parents, disappointing court appearances, illness, or recent changes in foster care, can disrupt the children's ability to respond as they "typically" would. We evaluate the situation at the beginning of the session, and are prepared to reschedule if necessary.

- Offer additional support. Although not typical, some children struggle to contain the emotions triggered by an assessment. In such cases, clinicians should stay with the child until he or she has calmed down, and the clinician should be available for further discussion if needed. Letting the child's foster parents know that the clinician is available and willing to return or talk by phone is part of what can be done to ensure that the child receives any necessary support following the assessment.

- Lay the groundwork for the intervention. In some circumstances, the adult conducting the assessment also conducts the intervention. If this is not the case, then assessors should keep in mind that they have the first direct contact with the child. Positive interactions during the assessment can support relationship-building with the clinician conducting Life Story Intervention.

From Assessment to Intervention

An assessment provides specific information on the level and nature of children's trauma symptoms and any other emotional or behavioral issues, as well as their perspectives and strengths. It considers children's developmental histories, what they have experienced in foster care, and how they relate to other important people in their lives. It also looks at how they are doing in school and other areas of their lives, and whether they have other significant needs (e.g., medical). Based on a synthesis of all information, domains in need of particular attention are identified (Herbert & Harper-Dorton, 2003; Meisels, 2001) and priorities are set. Prioritizing interventions is important when children have multiple needs. What the clinician addresses should be guided by how realistic it is to address the area and how likely the child will respond. Pacing is another critical consideration; for example, it may be less threatening for a child if less difficult issues are tackled first. The following case summary is an example of successful pacing:

> Lucy was seen in Life Story Intervention for a 6-month period. The assessment revealed that she denied most trauma symptoms, but an under-reporting scale suggested that she likely had many more trauma symptoms than she could acknowledge. The assessment provided a road map for the intervention. It was clear that Lucy would not be able to talk easily about trauma and about situations in which she felt frightened and helpless. Focus was therefore given to helping her feel safe and comfortable with the community clinician. As the topic of trauma emerged spontaneously, but indirectly, the community clinician told Lucy that most children feel very frightened and overwhelmed in such situations. By helping her to feel safe, and by normalizing some of the feelings that she was denying, Lucy was able to participate more actively in Life Story Intervention.

We see the relationship between the assessment and intervention as fluid and mutually informative. In conducting the assessment, attention is given to establishing a relationship with the child that is based in reciprocity and trust, so as to enhance the child's interest and willingness to participate in the intervention. Material from the assessment informs the intervention, but material that emerges from the intervention also refines our assessment of children's functioning (Meisels, 2001). For example, over the course of the intervention, we informally track a variety of aspects of children's functioning: children's level of trust in the clinician, the children's ability to regulate their emotions, children's abilities to articulate and understand their feelings and experiences, children's sense of self (value, self-esteem, belief in own abilities), children's ability to engage in meaningful activities, and children's ability to engage in meaningful and safe relationships with others (peers, friends, adults). The focus of the intervention may change accordingly.

Phases of Life Story Intervention

Life Story Intervention lasts for a period of 6–8 months, depending on the child's needs. During this period, the participating community clinician meets weekly with the child in 1-hour sessions, although, in emergencies, more frequent sessions may be scheduled. The intervention includes four overlapping phases:

Phase 1. Orientation and Relationship-building (Months 1–2)

Prior to beginning the intervention, the community clinician meets with the child and his family. The clinician describes the intervention and discusses any concerns or fears they may have about participating. For example, the clinician might comment to the child, "Some people find it helpful to talk about their lives. Telling their stories can help people to understand what's happened to them. I can help you better if you can let me know about your life—where you've lived, who your parents are, what you are like as a person, how you feel. You could tell the story in any way you'd like. We'll talk each week with each other about how you are feeling and what you are thinking about, but there are other ways to tell stories too. For instance, by writing, drawing, or taking pictures. How would you feel about that? Telling a life story can take some time, so I'd like to meet every week for about 6 to 8 months. What questions do you have for me?"

Relationship-building occurs throughout the intervention, but is of special focus during the first phase of the intervention. During the first 4–8 weeks, the clinician focuses on establishing a safe and trusting relationship with the child. During this introductory period, the clinician and child, essentially, meet and get to know one another. They may go out to eat, visit the park, go to the library, or engage in some other activity of the child's choosing. The clinician is respectful of the child's boundaries, shows a genuine interest in the child and her world, and accepts the child, imperfections and all (Axline, 1989; Bowlby, 1988). The clinician also allows the child to explore and express her feelings, positive or negative.

Children who have experienced parental methamphetamine misuse vary greatly in how they respond to adults. Some will be friendly and enjoy talking with an adult. Others will be overly friendly and show a lack of boundaries. Yet others will be guarded and reluctant to interact, or even fearful of engaging in a relationship with a clinician. There are a variety of reasons why some children may require a longer period of rapport-building before they feel safe enough in a relationship with a clinician to begin talking about their life stories. As described in Part 2, some parents who engaged in illegal activities, such as methamphetamine production, explicitly instructed their children not to talk about the family to outsiders, and some even punished them for doing so. In addition, some children who have told their stories to child welfare professionals were then removed from their families and placed in foster care, a traumatic event for many children. Other children may be more than willing to tell all, but then regret it afterward, feeling that they exposed themselves too much. Others have been threatened, and fear that telling the story will result in them or family members being harmed. It is therefore critical that the child have some trust in the clinician before beginning in-depth with the intervention. Much of the advice for conducting the assessment, especially rapport-building and supporting the child emotionally, also applies to the intervention. Listed are some general guidelines for encouraging the development of a positive and supportive relationship:

- Define your relationship and role to the child soon. It is important early on to define your relationship with the child in a manner that is connected with the child's experience and also identifies the relationship as temporary. Communicate that your first priority is to be there to support the child's well-being through talking. Children may not have encountered mental health clinicians in the past, and many may come from families whose beliefs with respect to mental health clinicians are negative. Some community clinicians introduce themselves by describing their professional roles in relation to the intervention, for example, as a social worker who helps children and families. It also is important to recognize that many children have experienced multiple disruptions in close relationships with adults. One clinician approached the short-term characteristic of the relationship by describing her role in the child's life as "Kind of like a favorite teacher. We'll be working closely for a period of months. We'll be talking about things that are important to you. Then we will move on to work with other people, but we still may see one another on occasion around town."

- Recognize the child's individuality and strengths. Show genuine interest in the child through comments, for example, about the child's pets, artwork, or baseball team. Take the child's lead—if a child expresses an interest in baseball, talk with him about his team. Avoid, however, making evaluative comments about topics of interest. For example, if a child comments, "My dad doesn't do drugs," an appropriate response would be a neutral acknowledgement such as, "OK," and not an evaluative comment such as "Good." Comments that convey judgment, even positive judgment, could inhibit the child's ability to be forthcoming about drugs or other antisocial behavior in the future. The aim is to help children to reflect on memories and feelings, not to help children to judge them. Keep initial references to drugs to a minimum, as they can lead to defensiveness in the child. For example, during one interview, the foster mother began with the comment: "She doesn't want to talk to you because she doesn't think her dad has a drug problem." The child then shook her head and crossed her arms in front of her chest. The interviewer replied: "I don't know your dad. I'm really interested in hearing from you."

- Convey interest and attentiveness. Convey your interest in the child by listening to the child. Communicate a focused attentiveness. For example, at the beginning of one session, a clinician's cell phone rang. She reached down and turned it off. The child expressed surprise that she did not take the call, but was delighted when the clinician explained that during their sessions together she was her priority.

- Respect the child's autonomy. Let the child take the lead and share what she chooses to share with you. The relationship between the child and clinician is co-created and reciprocal. Within the bounds of this relationship, respect children's individuality and ability to make sense of their lives and to solve problems.

- Model open communication. For children who are very defensive or unsure about disclosing their lives, some strategic use of limited self-disclosure may be appropriate. The challenge is to keep the focus on the child's story, feelings, and experiences. For example, one child expressed embarrassment at her family's lack of routines for eating, bathing, and the like. The clinician mentioned that when he was being raised by his mother, who was an alcoholic, he didn't realize that some people bathe everyday until he went to school. The child smiled and then revealed a personal narrative involving a time when she and her brother were left unsupervised for a week and didn't bathe once during the whole time. The clinician's account allowed the child to identify with him, and modeled permission to talk about substance misuse, a taboo topic in this child's family. Keep in mind, however, that the focus is on the child's, not the clinician's, experiences. Keeping personal narratives to a minimum is therefore essential.

- Practice flexibility. If the clinician arrives and the child is reluctant to proceed as planned, practice flexibility. Explore first with the child what is bothering her and give the child time to open up. Focus may be given to present concerns rather than the past, but the child should be given room to explore and choose. The clinician may offer to reschedule, especially if a child feels that he or she cannot talk at all on that day. In other circumstances, the clinician may stop the session earlier or later, depending on the particular circumstances.

Challenges and Strategies. A challenge that may emerge during the first phase of the intervention is encouraging the child to engage in the program. Some children have learned to be suspicious of adults in positions of authority, for example, to lie to teachers and child welfare professionals regarding events that occurred within their families. Open discussion with the child about choosing to talk or not to talk about family, as well as patience, can be effective.

Another challenge may be balancing the clinician's own enthusiasm for the intervention with a need to let the child freely choose to participate or not. In an attempt to engage the child, it may be tempting to over-sell the intervention or to over-promise what can realistically be accomplished during the intervention. This can lead to a disappointed child or an exhausted clinician.

The clinician also should keep in mind that children reveal their stories in many different ways—in words, movements, and facial expressions.

Often, stories are revealed only piecemeal. Although it may be tempting to elicit the "whole story" in one session, such sessions generally are not effective. Children will and do reveal their stories if time is given to listen to them within the context of a supportive relationship. If a child is rushed or pushed to tell a story, or questioned repeatedly, the result is a foreclosure of important information. Important ground is lost, as the child will likely close down and reveal very little.

Phase 2. Co-constructing the Child's Life Story (Months 2–7)

Once the clinician and child have established a sense of comfort and trust in their relationship, they may begin to spend more time on co-constructing a narrative of the child's life. The means of telling the story, for example, through oral narrative, conversation, play, and similar activities will vary depending on the child's developmental level, readiness to talk, and individual preferences. Depending on the child's age and interests, the clinician can make available writing and drawing materials, cameras, computers, puppets, or doll-house toys. One strategy for beginning the process with school-aged children is to construct a lifeline of the child's life, similar to the timelines the child may be familiar with from school history texts. Over a period of weeks, the clinician and child can elaborate various narratives in relation to this lifeline. Children are encouraged to take the lead in where to start their narrative (e.g., birth, present day, or some relatively happy period) and pace the story in relation to their level of comfort. Some children will become absorbed in the mechanics of writing a story or portraying experiences through drawings. The challenge is to engage children in telling the story through a medium of their choice, while keeping the focus on the *process* of storytelling, not on the medium or the resulting product.

The clinician supports the child's story by providing scaffolding, empathy, and coherency. The focus is on the content of the child's story, but also on its style and form, as they may reveal the child's self-perception as well as aspects of the child's past experiences (Holmes, 2001). For instance, children whose stories go on without focus may feel overwhelmed by their experiences. Similarly, children who participate minimally in personal storytelling may have been consistently discouraged from talking about their experiences.

As the child reveals stories, the clinician reflects on the story and its meaning with the child and also may pause it, help the child to tolerate emotional intensity, or help the child to elaborate or recognize inconsistencies and incoherencies. Most importantly, clinicians help children to feel that their experiences are shared and understood.

Several goals are to be met during this period of intervention:

Help Interpret the Meaning of Trauma Within the Context of the Child's Life, Including Strengths. The child controls to a large degree what is told during the story, but the clinician can gradually address trauma if the child fails to do so. Similarly, the clinician can address more normative aspects of the child's life, if the child only discusses trauma. Without minimizing issues of trauma and loss, the clinician should support the child in telling a complex life story, with positive as well as negative elements. For example, one young teenager was adopted during the intervention by loving foster parents with whom he closely identified. He was very angry with his mother, who became involved with methamphetamine while grieving the death of her own parent. Although he clearly was very conflicted in his feelings about his mother, he adamantly portrayed her as "all bad." Helping this child to remember more positive characteristics of his mother, and acknowledge his loving feelings toward her, actually helped him to become more comfortable with the adoption. Accessing strengths also helps the child to put traumatic events in perspective and discover not only "ghosts" from the past, but "angels"; that is, beneficent influences or protective sources (Lieberman, Padrón, Van Horn & Harris, 2005). Accessing positive influences also can help a child feel more strength to look at negative influences.

Important lines of development that the clinician can encourage include viewing the trauma as one part of the past and not the entire "storyline," helping the child to reestablish trust in her ability to understand past experiences and feelings, helping the child to place traumatic experiences in perspective, and focusing on the child's ability to actively create a healthy life rather than being a victim (Lieberman & Van Horn, 1998; 2005).

Address Trauma Through Containment. The clinician also will serve as a source of containment for regulating intense emotions associated with trauma through emotional comfort and helping the child to understand overwhelming experiences in a way that supports a positive self-concept, trust in others, and hope for the future. A clinician who contains the child's emotions listens to what the child is saying and makes sense of it in light of all that he knows about this specific child. The clinician then helps the child to interpret intense feelings and experiences in a way that the child can understand and accept. We use a variety of different intervention strategies, adapted from existing relationship-based therapies (Lieberman & Van Horn, 1998; Lieberman, Compton, Van Horn & Ghosh-Ippen, 2003), such as identifying and linking the child's feelings with past experience and current behavior and directly addressing issues of trauma.

The following is an example of containment:

John, age 10, tells the clinician that he would like to get revenge on his mother's paramour, who had beaten his mother several times when they were living together. He then talks about finding this man when he turns 16 and punishing him. As John talks about his anger, he balls up his fist and laughs uncomfortably. The clinician listens to John and rather than responding with shock and telling him that his thoughts are dangerous and inappropriate, she articulates to him that it must make him feel very helpless to have witnessed this man's anger and violence. She then interests John in working together to look at his anger and find appropriate and safe ways to deal with it. John calms visibly and no longer laughs. He cries when he tells the clinician how no one had been there to help him when he was with his mother.

In this excerpt, the clinician relied on her understanding of John's anger in the larger context of his history and in the context of her relationship with him. John's aggressive thoughts appeared to be a defensive response to intense fear and a profound sense of vulnerability. From prior sessions, the clinician recalled that John had not been protected from the paramour on many occasions by his mother and had not learned age-appropriate ways to manage his intense anger. As a result, his thoughts of anger appeared to be based on a "flight-or-fight" survival mode. John's visible relaxation suggests that the containment was successful and helped him to better understand his feelings.

Help the Child to Develop the Ability to Independently Regulate Intense Emotion. Helping children to find ways to regulate strong emotions and to self-soothe is another central aspect of this phase of the intervention. As children begin to tell their stories, they may experience symptoms of PTSD during the session or when they return home. The clinician should be prepared to slow down the pace of the session and help the child focus on a manageable part of the story. Sometimes, it can be helpful if the clinician teaches the child how to self-soothe, so that the child can better tolerate the negative emotion associated with trauma that may surface during the intervention or when the child goes home.

One way to help the child to self-soothe is to initiate a conversation with the child about caring for physical needs. This strategy has the advantage that it can be used with children of different ages and appeals to children's desire to be independent. Some questions that initiate these conversations are the following: What does your body feel like when you are thirsty? How do you act when feeling thirsty? Is it okay to feel thirsty? What's the plan for taking care of yourself when you feel thirsty? Who can you ask for help if you need it? The clinician affirms that it is normal to feel thirsty and that the child can take care of it. In subsequent discussion, clinicians may ask children about self-care when they are tired, hungry, hot, or cold.

From these types of questions, the clinician lays the foundation for understanding that, as with physical needs, we have emotional needs and our bodies also give us information about those needs. The clinician helps the child to understand that, to take care of ourselves emotionally, we need to be able to identify and take care of emotions. Some questions to initiate these conversations are: How does your body feel when you are sad? How do you act when sad? Is it okay to feel sad? When was the last time you were sad? Did you tell anyone? Does telling someone help you not to feel sad? Do you ever pretend to be happy, but are sad inside? Clinicians and children then can discuss how to take care of themselves when sad. If children cannot come up with any suggestions, clinicians may ask them how they feel when they are happy, what makes them happy, and then feed those items back to them as a means to relieve their sadness. The discussion should end with the message that "this is another way you can take care of yourself—knowing when you are sad and then knowing what to do to feel less sad." In other sessions, the clinician may move on to other feelings relevant to the particular child, such as anxiety or anger.

This scheme can be adapted to children at different developmental levels. The technique is flexible, as it can be covered in one session with an older child or slowly built upon with younger children by discussing different aspects over a period of time.

Provide Education Regarding Parental Substance Misuse. Part of the child's story will involve methamphetamine misuse by parents or experiences in which parents used or misused other substances. Since many children of parents with substance misuse problems have learned to avoid talking about family problems, it may take time for them to actively engage in a discussion of their own thoughts and feelings on the subject. Claudia Black (2001) underscores that the very fact that a clinician begins to talk with a child about a topic that has been taboo or kept silent begins an important process. In this discussion, it is critical to find out what the child is feeling. Some children are worried, others are angry or feel numbed by past experiences when their parents were misusing substances. Discussions should occur over time and clinicians may return to this topic on different occasions. In discussions, clinicians can help children to understand that:

- Addiction is an illness that is very hard to recover from.
- They are not to blame for their parents' addiction.

- Their parent is ill, not bad.
- An addiction in a parent can make a child feel confused and rejected.
- It is important to talk about their experiences with a person they trust.
- Parental addiction has far-reaching effects on children and families.

Opportunities to discuss parental methamphetamine misuse may arise naturally and spontaneously, but sometimes the clinician may want to introduce the topics in conversation or through a book about addictions. One book that has been quite popular with younger children is called *Our Gracie Aunt* by J. Woodson (2002). In this beautifully illustrated book, two children develop a secure and loving relationship with their aunt following their removal by child protective services from their mother's care, apparently due to substance misuse.

Confront and Correct Erroneous Beliefs. In this phase of the intervention, the professional challenges certain of children's assumptions and corrects misinformation related to important life experiences. Many children who experience trauma may have received harmful misinformation, for example, that they are responsible for the trauma or the family's problems, or they may draw other incorrect conclusions, for example, that other families do not also experience parental methamphetamine misuse. Such erroneous beliefs can block understanding. Therefore, as part of the intervention, the clinician should be alert to any utterances on the part of the child that suggest self-blame, condemnation, or other harmful beliefs and should directly confront them.

Challenges and Strategies. The clinician and child may encounter a number of challenges to the co-construction of the child's life story. Some children may not be familiar with telling stories about themselves, or may not have the language to convey their emotions. For other children, trauma stories, for example, those involving their parents' substance misuse, may be forbidden topics within their families of origin. In addition, the topics may be painful or embarrassing. Some children may deny their experiences of trauma. Others may struggle to even tell any story, "shutting down" and telling only fragmented bits of experience.

A variety of strategies are available for supporting the child when storytelling becomes difficult. Sitting quietly for a short period, slowing down, focusing on only one part of the story, and openly acknowledging the difficulties of the topics under discussion are possible responses. In some cases, the clinician works with only a few words and reflects them back while encouraging the child that such words are important. The clinician may strive to provide the child with a sense of safety. For instance, a clinician can let the child know that together they can begin to look at these issues, so that the child does not feel as overwhelmed or alone.

Clinicians often have strong reactions to children in foster care (Jacobsen, Levy-Chung & Kim, 2002) and to children who have experienced trauma, loss, and separation. Common reactions that we have experienced in Life Story Intervention are a wish to provide more to the child than is realistic, or to retreat from the child. Some clinicians have wanted to provide more sessions to the child each week, to spend several hours per session with the child to make up for all of the negative experiences the child has had, to continue the therapy beyond what is realistically possible, or to step in to become a foster parent to the child. Other reactions include the community clinician's feeling that the child has nothing to say, is disinterested in them, or that they can't reach the child emotionally. Understanding these reactions and being alert to their influence is key to ensuring that they do not divert therapeutic progress. Such feelings should be discussed in supervision (described later).

Phase 3: Endings (Months 6–8)

Endings are an essential and difficult part of all interventions. In endings, feelings of sadness, regret, and hope may be experienced. Accomplishments are acknowledged, as are disappointments; losses and gains are discussed (Holmes, 2001). If this phase of the intervention is successful, the relationship between child and clinician is brought to closure in a manner that allows the child to find a healthy way to deal with loss. A child who is able to come to closure will inevitably feel and express sadness at the ending of the intervention, but realize and readily acknowledge the gains made. The child does not feel that she is to blame for the ending.

The following goals comprise this third phase of the intervention:

Discuss the Separation with the Child. Children should know at the outset that the intervention is limited in time. Children typically approach the end phase of the intervention with preconceptions about past separations or losses. Although separations often are difficult, if a child has not been helped to grieve past losses, the ending phase will be particularly challenging. In this phase, children will need help to interpret and cope with the end of their relationship with the clinician.

Often, the ending phase is one in which feedback about the relationship and about the child is synthesized and directly communicated to the child. This feedback has occurred throughout the intervention, but more emphasis is given to it in the ending phase. This feedback is intertwined with the notion that the ending also bridges the possibility of a new beginning. The child needs to know she also proceeds with strengths, and that others are there to help.

Create a Memento of the Intervention. During the final weeks, the child and clinician may work together to create a memento of their time together. The child, for instance, may choose to create a story or drawing, or to illustrate a timeline as a memory of the intervention. Alternately, the child may take photos of something the two did together or of a place they visited.

What the clinician and child create together may vary greatly depending on the child, the clinician, and their specific relationship. Annie, age 8, worked with a social worker from a Japanese background. Annie loved jewelry. At the end of intervention, the two created a colorful origami necklace for Annie to keep. Before the paper squares were folded, Annie and her clinician each wrote important thoughts or memories on the inside. For instance, on one paper fold, the clinician noted, "I remember how you smiled when you talked about your grandmother." Annie also communicated important memories and feelings to the clinician. Other clinicians and children have created mementos in the form of memory books, photo albums, drawings, and videos.

Identify a Natural Mentor. Children also are helped to identify a trustworthy, supportive adult in their current social network. This adult can be a relative, foster parent, or educator. Learning to identify such individuals is an important life skill, and also will increase the likelihood that children will continue to receive support after the termination of the intervention. This adult has a healthy interest in the child and serves as a "bridge," consolidating the gains the child has made over the course of the intervention.

Meet with the Child and the Child's Natural Mentor(s). In the final session, the clinician meets with the child and mentor to review the child's progress, share the memento, and say good-bye.

Provide Referrals. The child and foster parent will be provided with contact information should the child require further support.

Challenges and Strategies. Clinicians should be alert to a denial of feelings by children during the ending phase of intervention, or to highly self-reliant strategies. Helping the child to acknowledge strengths is important, but so is underscoring their sadness and loss.

Clinicians also need to be aware of countertransference about separations in general, and about this ending in particular. If a clinician has difficulties in coming to terms with separations, it will make it hard for the child to do so. The topic may be avoided, dwelt on too long, or the clinician may confuse his or her feelings with those of the child. Separations are an important topic for supervision (see later discussion).

Post-test and Follow-up Assessments

Within 2 weeks subsequent to termination, and again 6 months subsequent to the termination of the intervention, the individual who conducted the pre-test assessment readministers the battery of standardized developmental, mental health, and substance use/attitude measures. The assessor meets with the child and foster parent (separately) to express a continuing concern and interest in the child and family, and to discuss the child's functioning at home and school and the presence of any trauma symptoms. Referrals will be offered based on the post-test and follow-up assessments, and should the child need additional support in the future.

Caregiver Component

The child's caregiver, typically the foster parent or kinship care provider, also is seen over a 6–8-month period by the clinician. Caregivers typically are included in mental health treatment for children for a variety of reasons. Obtaining multiple sources of information may be critical to the initial and ongoing assessment of the impact of the intervention. In addition, parents, including foster parents, may be vicariously traumatized by their child's exposure to traumatic events and require support. Significant empirical evidence suggests that trauma-related parental distress is related to the child's symptoms, and that parental support of the traumatized child is a significant factor in successful treatment (American Academy of Child and Adolescent Psychiatry, 1998).

Foster parents are seen by the clinician either before or after sessions with the child. The overarching goals of these sessions are to provide emotional support to the foster parent, provide appropriate information to the foster parent regarding the child's intervention, and share information with the foster parent regarding child trauma and parental methamphetamine misuse. In addition, the foster parent can provide valuable assessment information on the child's functioning and significant feedback regarding the implementation of Life Story Intervention. Weekly meetings are encouraged, especially at the beginning of the intervention and in times of crisis, but clinicians typically have a monthly session with foster parents.

Phase 1: Rapport-building and Introduction to the Program (Month 1)

Clinicians schedule sufficient time to talk with foster parents to begin establishing a mutually respectful, trusting, and collaborative working relationship. They describe the program rationale, goals, methods, and timeline to foster parents. They explain to foster parents that they will be keeping them informed of the various activities the children engage in during the intervention session and their rationale, but will respect the children's confidentiality. They also actively listen and respond to foster parents' concerns and observations of the child.

Phase 2. Continued, Monthly Debriefing (Months 2–5)

Clinicians meet the foster parents at least once per month to actively listen and respond to their observations and concerns. Clinicians also share information with foster parents regarding activities engaged in with children during intervention sessions. They do, however, respect the child's confidentiality and do not provide specifics regarding memories, feelings, or perceptions reported by children. Clinicians also share with foster parents more general information regarding a variety of child responses to trauma and intervention and the impact of parental methamphetamine misuse on children. They ask foster parents if there is any information they should be aware of in working with their family, for example, religious practices. Finally, clinicians support foster parents and their families. They provide referrals for foster parents, for example for homemaker services, or to provide coaching for how to approach medical, educational, and child welfare systems to obtain services for children.

Phase 3. Endings (Month 6)

Foster parents will be offered a list of mental health, health, and educational referrals should children require further support then or in the future. Foster parents also are offered a list of community supports available to them should they require respite or other support.

If the foster parent is identified by the child as the "natural mentor," then the foster parent attends a final meeting to review the child's progress and say good-bye to the clinician with the child. If the foster parent is not so designated, then the clinician meets separately with him or her to discuss the child's progress and to say good-bye.

Challenges and Strategies. Clinicians may face a variety of challenges at any point in the intervention with foster parents. Although communication with the child's caregiver is vital, it can present a significant challenge, especially if the child has difficulty trusting adults. It is a balancing act to maintain a relationship with the foster parent while not giving the child the suspicion that the clinician is "talking behind her back."

In addressing this challenge, we openly discuss with children what we will and will not share with their foster parents. We discuss confidentiality and its limits. The priority is child safety. For example, a child returned home during the course of the intervention. After several months, the community clinician began to suspect that the child's mother had relapsed. She had discontinued her participation in Narcotics Anonymous and lost her job. During one session, she was sleeping, unresponsively, on the couch when the clinician arrived, and on another she seemed to be high. As a mandated reporter, the clinician had to report her observations to the child welfare caseworker to the detriment of her relationship with the family. She did, however, share this with both the mother and the child, thereby preserving a working relationship.

In assessing crisis situations, clinicians should examine the situations from different perspectives and understand what is happening, especially in situations in which a parent or child may not view the situation in the same manner as the clinician or others from the dominant culture. However, when clear risks emerge, swift action to keep the child safe from harm is essential (Lieberman & Van Horn, 1998, 2005).

Child Welfare Professionals

The children served were all in foster care and had monthly contact with their family caseworkers. The community clinician working with the child spoke with the child's caseworker prior to the beginning of the intervention, and the caseworker signed a consent form stating that the caseworker believed the intervention would be beneficial for the child and, more specifically, confirmed that there was no information about the child that would suggest the intervention would be harmful. This information was used by the child's legal guardian, a lawyer employed by DCFS, to grant official permission for the child's inclusion in the study.

Maintaining contact with the caseworker during the course of the intervention proved to be challenging, as child welfare workers have extremely busy schedules and are not always able to take on new projects. This is not to say that caseworkers were unconcerned or difficult to work with, merely that the daily work load is very time-consuming and does not allow much time for philosophical reflection.

In spite of this challenge of finding time, in the case mentioned previously in which a foster child was experiencing difficulty with a foster parent, the caseworker responded swiftly and appropriately upon receipt of this information. It almost goes without saying that any intervention with children in foster care is highly dependent upon the support and cooperation of the caseworker.

Supervision

Foster children from methamphetamine-involved families typically have complex life histories and multiple, unmet needs. For community clinicians to function adequately, supervision is an integral part of the intervention. The goals of the Life Story Intervention include the continuing education of community clinicians regarding children's development and responses to multiple traumas, the maintenance of program fidelity, problem solving, reflection, and support for any secondary trauma that community clinicians may be experiencing as a result of the disturbing life stories told by the children. Supervision occurs on a weekly basis, typically in person, but in some circumstances via telephone.

The main characteristics of the supervision are:

- **Transdisciplinary**. Given the complexity of the cases, we prefer to provide clinical supervision within a transdisciplinary team setting. It is necessary that the team include an experienced, licensed mental health clinician such as a licensed clinical social worker (LCSW), clinical psychologist, or psychiatrist who has expertise in working with children who have been exposed to trauma and substance misuse. In addition to supervision, the licensed mental health clinicians provide telephone backup or crisis intervention for community clinicians. The team also should include a child welfare professional to educate professionals and team members regarding child welfare policy and practice, and to strategize regarding interaction with the child welfare system. Other members who can provide important perspectives include developmental psychologists, educators, and experienced foster parents.

- **Group setting**. We also prefer to provide supervision within a group setting. This is not only efficient, but it allows community clinicians to learn from each others' experiences.

- **Reflective**. Supervision also is reflective. According to Shahmoon-Shanok and colleagues (1995), reflection involves "stepping back from the immediate experience to sort through thoughts and feelings about what one is observing and doing with children and families" (p. 9). Emphasis is placed on the community professional's continued professional development.

- **Collaborative**. The relationship formed by the community clinicians and supervisory team members is collaborative. Reflective supervision involves a reciprocal relationship that is built on empathy, respect, validation, and shared experience. Critical thinking and accountability are other essential aspects of the relationship.

- **Monitoring**. Supervision also provides an important monitoring function regarding treatment fidelity and any needed referrals.

- **Educational**. Participating community clinicians are provided with information regarding children's development and responses to trauma. They also share resources with one another regarding helpful articles in the professional literature and resources for children.

Challenges and Strategies

There are a variety of challenges to supervision. For example, reaching consensus across diverse clinicians in complex and urgent situations is not always realistic. To address this issue, each case is assigned a primary supervisor, who may respond in emergency situations. Respect and clear communication among supervisory team members is essential.

Conclusion

In conclusion, Life Story Intervention is a flexible and individualized intervention to support the psychological development of foster children from methamphetamine-involved families. Each intervention will share a number of characteristics that are important to underscore:

Life Story Intervention is Embedded within a Sociocultural Context

Life Story intervention is designed for use in the cultural context of rural Illinois, and takes into account the community strengths and limitations, as revealed in our ethnographic research (Part 2), as well as clinical and child welfare experience with children subjected to trauma and parental substance misuse. Rural Illinois has a rich tradition of oral narrative, but not of widespread use of traditional mental health services, especially within lower-income communities and for problems viewed as "family business." We provide education and supervision for adults who work professionally with children and families, and who live within communities with few existing resources for providing high-quality mental health interventions for children exposed to multiple traumas and parental substance misuse. By using community clinicians, we aim to facilitate communication between the child, the child's family, and the clinician, and ensure that the intervention "makes sense" given local understandings and socialization practices.

Life Story Intervention Directly Addresses Traumatic Events

Research indicates that those interventions with traumatized children that address trauma are more effective than nondirective treatment (Cohen & Mannarino, 1996; Deblinger, McLeer & Henry, 1990). Further, treatment designed to support a sense of mastery over the traumatic event is more efficacious than techniques designed to merely help children express their feelings (Corder & Haizlip, 1989; Galante & Foa, 1986; Shelby, 2000). In addition, children benefit most from having adults help them share and cope with their subjective feelings of distress, rather than avoiding, distracting, or minimizing their emotional pain.

Life Story Intervention Contextualizes Traumatic Events and Relationships

Life Story Intervention focuses on the meaning of traumatic events within the context of the child's life. Without minimizing the negative impact of traumatic events, the child is encouraged to understand the emotional impact of any trauma events and to separate concepts of self from them; in other words, to define the self as separate from what others have done to the child and separate from other traumatic events that the child may have experienced. This perspective-taking is facilitated through the development not of a "trauma narrative," but of a life story, which includes traumatic as well as other events.

Life Story Intervention is Relationship-based

In the context of a supportive relationship with an adult, many children will share difficult components of their personal history. Other children may be angry, distrustful, and reluctant to engage with an adult; superficial and overly friendly; or so "choked" with emotion that they are unable to communicate.

Throughout the intervention, clinicians build a healthy relationship by balancing "following the child's lead" (i.e., engaging in activities and conversations that the child initiates and finds enjoyable) with initiating and facilitating the telling of difficult life stories.

Life Story Intervention is Sustained

Establishing a healthy, trusting relationship with a traumatized foster child is likely to require a lengthy period of time. Many foster children have been betrayed by adults whom they once trusted, for example, abusive parents. They all have experienced disrupted relationships with parents, as well as maltreatment. This intervention is designed for use over a 6–8-month period. In our experience, most children can develop a positive relationship with the clinician and begin meaningful discussions of their lives within this period, but some traumatized children may require a more extended period. For all children, an essential component of termination is helping the child to identify and approach a "natural mentor"—a trustworthy and supportive adult in the child's own social network who may serve as a long-term, ongoing source of support for the child after the intervention is concluded.

Life Story Intervention is Strengths-based

Life Story Intervention also allows the clinician and child to co-construct an interpretation of the child's life story that supports the child's strengths, ability to help herself, understanding of which relationships are safe and trusting, positive sense of self, and hope for the future. Life Story Intervention also allows the clinician to correct the child's misinformation, for example, that the child is responsible for the trauma or the family's problems, or that other families do not also experience parental methamphetamine misuse.

Life Story Intervention is Individualized

Children choose to tell their stories in many ways. Different children may respond to very different conversational or activity contexts, for example, direct questioning, playing, or talking. Some children, for example, may prefer to communicate their stories through drawing, lifelines or genograms, play writing, puppet-play, video movies of their lives, or other creative activity. Some children may combine different expressive contexts depending upon the particular narrative within the life story. How the child chooses to tell the story, or what the child uses as a springboard, is not the emphasis. What is emphasized is the child's understanding of complex life events in a way that allows for a more positive future.

Life Story Intervention is Child-paced and Responsive to the Child's Developmental Level

Some children will move quickly through the intervention, whereas others with different personal characteristics or more complex trauma histories may require a slower pace. The goal is to "walk beside" the child through difficult memories, sharing and providing an adult perspective, not to "fix" or "instruct" the child. Some older children may prefer to tell their life stories in the context of gentle, direct questioning from the clinician, whereas younger children may prefer to construct their life stories in the context of pretend play.

Life Story Intervention Includes Foster Parents

Interventions with children are more effective when they include parents (or foster parents) as well (Cohen & Mannarino, 1996; Deblinger et al., 1990). At least once a month, the clinician meets with foster parents to listen to and discuss their concerns and observations; check in regarding how the child is functioning at school and home; communicate about the intervention (the rationale and activities, but not about the child's specific responses); and provide educational information as needed, for example, about some common child responses to trauma and intervention.

Life Story Intervention Includes Communication with Child Welfare Workers

The clinician also meets with the child's case worker as least once. Child welfare workers are presented with recent research on methamphetamine and its effects on children and families. They are encouraged to provide feedback to the clinician and to share their perspectives.

In summary, Life Story Intervention is an evidence-informed, culturally sensitive intervention designed through the collaboration of researchers and clinicians for rural children affected by parental substance misuse. Assessment of the effectiveness of Life Story Intervention is ongoing. In Chapter 12, we describe pilot testing of the intervention through several case examples of children's responses to Life Story Intervention.

Chapter Twelve

Children's Responses to Life Story Intervention

Alice, a 10-year-old girl who participated in Life Story Intervention, loved listening to popular music—on the radio, CDs, and TV. During one session of Life Story Intervention, she talked in an animated way with her community clinician about a song from a popular group, the Cheetah Girls, that she "loved." She asked if she could sing the song into the tape recorder, "for the teachers at the college." The song referred to Cinderella, but, unlike Cinderella, the Cheetah Girls had no intention of waiting for someone to set them free. The Cheetah Girls intended to rescue themselves.

Other children who participated in Life Story Intervention also played songs on CDs that they brought to sessions, or they turned on radios as they drove with their community clinicians on their way to a nearby park or library. They voiced the words as they were sung or sang along, often with intensity, clearly identifying with the words or remembering past places and experiences.

In this chapter, we have selected three children to illustrate a variety of child responses to Life Story Intervention, their struggles, and our attempts to help. The children depicted here are similar in age, length of time in foster care, past experiences, and history of involvement with parental methamphetamine misuse, but they show individual variation and variation over time in their responses to Life Story Intervention. For example, children sometimes communicated about their lives through play, oral narratives of personal experience, or, as in our opening example of Alice, through songs associated with a particular memory of a time when the their families were together. In telling the stories of Jake, Alice, and Mark, we have altered important details of children's profiles both to assure their anonymity and to reflect larger patterns observed in the children we worked with as a whole. Cases were constructed using weekly notes provided by community clinicians,

Many children from methamphetamine-involved families formed meaningful relationships with community clinicians. Photo by Carl Kingery.

notes taken during weekly supervision sessions, audiotapes of sessions, and standardized assessments.

Jake: The Child Who Had No Story to Tell

Jake, age 10 years, was referred to Life Story Intervention by his child protective service caseworker. Mrs. Bernard, Jake's foster mother, was overwhelmed with Jake's many needs. She described him as too dependent, demanding too much attention, arguing a lot, destroying things, and failing to finish things he started. Mrs. Bernard was particularly frustrated because Jake hoarded food and had problems with bedwetting. She also noted that Jake was sweet and smart.

Jake had been taken into custody 2 years prior because his parents were found producing methamphetamine in the home where they lived. The child protective agency investigation revealed that the children were living in a small trailer, described as chaotic, cluttered, and dirty. Importantly, investigators found hydrochloric acid, a precursor of methamphetamine, in the living room. Jake apparently had observed sexual activities between adults in the home and had been molested sexually by an older woman. He had not talked about these experiences except with a sister. Jake was first placed with relatives, where he lived for about a year, but was subsequently moved to his current home because his relatives found his behavior hard to manage.

When we saw Jake, his parents were losing their parental rights, and his foster parents had decided to adopt him.

Assessment

Jake had significant emotional and behavioral problems. When Mrs. Bernard completed the Child Behavior Checklist (CBCL), she used a black pen to heavily underscore that she needed "help." She was particularly concerned because Jake lied, stole, blamed others, snuck out of the house, picked fights, and broke other children's toys. On this measure, he scored in the clinical range on externalizing and internalizing behaviors including attention, anxiety, social problems, delinquent and aggressive behaviors. On the Trauma Symptom Checklist for Children (TSCC), Jake scored in the clinical range on scales assessing anxiety, anger, and dissociation. He noted that he "very often" felt afraid that something bad would happen, and he felt he did something wrong. In addition, he described frequently daydreaming, wanting to yell and break things, going away in his mind, trying not to think, and pretending he was someone else. Jake scored within the normal range on a measure of receptive language, the PPVT.

Jake was guarded throughout most of the assessment. He was able to briefly express some feelings of vulnerability, however, and to share them with the assessor. He noted, for instance, that he did not want to be "tooken from Mom," and told the assessor that he was afraid a stranger might kill him with a gun. When asked about memories of sad or unhappy times, Jake said simply that he had "lost them." He had no memories.

Initial Phase

Mae worked with Jake as his community clinician. She was a long-term resident of the area and had reared four children there. She had a master's degree in social work and a position with the local child protection agency. When she arrived for the first session, Jake was waiting in the living room of his foster home. Although interested in participating, he was also doubtful whether Mae would really be available for him. He asked Mae repeatedly if she was coming back again. On one occasion, he expressed a fear that he would get lost and that Mae would not be able to find him. Jake also did not quite believe whether what Mae said was true, possibly reflecting his belief that he could only minimally trust what adults told him. For instance, when Mae complimented Jake on his handwriting, he looked at her skeptically. Jake's hunger for attention also stood out. He longed for positive feedback, and beamed when he received individual attention.

Mae worked to define what Jake wanted to address during their work together. His list consisted of several items, all linked to issues in his foster home. He wanted to be more honest, get help to stop stealing, and do things right. Jake's foster mom had come up with a similar list.

Early sessions took place in the library near the house, as well as a room in Jake's home. Both places afforded enough privacy to talk. Jake avoided mention of his family of origin and did not talk about past experiences of trauma. He dealt with even brief questions about his past by averting his eyes and quickly changing topics. In this and all sessions, Mae worked to create the essential parameters to support a safe and collaborative relationship by being consistent, emotionally responsive, empathetic, reliable, and by setting the clear boundaries needed for a safe relationship.

When Mae inquired in a later session if Jake could talk about his past, he stated that his parents were "drug addicts," but did not elaborate. At times, he would spontaneously tell Mae about nightmares that "weren't so nice," but he was unable to elaborate. Jake gave a minimal account of his past by drawing a timeline on a large sheet of construction paper that Mae brought to a session. He marked a notch on the sheet and wrote below this "Sam," referring to a relative whom he had lived with before coming to his current foster placement. When asked about why he moved from Sam's place, or what it was like there, he simply said that he "couldn't remember."

Mae approached sessions by not pressing Jake and by listening to what he had to say. She gave Jake "permission" to talk by listening to him in a focused, empathetic way and by telling him that she would be there for him. She did not pressure him about past trauma, but let him know that it was "okay" to talk about painful things, but it was also "okay" if he didn't want to talk.

Jake responded to Mae by talking obliquely about children who appeared to be lonely. During several sessions, he held a mother dog and taught Mae the names of her puppies. He then taught her how to call the puppies, so that they would not get lost. He smiled when Mae called them and the puppies responded. These and other interactions seemed to capture Jake's growing trust and confidence in Mae. Some of the story fragments of Jake's past that emerged were becoming more elaborated, invested with feeling, and expressive of Jake's own perspective. At the same time, formidable barriers remained. Mae summarized her thoughts about the early sessions by noting that, although she felt she had established a meaningful relationship with Jake, "I don't know how to break through the walls that he has put up."

Mae also met regularly with Mrs. Bernard, Jake's foster mother. Overwhelmed with Jake's many needs, Mrs. Bernard appreciated Mae's support and came to better understand his need to hold onto someone or something tangible. With this perspective on why Jake was hoarding items and why he was so clingy, Mrs. Bernard responded by being less punitive and more responsive to Jake's needs.

Although Jake thrived on the individual attention she gave him, Mae struggled with Jake's silences. She felt that more time with Jake could help him and that she could help to compensate for his painful past. Mae also struggled with the pervasive sadness that Jake exuded. In supervision, she frequently spoke of wanting to cheer him up. Mae also brought up the idea of seeing Jake for several hours per week in more intensive therapy. Mae brought in various materials, including a computer and camera, to help Jake tell his story and make a memento. Supervision focused on exploring why Mae felt such pressure to take care of Jake and on helping her to contain his feelings rather than trying to elicit a story through any means. Emphasis was also placed on putting the relationship first and making it realistic within the needed boundaries of the intervention. Mae thus worked on being available, consistent, reliable, sensitive and responsive (Holmes, 2001), thereby creating the essential conditions for a story to emerge.

Middle Phase

In the middle phase of the intervention, Mrs. Bernard began to tell Mae more about struggles Jake was having at school. By coordinating a school meeting that included Mrs. Bernard, his teacher, child protective caseworker, the school psychologist, and herself, Mae facilitated communication between all members about Jake's difficulties with homework. The school offered Jake additional academic services.

Jake began to reveal much more about his past in Life Story Intervention sessions. Sometimes this occurred unexpectedly after long periods during which he had been silent, but when Mae had provided considerable containment; that is, when she tolerated his feelings and provided the emotional support for him to consider and understand them.

At first, Jake's story emerged nonverbally, in pictures he drew on large sheets of construction paper that Mae brought to sessions. Jake first drew a house and then barred all of the windows, leaving the viewer little access to its interior. He then focused on Belle, the mother dog with puppies, in his drawings. Jake's drawing of Belle was well rendered and contained many details—her long tail, paws, white face, and frightened, alert eyes. In supervisory sessions, we wondered whether Jake himself identified with the dog, and whether he might be projecting fears regarding his mother's absence from his life and aloneness onto the dog.

In other sessions, Jake used language to talk about experiences. For instance, he recalled his favorite teacher, Ms Thomas, who taught him how to button up his coat in kindergarten. His voice became more animated as he talked. Mae continued to "contain" by listening to Jake, and helping him to interpret his experiences. She commented on the happiness and animation in his voice as he recalled Ms Thomas. In this same session, Jake talked about the grandmother with whom he had lived briefly after being removed from his home. He also recalled his second grade teacher, and remembered playing outside and eating lunch. These topics were not too threatening, and the animation in Jake's voice underscored his sense of connection to his own narrative.

The following week bridged more painful themes. Jake talked about a cousin who had died. In this context, Mae helped him to feel safe in talking about his feelings. He spontaneously said that he felt "a little sad," minimizing the pain that was evident in his facial expression and posture. Mae underscored that such experiences did make people feel sad, often very sad. Jake recalled other early memories during this session as well, including experiences he had enjoyed. He then referred briefly to the sexual abuse before closing down. Mae underscored that they could talk about anything painful together, but only if he wanted to share it.

In the following sessions, Jake began to move a bit more fluidly between present and past. During one session, he talked about being down in the dumps about himself because of the recent bad grades he had received at school. He then sang a ballad that his mother sang when she was sad, noting that the song spoke about winter coming and about death. Jake was calm when he said this and was able to maintain eye contact with Mae, who noted that Jake seemed to be including feelings and memories into his story. As he told different stories, Mae listened calmly, commenting on the underlying emotional themes.

Other sessions seemed less productive. Although Jake appeared happy to see Mae each week, what he talked about seemed peripheral to larger themes in his life. On one occasion, he said he couldn't remember any more and didn't have any more stories to tell. Mae listened, but she did not intrude on or try to control what Jake said. In the next session, Mae continued to keep the thread of the narrative alive and encourage Jake to become more reflective, noting "You started off last time feeling. . . ." Sometimes Jake would show some realization of past topics he had brought up or of past feelings. He might note, for example, "Oh, yes, I was pretty sad." These exchanges seemed to help Jake develop more continuity and awareness of the various feelings he had shared with Mae.

Jake's periods of silence and his continuing avoidance of stories of personal experience remained challenging to Mae. Mae did not want to dominate sessions, intrude on spaces Jake could not yet enter, or inquire too much into painful areas of his life. At the same time, Mae had difficulties with long silences. Imposing her own narrative or story to fill the spaces would have been risky, as it may have filled her own need to have "something happen" in the sessions. As Jake often said little, Mae became discouraged at times and wondered if Jake really had forgotten about his life. At times Mae wanted "rules" about what to do in therapy so as to make things happen. On other occasions, Mae noted that Jake's underlying sadness made her want to cheer him up.

Supervision focused on what Mae could realistically offer and on the challenges she was experiencing in "holding" the intense sadness that pervaded Jake's stories. It also focused on helping Mae to see her role as facilitating conditions for Jake to tell his story, whether negative or positive (Winnicott, 1965). Tolerating undefined or unarticulated feelings was part of this process.

In this phase of the intervention, Jake's stories began to include Mae. Jake, for example, spontaneously recalled their first session and smiled as he talked about this memory. In this and other sessions, Mae wrote in her notebook that Jake seemed to take more initiative in remembering. She described their conversations now as going "two ways," suggesting that she had to some extent helped to create a reciprocal, collaborative, and safe relationship with Jake.

Overall, Jake seemed to be more connected to memories and feelings in the middle phase of the intervention. He began to link memories and feelings together into a larger story. Given that he hardly had any story to tell in the initial phase, what he said in this phase seemed more elaborated and spontaneous.

Ending Phase

As Jake and Mae began to talk more about endings, he responded by forgetting that Life Story Intervention would end. His denial that the end of Life Story Intervention was approaching echoed his initial approach to narratives: He had insisted that he had no story. Forgetting that Life Story Intervention was coming to a close was less painful than realizing that it and the relationship with Mae had been meaningful to him.

In the last weeks of the intervention, Jake remained engaged with Mae. He sometimes said that he had no story to tell, but nonetheless recalled some positive experiences he had both with an uncle and with Mae. Mae described communications being more like a "normal, two-way conversation." Jake continued to need considerable scaffolding to tell a story, but when that was provided, he could articulate important events or feelings in a shared context. On one occasion, Jake revealed some negative experiences he had had at school. He then sang bluegrass songs for Mae and noted that the songs came from his mother. As he sang, his eye contact with Mae was good. Jake also listened to what Mae said and remained calm as she discussed how many sessions the two still had left.

Jake wanted soda and pizza on the last day, to celebrate their work together. As they ate, Mac and Jake reminisced about their time together. Jake smiled. His affect seemed genuine and was expressed calmly and openly. Mae talked with him about saying good-bye. Jake asked whether this really was the last day, suggesting that he didn't want it to end. Mae spent time with Jake and his foster mother before saying good-bye.

Jake's mentor was Mrs. Albert, a new counselor that he was slated to see. His continuing behavior problems and trauma symptoms required more intensive therapy. Mrs. Albert had worked with many children in foster care. She was eager to work with Jake, both to break new ground and to maintain the gains he had made.

Mae noted that working with Jake was a unique challenge. She recalled that he had an extremely hard time in remembering details of his life. According to Mae, Jake now was able to have more coherent conversations regarding recent experiences in his life, even though he continued to have some difficulty sharing stories about past life experiences. Mae also commented on the benefits to Jake of receiving one-on-one, individual attention from a caring, concerned adult. He seemed to flourish with this attention. During this time, his grades improved, and Mrs. Bernard noticed his improved ability to concentrate on his homework. Over the course of the intervention, Mae talked with Jake about confidentiality and about the fact that talking can be healthy. Mae hoped these conversations might help Jake to open up in the future should he so choose.

Follow-up Assessment

Jake continued to evidence trauma symptoms when he was reassessed 2 weeks later. On the TSCC that Jake himself completed, he continued to have elevated scores on scales assessing anxiety, anger, and dissociative symptoms, although they were no longer in the clinical range. Mrs. Bernard continued to note some behavior problems on the CBCL. For instance, she wrote that he "very often" failed to finish things he started, that he was obsessive, couldn't sit still, and demanded a lot of attention. In addition, he continued to wet the bed and to have nightmares. On this measure, he continued to score in the clinical range with regards to internalizing and externalizing problems including attention, anxiety, social problems, delinquent and aggressive behaviors.

On a more positive note, when asked about Life Story Intervention, Mrs. Bernard underscored that it was "worth it all." She described Jake as a happier child and as being "more open and willing to be a part of our family." The clinician who assessed Jake also described him as cooperative and more open than during the initial assessment. She noted that, during the assessment,

Jake was able to elaborate on some past experiences from his own perspective. However, in so doing, he talked very softly and gave short answers. His demeanor did suggest that he was in emotional pain as he spoke about past experiences in his life. This contrasted with the first assessment, when Jake had insisted that he had no story or memories. Now, he was beginning to speak about the topics that he hitherto had forgotten or could not address.

Six Months Later

Six months later, Jake continued to have behavioral and emotional problems. He scored in the clinical range on externalizing and internalizing behavioral problems as assessed with the CBCL completed by his foster mother. As with previous assessments, his scores on attention, anxiety, social problems, delinquent and aggressive behaviors fell in the clinical range. According to Mrs. Bernard, Jake still was arguing and worrying a lot, demanding a lot of attention, and destroying his own things. He couldn't sit still, complained that no one loved him, got in many fights, and lied. He also did poorly with school work, screamed a lot, hoarded food, and wet the bed almost every night. In contrast to earlier assessments, Jake also showed elevated scores on depression. Jake also continued to have elevated trauma symptoms on the TSCC, especially with regard to anxiety, anger, and dissociative symptoms. On a more positive note, the clinician who assessed Jake noted that he was more able than before to recall and relate experiences from his past. By this account, then, this boy who had no story or memories showed some change in his ability to remember and talk about experiences from his past. We relayed to his guardian our recommendation that Jake continue to receive mental health services.

Alice: A Girl Who Lacked Boundaries

Alice was almost 8 years old when she became a part of Life Story Intervention. Even before her initial assessment, her behavior stood out as unusual. She immediately hugged the assessor and told her that she had been sexually abused. She warmed up to a second assessor in no time and asked to go home with her. She told both women that she "loved" them.

Alice's willingness to reveal anything, even to strangers, was much akin to what has been described as *reactive attachment disorder* in the Diagnostic and Statistical Manual of Mental Disorders–Fourth Edition (DSM-IV-TR, American Psychiatric Association, 2000). According to the DSM-IV-TR (p. 127), this disorder is characterized by "markedly disturbed and developmentally inappropriate social relatedness in most contexts that begins before age 5 years and is associated with grossly pathological care." In one subform, the disinhibited type, the child is indiscriminately sociable, something we observed in Alice. In this disorder, the child's disturbance is not due to delays in development, but rather to grossly pathological care and/or to repeated changes of primary caregivers.

Alice's history involved neglect, along with repeated changes of care-givers. Her mother, Lucinda, had a long history of substance misuse dating back to Alice's first years of life. She became involved in methamphetamine when Alice was 6 years old. After cooking methamphetamine with her boyfriend on outings that included Alice and her sisters, Lucinda would smoke it in pipes or deliver it to other people for money. Eventually, Lucinda was unable even to meet her children's most basic needs. On one occasion when her mother was high, Alice was sexually abused by a man frequenting the home. After she was removed from her mother's charge, Alice lived in four different foster homes. When Life Story Intervention began, Alice had been in foster care for 2 years. Her current foster parents wanted to adopt her.

Assessment

Alice readily acknowledged experiencing trauma symptoms when she was assessed. She spoke openly about having nightmares at about the time when she was sexually abused and worried that someone wanted to kill her. In addition, Alice observed that she was unhappy, wanted to yell at people, and had thoughts of killing herself. She dreamed about being wealthy and living in a mansion. On the TSCC, Alice had elevated scores on scales assessing anxiety, posttraumatic symptoms, and dissociation.

Alice's foster parents noted problems when they completed the CBCL. According to the Weavers, Alice wet the bed, had psychosomatic headaches, argued, showed off, and daydreamed. In addition, she hoarded food, stared blankly at times, and had sudden changes in mood. On this measure, Alice scored in the clinical range in rule-breaking, attention problems, and aggressive behavior. Her receptive language skills, as assessed by the Peabody Picture Vocabulary Test (PPVT-3), were average.

When asked about her family of origin, Alice recalled family violence. On one occasion, she reported stepping in to help her mom when her dad was choking her. She also recalled her mom hitting her dad on the head with a bottle. On that occasion, Alice recalled "glass flying." It took some time for the assessor to surmise that her mother had also broken a window. At times, Alice's recollections took on fantastic elements, making it difficult to discern what actually happened from Alice's own hopes or dreams. For instance, in one story, Alice's parents were "doing meth" in the shed. When Alice discovered this, she screamed, telling her mother to stop. Per Alice's report, her mother listened to her and stopped taking meth all together, something that seemed implausible especially in light of what was known about her mother's continuing methamphetamine misuse.

Initial Phase

Marie, a teacher who had also been a foster mother for several years, worked with Alice. Marie described the initial session as "complex." When Marie arrived, Alice told her that the assessors had promised that she (Marie) would take her to a local department store to buy her make-up. Marie was uncertain about this, and called the assessors, who assured her that they had made no such promise. Seeing that her attempt at manipulation had been foiled, Alice promptly told Marie that she wanted to kill herself, insisting that it had always been her "dream" to buy make-up. Attempts to get Marie to buy material goods for her were a recurrent theme.

Alice was eager to talk about her past. To facilitate this, Marie helped her to construct a genogram of her family. Briefly, a genogram provides a visual overview of a family's history and structure, including relevant marriages, children, deaths, and births (Hartman, 1978; McGoldrick, Gerson & Shellenberger, 1999). Together, the clinician and child can explore what different individuals were like and how the child related to them. Alice listed only her mother's side of the family. On the genogram, Alice wrote "I love you" by her mother and drew a large heart beside it, embellishing it in red.

Alice talked a great deal in the next sessions. She noted that she was ashamed about her looks, and she also recalled a time when her father was drunk and told her to drive his car home. She described her terror as she veered off the road, and then concluded that this experience had been "fun." Later in the session, Alice noted emphatically and angrily that she "hated men." Marie listened to Alice and nodded, but getting a word in edgewise proved difficult.

Alice also discussed her ambivalent and confused feelings about her upcoming adoption. She noted that her foster mom wanted to change her first name to another name when the adoption was completed. To encourage Alice to reflect on her thoughts and feelings, Marie asked Alice what she thought about this. Alice shrugged off the question, stating that it was her new mom's choice.

By the fifth session, Alice eagerly looked forward to Marie's arrival. This day, Alice and Marie met in a park, where Alice began to talk about a story of an abused child she had read, but soon noted that she'd prefer if they could go "buy stuff." It was as if buying could distract her from her psychological pain. With Marie's support, Alice was able to stay involved in the session, and she even listed things she wanted to talk about in Life Story Intervention. Her list included talking about her rabbit, her older sister who was in another foster home, her foster parents, and gifts her biological mother had given her.

Later, Alice talked about fears she experienced when she was raped. This topic came up unexpectedly and was elaborated only briefly. Alice said she was teased later about the experience by students at her school, who taunted her by telling her that she was pregnant. Alice talked about these events in a detached manner. Marie attempted to contain Alice's feelings by commenting, "It is hard to talk about such painful things but we can go slowly and stop if you need to." In this way, she let Alice know that she could understand and empathize with her feelings, and that Alice had control over the telling of her story.

The topics of loss, family violence, self-hatred, and belonging dominated the next session. Marie heard from Alice how her father used to hit her with a belt, how he could not say "no" to drugs, and how quickly he had given up his parental rights. She then expressed a wish to know more about her biological mother. Marie commented on how important it is to know about someone you love. Alice again worked on genograms, this time drawing two trees, one representing her "real family" and one her foster family. She then talked about her feelings about her self, noting that she felt unimportant as a person, that her drawings "stink," and that nobody cared about her except her biological mother and foster mother. Later in the session, Alice told Marie that her foster mother had selected the name "Linda" for her. Marie attended carefully to what Alice said, and asked Alice what she felt about this. In this way, Marie attempted to understand and give Alice room to reflect and voice her thoughts.

In summary, Alice viewed herself in a negative, shameful, and blaming light. She longed for closeness, and sought it out almost indiscriminately, suggesting that she had serious difficulties in protecting herself from potential abuse. She was also fearful of men and doubted whether others would actually be there to recognize and meet her needs. Alice could recall numerous details about past experiences, but struggled to find larger overriding themes or to identify which were her feelings and experiences versus those of others with whom she was close. When she spoke, she did not always clearly mark linguistically who she was taking about. Her stories thus did not clearly differentiate her own feelings and experiences from those of others. Neither did she differentiate her experiences from dreams. Often, her experiences were marked as dreams, or the boundaries between dreams and reality were blurred. Alice also had difficulties in looking more objectively at her past and in reflecting on what she said. Her sentences came rapidly, with quickly shifting themes. Slowing down and reflecting on what she said was difficult. In short, she could not contain her feelings, but acted out and became angry and manipulative when disappointed.

Marie had to constantly balance her empathy for Alice with the need to set clear boundaries. Alice's high level of neediness, evidenced, for example, in her constant wish to go shopping, was a challenge encountered each week in different guises. It was as if, by going shopping or eating, Alice could avoid the need to think about or make sense of her experiences. It was clear that Alice was struggling to come to terms with the painful separation from her biological mother. She was also struggling with the adoption, which she both looked forward to but also feared. Alice was also beginning to talk about her rape and her deep-seated anger toward men, including her father.

Middle Phase

Initially, Alice was very engaged in the middle phase of therapy. She waved when Marie arrived and immediately told her what her needs were. Often, the first need expressed was hunger, something that was met for all children in the study in the form of a snack or small meal.

During one session, Alice mentioned that she knew the word "dependable" meant that you could count on a person. After a brief silence, Alice became somewhat reflective, commenting that it is not good to always be independent which, for Alice, meant not being able to count on anyone. For instance, she wanted a family to adopt her, rather than "wandering" around different foster homes. She then noted that she cannot count on her mother because she is in jail. Marie nodded, noting that this must be painful. Soon after noting this, Alice felt a need to stress that she "really loved" her mother.

As the community clinician, Marie worked hard to contain the many worries expressed by Alice. She told Marie that her father might kidnap her, especially if he found out that she was being adopted. She then talked about her new name and said that her old one will not be gone because she could still use it as a nickname. She later noted that she could also give her old name to her children. She seemed to be actively searching for ways to integrate her "old" and "new" identifies in some meaningful way. She then talked about herself, noting that she likes to grow up fast. Alice then talked about wanting to wear make-up. When she recalled putting on her mom's make-up, Marie noted that Alice had wanted to shop for make-up in the first session. Alice responded that, at the time, she was possibly missing her mother.

As the adoption moved forward, Alice began acting out so much that she was sent to a respite home. She talked with Marie about this, however, and worried that her acting out might affect the adoption. Marie validated her feelings of being afraid and confused. Alice seemed to calm down. Marie spent more time with Alice's foster mother in this period, checking in and providing support. This was often difficult, as Mrs. Weaver did not feel that she had much need for help. Perhaps it was too threatening to admit needing help at a time when she was assuming the role of Alice's adoptive mother.

Alice's anger and disappointment soon undermined her trust in Marie. Alice's anger was triggered by Marie arriving late to one session due to a severe Midwestern thunderstorm. That day, Alice was short-tempered and irritable. She told Marie, "You don't understand." As the two worked on a memory book, Alice told her, "I hate this."

Other factors appeared to be influencing Alice's bad mood. Alice talked about anger she had felt toward a foster sister who smacked her, and then underscored that she loved her new family, "no matter what." It seemed to us that Alice was struggling to integrate negative with positive feelings and to bring closure to her relationship with her biological mother while coming to terms with all the feelings involved in the adoption.

Alice told Marie that she was wanted to skip the next session because she was "too busy." As Marie explored this, Alice told her that "past is past," and that she didn't want to work on her life story project anymore. She reiterated this in a more forceful way, stating that she didn't want to meet with Marie again. She then added that members of her new family are "the most caring people I know."

Alice did not greet Marie spontaneously when Marie arrived for the next sessions. Instead, she waited until Marie took the first steps. The anger, disappointment, and fear of trusting were not easy to address. Marie helped Alice to verbalize a bit more what she felt toward Marie. In this context, Alice told Marie that she wouldn't have told her stories if she hadn't trusted her. Marie talked about how telling stories can trigger fearful memories and assured her that she would keep the stories safe. Alice later told Marie about a coyote family she had seen in the neighborhood. She then described being chased and frightened by a big coyote. The session ended with Alice telling Marie, "I hate you!" Marie did not retaliate but commented that Alice must be very angry and that they could talk about this together to understand why.

Core topics and feelings that were touched upon, addressed, and readdressed in this phase of therapy were those of anger, yearning, and loss; disappointment, anger, and fear; yearning for closeness; and guilt about giving up her family of origin. These topics were played out in Alice's relationship with Marie. Even small breaks in the therapeutic bond were devastating to Alice, who had only tenuous relationships with others to begin with. Alice's intense, negative emotions were formidable, and Marie often felt criticized and undermined. Supervision focused on Marie suspending her own feelings, so that she did not feel hurt and on the need to use her understanding in the intervention sessions.

The stories Alice told of her past life usually included danger, threats, and violence. For instance, she repeatedly spoke of car wrecks, guns, attempted stabbings, and threats between her parents, the adults who were responsible for her well-being and care. Adults were either passive or invited violence. Alice, for instance, recalled her mother saying at one point to her father, "Go ahead . . . shoot me." In her storytelling, Alice often blurred the distinction between dreams and reality. For instance, she thought that a dream she had involving her mother's death meant that her mother was going to die.

The manner in which Alice told stories also was striking. While talking about memories involving incidents in which she was violated or abused, she spoke in a robotic manner, with little or no feeling. In contrast, in other stories, she was the brave heroine "stepping in" to make them apologize when her parents beat each other up, threw hammers, and slammed each other into the wall.

Ending Phase

Alice closed down, opened up a little, and closed down during the final phase of Life Story Intervention. Some of the difficulty in talking about her past was that these memories triggered nightmares. When Marie came for sessions, Alice would tell her that she had had nightmares, but insist that she was "fine." When asked about the content of her troubling dreams, she would say that she couldn't remember. On such occasions, she would frequently say in mantra form "past is past" or "what happened has happened," perhaps as a way to cope and to put the nightmares behind her.

Marie worked to contain Alice's anxiety when she revealed that she was having troubled dreams. She would listen to what Alice said and try to relieve her of some of the anxiety it triggered. She did this by noting how frightening dreams can be and by underscoring how she (Marie) and others in her foster family are trying hard to make Alice feel safe. Marie did not press Alice to explore the nightmares or to reveal their content, but let her know that she was available to talk and listen if Alice wanted to take that route.

The adoption moved forward quickly during this phase of the intervention, resulting in another ending for Alice to face with her biological family. This, along with the games she played, the food she demanded, and the resistance to telling her story became the content of the final phase of the intervention. On one occasion, Alice began talking about her being her "Mommy's baby girl," words that seemed to refer to her biological mother; but before she could elaborate, she talked about the new name her foster mother wanted to give to her at the time of the adoption. Alice also told Marie that she didn't want to participate any more. Alice did share songs with Marie. One song, entitled "So Sick" seemed to express many of the painful and unresolved feelings she had about her past. Marie underscored how hard it can be to talk about the past and how important it is to feel understood.

In this phase of Life Story Intervention, Marie taught Alice how to fold paper airplanes. Before folding them, they would write their memories or feelings on the pieces of paper. In this context, Alice's feelings toward Marie became more transparent. She told her that when she first met Marie, she was sure they were, "Gonna bond right away and have fun," but that it didn't always work out. Marie noted that it takes time to trust. Alice then insisted that she trusted Marie. She then told Marie how her mom and her friends were "stupid" because they got arrested for taking drugs, and that her parents gave her a cigarette to smoke when she was little. Alice revealed that she had never told this story to anyone. She insisted that telling it proved that she trusted Marie. Alice then told Marie she would bring a picture of her and her real mom to share in the next session. Later on, Alice wrote, "Marie is the best" on a paper airplane, noting that she liked talking and laughing with Marie. Marie also wrote down memories of sessions with Alice and sent them to her via paper airplane.

With five more sessions remaining, Alice's anger at the upcoming separation was evident. She started the next session by telling Marie that she hated her. She also talked about a story involving an abused dog and his owner. A boy rescued the dog, but when the owner got hurt, the dog rescued him. This changed the owner, who became nice and cared for the dog. It was unclear what the story referred to, but Marie and the supervisor speculated that it represented some amalgam of her own feelings toward her mother, her upcoming adoption, and her community clinician. Perhaps she wondered whether she could have made her biological mother change or whether the community clinician might stay and care for her.

On the last session, Alice was hypervigilant. Once or twice she noted that she saw a man walking behind them whom she thought might want to kidnap her. Marie took this seriously and checked out the situation. When Marie was sure that nothing was happening, she assured Alice that the situation looked safe. Marie also told Alice that she would miss and remember her.

Before Life Story Intervention came to a close, Marie and Alice identified Alice's teacher to be her mentor. Marie had met Mrs. Johnson on several occasions when she had picked Alice up at school for sessions. Moreover, Alice had often talked about this teacher and was developing a relationship with her. Mrs. Johnson was willing to step into a mentoring role for Alice. She had already spent some time with her, as Alice had participated in an after school program.

Follow-up Assessment

The individual who assessed Alice noted that Alice "lacked boundaries." Within several minutes of meeting this clinician, Alice hugged her. During this session, Alice also told the clinician that she wished that she was her "mommy." As earlier, Alice's scores on the TSCC scales assessing anxiety, post traumatic symptoms and dissociation were elevated. In contrast to the initial assessment her scores on the CBCL were within the normal range including rule breaking, attention problems and aggressive behavior. Mrs. Weaver did note some continuing concerns that Alice had difficulties in working and playing alone, and telling stories that were not true. On the positive side, she was getting average grades and got along adequately with other children.

Six Months Later

Alice did not evidence significant emotional or behavioral problems when she was reassessed. On all of the measures, she scored in the normal range. She continued to have some difficulties, but they were not enough to place her in the clinical or subclinical ranges. For instance, Alice noted that she sometimes argued too much with her foster sister about "stupid little things." She also continued to have "some" fear of men, but stated that she felt safer because her name had changed. With regard to her nightmares, Alice noted that she had only had one since being adopted. Alice's coping skills did not seem optimal, although they were not negative either. For instance, she stated that she dealt with anger by singing "lalala," thus blocking her anger out of her mind. We thought that her singing might help her from acting on her anger, but it did not necessarily help her to understand what she felt or why.

The clinician who assessed Alice noted changes with regards to her interpersonal boundaries. With this clinician, Alice was more subdued and not overly friendly. Alice's stories too had changed. She was able to talk about past experiences in a coherent and serious way. Mrs. Weaver described Alice as a well-adjusted child, but noted that she still told stories that weren't true or contained made-up details.

Mark: A Polite and Adult-Like Child

Mark, a 10-year-old boy, had become involved in the foster care system at the age of 8 years. His mother was deeply involved in methamphetamine along with her paramour, Seth, who sexually abused Mark. When a clandestine methamphetamine laboratory in the home exploded, Mark was taken into custody along with his 6-year-old brother. The reports from that time underscored that both children had poor hygiene and had received inadequate food. Mark's language was noted to be quite delayed as well. There also was evidence of physical abuse. Seth had repeatedly hit the children, leaving marks on their bodies. According to Mark, he also had covered their mouths to make them stop crying. When we saw Mark, he was in foster care with a family who lived in a neighboring village.

Assessment

Despite his initial delays in language, Mark scored in the average range for children his age on a measure of children's receptive vocabulary knowledge. At the same time, he was experiencing many mental health symptoms. On the TSCC, he noted, for example, that his mind often went blank, that scary ideas popped into his head almost all of the time, and that he remembered things he didn't want to remember. He acknowledged frequent daydreaming, getting very angry and not being able to calm down, and feeling that nobody liked him. He scored in the clinical range on anxiety and dissociation scales. His foster mother, Mrs. Karny, reported somatic complaints and attention problems on the CBCL. His scores on these scales fell within the clinical range. Mark scored within the normal range on a measure of receptive language, the PPVT.

In an interview, Mark readily noted that he had a "huge temper" and that his nerves seemed to "explode." He then added that, when this happens, he wants to punch people "softly." When asked about his family of origin, Mark's voice grew quiet. He noted that he wondered a lot about his dad and didn't know if he was alive. He did know his father's full name and date of birth and this was important to Mark. It was a tangible connection to a person who had been absent for most of his life.

Initial Phase

Mark eagerly awaited the first session of Life Story Intervention. Jane, his community clinician, had worked for over 20 years with the state child protection service agency, first as a caseworker and then as one of the heads of a local office. She had her master's degree in counseling. After the first session, Jane described Mark as being anxious, "very talkative," and as "skipping from one subject to the next." Some of the themes he covered briefly, with little pause for thought or discussion, included computers, games, school, his mom's boyfriend, and monsters. At all times, he was polite and enjoyed praise. Jane listened attentively to what Mark said, stressing that it is important for children to tell their stories. She added that telling stories helps children to move on and feel better, but that it can also bring back memories that can be painful. Mark nodded.

In the next sessions, Jane again listened to a wide variety of topics. Mark did note that something "disappointing" happened, but didn't want to talk further about it. Jane noted that to make sense of things that are disappointing, it is important to be able to feel calm and to soothe oneself. She then asked Mark how he soothed himself. Mark noted that he usually listens to the radio when he is upset. Jane commented that many children did this. Mark then spontaneously brought up his relationship with his foster mom, whom he said was "too concerned about his safety." Jane underscored that feeling safe is important. Mark relaxed visibly in this session. Jane's attentive listening, her reaffirmations of his feelings, and her allowing him to explore his concerns with her contributed to a sense of safety and sharing in their relationship.

In the next session, Mark told Jane that his younger brother had cried all night. "It doesn't matter," he said, as school was out. Jane explored these feelings more with Mark. He seemed to open up. Later, Jane suggested that Mark tell her something about himself—for instance, what his favorite things were because she wanted to know more about him. She then noted that they could list his favorite things on paper. Together, the two went through a long list. Mark told Jane, for example, that he liked the color black and that his favorite feeling was "happy." He asked Jane whether she had a CD of happy songs to make her happy when she was sad. Later on, he spontaneously told Jane how he liked to go skating. Jane noted that perhaps they could write down an experience about skating as a story. Mark seemed interested in this, but then backed away, noting that he could maybe write a story that was only one sentence or one word or maybe even just one letter. He laughed at this, as did Jane, who did not pressure him to continue. Instead, she took an interest in learning more about who he was and what he felt. At the end of the session, Jane remarked in her notes that Mark lacked energy and looked sad.

Some of the reasons for Mark's sadness and lack of energy emerged when Jane spoke with his foster mother, who had had a recent telephone call from Mark's mother that had ended in a heated argument. Mark, who had overheard the phone call and was acutely aware of an upcoming court date, had a long crying spell after the call. In the ensuing days, his foster mother found his urine-soaked clothing hidden under his bed.

In the next sessions, Mark told Jane he had thought of some stories he wanted to write. He wrote his name on the first sheet of paper, and then asked Jane if they could drive by his school to take a photograph of it. As they drove through the streets of the small town where he was living, Mark pondered several topics and wondered whether his family included his "real" mom or his foster mom. When Jane and Mark returned to the story he was working on, Mark chose to write about his biological mother. He jotted down several sentences about holidays. He then talked about his foster mother's visit to the court and about how his mom liked drugs better than she liked him. Jane noted that Mark looked sad as he spoke about these things and commented that they were probably very painful feelings. Mark quietly agreed. Jane had put words to feelings that Mark could not yet articulate.

During this time, Jane and Mark began to reflect upon the stories he told, typically in the public library. Mark was so easily irritated by noises, for example, that he would often tell other children to "be quiet," so that Jane wondered whether he had often been told to "be quiet." On one occasion, Mark saw his teacher in the library. He introduced Jane to her and was obviously pleased. Jane and Mark also took photos of houses Mark had lived in. As the two later put the photos into a scrapbook, Mark noted in a small voice that he had photos of his mom too, but he wanted to keep them. He was beginning to bring up important thoughts that he had not previously voiced.

As the initial phase of Life Story Intervention ended, Jane noted that the therapeutic relationship she had established with Mark was taking hold. Mark listened to what she said, looked forward to sessions, and had begun to rely on her for support. When asked what she saw as key components of his internal working model of self and other, Jane described Mark as a fragile and polite child with notable strengths, including his intelligence and thoughtfulness. Jane also described Mark as a small adult, who was prematurely burdened with responsibilities, for example, the care of his younger brother prior to entering foster care. He doubted his abilities to live up to these responsibilities, and was wary about whether adults would be available to help him.

Mark also had many questions about methamphetamine misuse and what it meant. He seemed to feel that his mother was evil for having gotten addicted to "meth," a view that had been reinforced by some adults in his life. Jane began to address this issue in the next phase of Life Story Intervention.

Middle Phase

Mark began writing his stories. He would help Jane carry the paper and laptop computer to the local library, where they worked together in a private room. Mark was attentive as he wrote down brief stories, usually about school. He often misspelled words, but saw no reason to correct them. Jane praised him, and Mark responded by looking more relaxed, responsive, and focused.

In this phase of the intervention, Jane worked intensely with Mark, so that he could learn to calm and soothe himself. This was important, since he was often anxious and worried that he had done things wrong. Jane began to address this area by asking Mark what he did when he was thirsty. Mark noted that he gets a drink from the refrigerator. She then asked what he does when he is tired. He noted that he goes to the living room, watches TV, and falls asleep. In this context, he talked about a recent time when he was sad. This occurred when his biological mother went to a court date. Mark again noted that she liked drugs more than she liked her children. Jane commented that he looked sad as he said this. They then discussed how Mark could take care of himself when he felt sad, and he suggested listening to happy music.

If Mark wrote his stories on Jane's computer, he would ask the following week if Jane had printed them out for him. He would then illustrate the stories or comment on them. The stories covered various topics: his sports team, his mother's relatives, drugs, and memories of good times and not so pleasant times in his family. As Mark brought up memories of his mother's drug use, Jane queried whether he wondered why she used drugs. Since Jane noted that Mark grew anxious at this question, she brought up his anxiety by asking him how he cared for himself when he is anxious. Mark said he didn't know how to care for himself when he is anxious, so Jane noted that they could talk about ideas together. At the end of this session, Mark reminded Jane to bring a camera to the next session, as he wanted to take pictures to illustrate more stories.

Mark was in good spirits when Jane arrived for the next session and promptly asked her whether she had remembered to bring things. He also told her that he didn't feel like doing a story and asked whether that was "okay." Jane said it was, and the two played some board games together. While in the park, Mark met some friends he knew and played with them for a while. He later apologized to Jane for keeping her waiting. He did tell Jane that one of the boys he had met had talked about his father and then noted that it is hard to write stories about your dad when you don't even know him. Jane agreed and commented that "maybe the story is that it makes me sad that I do not know my dad." Mark listened quietly and said "yeah," very softly when Jane had finished. He later thanked her. He seemed more spontaneous and less compliant in this session.

The following week, Jane brought books about children in foster care to the session. Mark browsed through one book in particular, and, in this context, talked about past experiences. He described how he and his brother had been left alone with nothing to eat and wondered if the parents portrayed in the book used drugs like his mom. Jane listened and noted that "it can be scary when parents use drugs." Mark then changed topics and decided to write a story about the park on the computer, but he soon lost interest in this and commented that he didn't know what to say.

Sticking with and exploring a painful topic was clearly difficult for Mark. Jane tried to maintain some continuity in thought if only for a brief time. For example, when Mark repeatedly changed the fonts and colors on the computer, Jane encouraged him to reflect on his own thoughts by noting that he might be avoiding talking about his father. She also asked him about his feelings, so that he could integrate what he was saying with important emotions. Mark was particularly lucid, and noted that he changed topics when his mind was "feeling funny." Jane listened and commented that she too had noted this. Mark looked surprised that someone else might know how he felt and wanted to know how she knew. Jane noted how he changed fonts or played games, thereby avoiding what they were talked about. Mark nodded and said, "Yeah, I guess I did." Not wanting to put too much pressure on him, Jane asked Mark whether he was ready to talk about something else. He said that he was.

During one session, Jane and Mark saw a man walking on the street who was drunk. Mark saw this, and told Jane he was drunk. Jane used this occasion to ask Mark whether he had seen people who were drunk. This triggered memories for Mark, who noted that he had seen people who were drunk and who had walked that way. They were around when he lived with his mother.

As the middle phase drew to a close, Jane spent time talking with Mark about addictions. He viewed addictions as evil and as something that someone could change with sheer will power. Mark listened intently as Jane talked with him about addictions being a medical condition and that staying away from drugs and alcohol is very hard for someone who is addicted. She also talked about the need to be responsible for seeking help. Seeing his mother's addiction as a medical condition might allow him to acknowledge the love he has for her and grief at their separation.

Mark also talked about his dreams for the future. In one session, for example, he asked Jane whether she had dreams about what she wanted to be when she was his age. She told Mark she had wanted to be a school teacher or a social worker. Mark noted that he wanted to travel in time, perhaps articulating a wish to go back to understand his past. Mark took more photos and talked about working on another story that he remembered.

Ending Phase

Mark took many photos during the third phase of the intervention. With the small, disposable camera that Jane brought, he photographed his foster family, friends at school, and previous houses. Snacks, games, and conversations about drugs were part of this phase of the intervention as well.

Jane brought up the issue of drug use herself using books (e.g., Black, 1989) that had been developed for children to help them understand parental addictions. She talked about the responsibility each person has for taking care of himself, about drug addiction being an illness, and about the difficulties individuals have in stopping. Mark heard all that Jane said, but changed the topic. At the end of the session, however, he picked up this topic spontaneously, telling Jane, "I don't think you got to finish what you wanted to tell me about drugs." Jane said that they could talk more next week about this if he wanted. Before the session ended, Mark told Jane about many things he worried about, including nuclear bombs. He worried whether his small town would be targeted. Jane contained these feelings by telling him that she also thought about this but kept the thoughts in the "back of her mind," trusting that the world would not come to this point, as there were many who were working to keep us safe. Mark relaxed and said that he could put these worries in the back of his mind as well.

In the next session, Mark spontaneously brought up the topic of drugs by telling Jane that he and his schoolmates were making antidrug buttons to wear. He wrote "stay away from drugs" on his button and hoped that this slogan would help him win the school competition. Later, Mark perused a book that Jane had in her car about children's feelings. Jane again talked about drugs, noting that people are not bad who use them. She underscored that people use drugs to make themselves feel better. They then become addicted and can't stop because their bodies want more. She also described how it is important to understand your own feelings and to identify them, so that you take care of yourself and not substitute drugs for making yourself feel better. When she asked Mark whether this made sense, he paused a long time looking at her. He then said, "No, why would you use drugs in the first place?" Jane talked about peer pressure, people feeling unhappy or stressed, and how drugs can temporarily make you feel on top of the world. Mark commented that it was "stupid" to use drugs. He then said he thought his mom used drugs because her boyfriends did. He then talked about painful times he recalled, when his mother smoked methamphetamine, and he recalled smelling the "meth." After talking, Mark seemed calm.

The final sessions passed quickly. Mark wanted to write stories, but then changed his mind. He continued to approach and avoid painful topics, but was more able to include painful feelings in his narratives. When talking about difficult topics, Mark could elaborate more than he could previously on his feelings and memories. While playing the card game, Old Maid, for example, Mark talked about people committing crimes when they were high on drugs. He then talked about what his mother's behavior was like when she was "high," and how she left him and his sibling alone on such occasions. Jane again talked about people who used drugs not being bad or evil, but as needing help. Mark listened, but changed the topic.

Mark did not want to face the ending of Life Story Intervention. He asked Jane if she was sure that they had worked together for 6 months and whether this was really one of the last sessions together. Jane confirmed this. Later that day, Jane and Mark worked on Mark's Life Story Book by pasting photos and stories into it. Jane helped Mark to write a timeline of his life. She noted that a timeline can help someone to remember and to understand events.

On the last session, Mark and Jane looked at photos that Jane had developed. Mark recalled a time when the two talked in the rain. He also noted that he hoped he would never have to be around bad people who used drugs like he was when he lived with his mother. Mark remembered some of the stories he had told Jane, and she commented on how telling stories could help someone to understand both good and bad things that happened. Mark was calm as he said goodbye to Jane.

In reflecting on her work with Mark, Jane commented that Mark had remained positive and enthusiastic throughout the intervention. She recalled how he actively sought out information about drugs to test out some of his thoughts about his mother's methamphetamine use. She also commented on his increased ability to process conversations and underscored that he appeared to have reached another level of acceptance of losing his mother. Mark had more understanding of drug and alcohol addiction and was more adept at talking about details of events in his life. She noted that he was still reluctant at times to elaborate, stressing that he "couldn't remember."

Follow-up

When asked later about the intervention with Mark, Jane felt the timing of the ending was "right." She observed that she had become more fond of Mark than she ever thought she would and described him as "very forgiving." To illustrate, she noted that he often rushed in to say things were "okay" if she forgot something or made an error. She saw him as a "vulnerable" child still, noting that others might take advantage of his dependability. She noted that Mark continued to give the appearance that he could handle any disappointment.

With regard to other aspects of the intervention, Jane felt that the regular contact with Mark's foster parents was essential. He loved taking photographs and reading books. She found the lack of a specific room in which to meet difficult, noting that privacy was hard to achieve in a community setting.

In contrast with the initial assessment, Mark's foster mother indicated on the CBCL that he had no significant behavioral or emotional problems. Mark continued to score in the clinical range on the TSCC on anxiety and dissociation.

Mark's football coach became his mentor. Mark had increasingly come to be interested in sports, and Mr. Jasper saw his fine abilities. He agreed to spend time in helping Mark in this area of his life and to be available on other occasions as well in the months to come.

Six Months Later

When assessed 6 months later, Mark continued to have no clinically significant emotional or behavioral problems, as indicated by the CBCL. His foster mother did note some continuing concerns, for example, with arguing, crying, following rules, and peer relationships. On the positive side, Mrs. Karny underscored that he was very well behaved, had good manners, and was very responsible. She described him as, "my little big man."

Mark continued to have some trauma symptoms. On the TSCC, he received elevated scores on scales assessing anxiety and dissociative symptoms. He noted that he felt the following "lots of times": afraid something bad might happen, pretends he is someone else, remembering things that he didn't like, wanting to yell and break things, getting mad and not being able to calm down, and feeling nervous inside. Mark noted that he "often" feels dizzy and daydreams. We were concerned that Mark might continue to let others use or hurt him and that his helpful, polite behavior belied his need for protection and help. He may also be somebody who struggles with re-emerging symptoms when he is under stress. We relayed to his guardian our recommendation that Mark continue to receive mental health services.

Conclusion

We saw Life Story Intervention as a bridge, bringing a needed intervention to children at a critical time in their lives, characterized by impermanence and flux, prior to engagement in a longer-term mental health intervention. Jake, Alice, and Mark had significant emotional and behavioral issues when they began Life Story Intervention, and it is not realistic to expect that they would all be resolved in a few short months. Indeed, many issues remained at the conclusion of Life Story Intervention. On the other hand, each child had been able to form a meaningful relationship with a community clinician and begin to explore and reflect upon their past experiences through personal narrative. Life Story Intervention also helped the children's foster parents to better understand their children's perspectives, and it helped children to locate a mentor who would continue to monitor and work with them as Life Story Intervention drew to a close.

Although Jake, Alice, and Mark had much in common, each had experienced significant neglect and trauma in their families of origin, they showed some unique responses to Life Story. Initially, Jake did not appear to have a story. What he told initially was brief and incoherent. He insisted that he didn't know his story, and his own perspective and experience was absent from much of what he said. He doubted whether adults would be available to help him, and he had a negative view of his own abilities. When the intervention began, Jake had scored in the clinical range on both externalizing and internalizing behavior, per his foster mother's report. He reported significant clinical symptoms in the areas of trauma symptoms, anxiety, anger, and dissociation.

Over the course of the intervention, Jake came to trust Mae, his community clinician. In the context of this relationship, he began to relate and develop stories of his personal experiences. His stories were still short, but with Mae's support, he began to share more and to elaborate upon his experiences and feelings. When Jake was followed up 6 months later, he continued to score in the clinical range on the CBCL and did report some trauma symptoms on the TSCC. The clinician who assessed Jake at follow-up described him as able to recall and relate some important stories about his life. His own experience and perspective seemed to be present when he told the stories, something that was absent earlier on.

Alice was a child who lacked boundaries. She longed for closeness, but sought it out almost indiscriminately and had difficulties in protecting herself from abuse. She was also fearful of her community clinician and lacked trust, doubting whether she and others would be there to recognize her needs. She viewed herself in a negative, shameful, and blaming light. At the outset of the intervention, Alice recalled numerous details about past experiences, but struggled to identify which were her feelings and experiences and which were those of others with whom she was close. An ability to look at her experiences and feelings in a reflective manner was largely absent. She scored in the clinical range on several CBCL narrow band scales, and had several elevated scores on the TSCC.

When Alice was reassessed 6 months after the intervention ended, she scored in the normal range on all measures. The stability that resulted from the adoption may have contributed to these gains, along with the work that was part of Life Story Intervention. Some mental health issues remained that may emerge again in times of stress. Alice's adoptive mother noted that Alice continued to tell some stories that were untrue, a concern shared by the assessor. The clinician who assessed Alice noted that she was not as needy or overly friendly. Moreover, the stories she told were shorter, more concise, and less enmeshed.

Mark was a fragile and polite child who seemed to carry many burdens. He doubted his abilities, and was wary about whether adults would be available to help him. He had a strong need to please. Just before entering Life Story Intervention, he showed significant dissociative symptoms and anxiety. He scored in the clinical range on internalizing behaviors on the CBCL.

Six months after Mark had completed Life Story Intervention, he continued to have some trauma symptoms, particularly anxiety and dissociative symptoms. His foster mother, however, did not report any clinically significant emotional or behavioral problems on the CBCL. Nonetheless, he continued to cry a lot, to feel guilty, and to be secretive. He continued too to be a "little big man," carrying more responsibility than was warranted for his age. He struggled in getting along with peers. Nonetheless, when he saw his community clinician, he proudly told her of some recent accomplishments. His relationship to this person, then, remained significant, providing him with a working model from which he could seek out help from a trusted adult.

Given that Life Story Intervention was limited in time, the community clinicians and children addressed only a fraction of the children's experiences. This process of developing narratives of personal experience within the context of their relationships with the community clinicians hopefully helped children to see that experiences and feelings can be shared and interpreted. By making sense of important feelings and memories, children seemed to discover strengths in themselves and to understand some of the overwhelming experiences and feelings that had been part of their lives. In this way, they were becoming more reflective about their past experiences, more able to accept them as being one part of their lives, and more able to look positively toward a future.

Chapter Thirteen

Narrative of a Community Clinician

The design and implementation of Life Story Intervention involved close collaborations with rural adults who worked in a professional capacity with children. These adults each accepted responsibility for one or two children and participated in weekly supervision. As rural community members, these professionals brought a depth of knowledge and experience to our team in engaging and communicating with the children. In this chapter, we again depart from a traditional academic or clinical presentation to present Linda Kingery's reflections on her experience as a "community clinician" for Billy, introduced in Chapter 4, and Jason.

My experience with Life Story Intervention involved two young boys, Billy and Jason. Both boys were raised in two-parent homes, in which both parents misused methamphetamine; both had extended family members in the area who loved them very much but who, for complicated reasons, were unable to care for them; and both had been in foster care for approximately 2 years prior to the intervention. In Billy's case, his parents were involved in methamphetamine production to the extent that surveillance cameras were part of the home décor; Jason was used to "smurf" or steal cold medicine to assist in his parents' meth lab. Billy was growing up in a very small town, where he and his brother explored their community without parental constraints. He was well known and liked, and his extended family had lived in the area for generations. Jason was part of a larger town, with less of a feeling of community, and his family had a reputation for criminality. Jason and Billy also differed in intellectual ability. Billy was exceptionally bright and felt success and acceptance in school, whereas Jason experienced some difficulty in school and felt the rejection that school failure can sometimes cause.

Billy was 13-years-old and in his second foster home placement when we began working together. Billy is a personable, Midwestern boy who was being raised in a small town where he played and interacted within his community quite well in spite of, or perhaps because of, his parents' addiction. Billy has a brother 3 years his junior and, during the course of his parents'

In-depth examination of complex cases can yield important insights into the design and implementation of culturally appropriate, effective interventions for children from methamphetamine-involved families. Photo by Carl Kingery.

addiction, Billy had accepted much of the parenting responsibility for himself and for his brother. Billy's level of parentification was extreme, even for a child raised in a substance-affected home. When Billy was taken into protective custody, he assisted the child welfare worker in obtaining information regarding family members who might have been willing to help during his crisis, and he played a primary role in discussing medical issues with the treating physician during his Healthworks exam (a medical exam required for all children entering the foster care system). Billy was well known in his small community, and school personnel gave a glowing report of his educational abilities and school performance. A 12-year-old boy who was in school every day, maintained excellent grades, and participated in extracurricular activities while being "parented" by a mother and father suffering from an addiction as devastating as methamphetamine was certain to gain positive reinforcement from most adults. Throughout our research project (described in Part 2), Billy's name would come up again and again from professionals interviewed, and he would always be referred to as exceptional.

Jason was 11-years-old and in his fourth foster home placement when the intervention began. Jason has an engaging smile and charming personality that endears him to most adults rather quickly. He was separated from his siblings during one of the foster home moves, because of relationship difficulties between him and his younger sister. Jason had been described as both physically and verbally aggressive. During our times together, I found him to be friendly and hungry for positive attention from adults. Jason could describe in great detail the day he was taken into protective cus tody by the local police as he was hiding in his grandmother's closet. His mother was extremely ill from the effects of methamphetamine, and he could have no contact with his father because of sexual abuse to his older sister. Although some of Jason's teachers were said to be drawn to Jason, his classroom behaviors frequently prevented him from receiving much positive feedback. However, his foster/adoptive family provided Jason with a loving and nurturing environment through their involvement in their church. Jason spoke of the church youth group leaders with great affection and ad- miration. He freely expressed his commitment to both God and the church family and would always turn my radio to a Christian radio station when he entered my car. He would then proceed to sing his heart out, stopping peri- odically to advise me as to the name of the song writer or why he liked a particular song. Although not referred to by others as exceptional, Jason is a resilient young man who has the ability to accept the care and concern of those people who have become a part of his life through the foster care system.

After explaining the purpose of the intervention to Billy and Jason, both boys found it challenging to understand how talking about their lives could be helpful to them. However, they seemed to quickly invest in the idea of helping others. When discussing the fact that their "stories" could help another child experiencing foster care, both Jason and Billy verbalized a willingness to participate in this project. Both of these young men felt a strong commitment to caring for younger siblings. Billy had pretty much parented his younger brother throughout much of their childhood, and Jason had a younger brother with a physical disability whom he felt so much responsibility for that he reported wanting to become a foster parent some day, so that he could eventually be the primary caregiver for this brother. Caring for others is often a coping mechanism developed in children of addiction, as the parental responsibilities they assume can lead to a sense of control over what are otherwise pretty uncontrollable lives.

Jason

When I picked Jason up for our first meeting, I asked where he might like to go to get something to eat. Jason eagerly named his favorite place, a drive-through hamburger shop. Jason took great pride in ordering for both of us and telling me what the best sandwich was, as well as how I needed to eat my fries (with ranch dressing). He delighted at ordering a chili cheeseburger with jalapenos and then watching intently as I ate each tasty and fattening morsel. He would make certain I had a napkin, and was eager to receive confirmation that I was enjoying the meal. This is an example of the care-taking skills that have helped Jason to deal with life experiences that would cause most of us to shudder. There is also much to be said about the simple act of "breaking bread together." As is true in many cultures, the act of shar-ing a meal brings a trust and closeness that is difficult to achieve under other circumstances. It is noteworthy that, as Jason and I continued our journey together, and Jason's comfort level increased, food became less important, although it was always a part of our sessions.

During the relationship-building stage of the intervention with Jason, I was continually amazed by his willingness to accept this gray-haired social worker into his life and to share his stories with me. I am sure it had some-thing to do with my personality and his, our both being children of addiction, and our common culture of growing up in small-town, mid America. During the first few sessions, conversations about the Cardinals baseball team (which happened to be the favorite team for both of us) were numerous. We also spent time driving by Jason's school, previous foster homes, and other famil-iar places for him. As I drove, he would talk, telling me of times of joy and sadness, separation from family, and the coldness of strangers who were designated by the state as caregivers.

The bond between Jason and I came easily and quickly. What proved to be more of an issue was maintaining appropriate professional boundaries. It is not like this was totally new territory for me, since I have over 20 years of experience in child welfare or counseling with children and families. One of the major differences was the setting for the sessions. Like most profes-sionals, I was accustomed to being in an office where a client would come to see me, and both the child and I were well aware of the boundaries of the relationship, although they were unspoken. With this intervention, I was picking Jason up, taking him to lunch, and we spent a lot of time chatting about what he had done at school, where he was going on vacation, etc. Once, as we pulled through the fast-food drive-through, he said, "I'll bet those people think you're my gramma." I am a grandmother, and would actu-ally count it a privilege to be Jason's gramma as well, but in supervision, my supervisor and I discussed boundaries and the complexities of dual relation-ships. When working with children in the child welfare system, it is tempt-ing to try and fix what seems to have gone wrong with the family and to fill the void in a child's life. In meeting with Jason on a weekly basis in an informal setting, it was easy for the lines to blur. This was an issue that was addressed in supervision more than once, as crossing that line could have been harm-ful for Jason or for me.

During the course of our work together, Jason's mother died from the health problems she had suffered as a result of methamphetamine addiction.

Jason requested that I be at his mother's funeral, and I was. During the weeks that followed, we would often drive by the funeral home where her services were held, and Jason would comment on his mother's death, the funeral service, and how much he missed her. These topics were not forced on Jason. He would see the building and casually mention what he was thinking or feeling. I am not sure Jason ever felt he was receiving therapy or counseling. He considered himself my friend, a co-researcher of sorts, providing information about his life in an effort to help these curious university people help other kids like him.

Jason chose to make a video to tell his life story, and each week he would provide me with pictures of his family of origin as well as his foster/adoptive family. We put the pictures on a CD and then added music. Jason chose this format because he had an older foster brother who was killed in an accident a year or so earlier, and there had been a video commemorating his life at his memorial service. Jason was very affected by the other boy's life and death, and he saw the commemorative video as somehow signifying the importance of his foster sibling's life. Jason's video took on a unique quality as we talked about both of Jason's families, his birth family and his foster family. He was in the process of adoption with his foster family at the same time he was grieving the loss of his mother, an arduous task for even the most stout of heart. As we talked about the timeline of Jason's life, he would at times focus on the past and his family of origin, and at other times enjoy telling me about what he and his foster family were doing now. He was certainly conflicted about his loyalty to his birth family and his love for his current family. We entitled his life story, "Jason, the Boy with Two Families." He liked that idea and took pride in remembering the "good times" in both families. We talked at length about how many of us have several families—the family we are born into, maybe a church family, and the family we create when we get married. Framing Jason's life as normal was surely one of the most helpful aspects of this intervention.

Saying "good-bye" to Jason was difficult for both of us. Jason had suffered many losses, and, as would be expected, he was apprehensive at the thought of going through yet another one. I talked about this in supervision, and even thought about continuing my relationship with Jason when the time for the project was complete. Jason and I talked about how we were going to stay in touch periodically throughout our last several sessions. Jason would try to think of ideas of how we could keep meeting a while longer, and we actually did extend our time once in order to address some of the separation anxiety as well as to assist Jason in working through the conflict he felt over his upcoming adoption. In group supervision, the idea was presented that our role might be compared to that of a favorite teacher, and we might run into one another in the community, at which time we would say "hello" and exchange updates on our lives. For Jason and I, it has turned out exactly as what was discussed during supervision. Shortly after the intervention concluded, I attended Jason's adoption party and celebrated with him the confirmation of his new family.

This year, on Jason's birthday, I gave him a call. We went out to lunch, and Jason caught me up on all the latest activities in his family's life. He had a cell phone, and received several text messages throughout our time together. He apologized for the interruption, but explained that he is now part of the popular group and these girls "just won't leave me alone." Jason has responded well to the love of a family, and there appears to be a truly happy ending at this time. As is inevitable in life, Jason will face challenges, but he has a strong support system in his new family, wonderful memories of his family of origin, and an inner strength that has developed during his confrontations with adversity. As we ended our lunch and prepared to separate once again, Jason said, "Hey, Linda. Let's meet every year for lunch on my birthday. Even when I'm married, I'll bring my wife and kids, and I'll tell them, 'This is what I do every birthday. I have lunch with Linda!'" I agreed that this was a grand idea, and I am so looking forward to meeting Jason's wife and children!

(At the time of this writing, I received a phone call from Jason letting me know that his disabled brother had passed away. Jason wanted to know what computer program we had used to make his video, as he would like to use the same program to commemorate his brother's life. I offered Jason my condolences, and he shared with me that his brother was very sick and that he saw this as God's way of helping his brother. It was apparent that the support of Jason's adoptive family and his religious faith were helping him to deal with this loss. As for me, I am so honored that Jason continues to share his life with me.)

Billy

Working with Billy was considerably different, because I was the investigator who actually took him and his brother into protective custody (see Chapter 4). Billy saw me as a helping person, rather than the "bad guy" since the police were the ones who had arrested his parents and actually taken physical custody of him and his brother before I was called. My role was to take Billy and his brother for the hospital exam prior to them going to their first foster home, and Billy actually lives in the same community that I do. He was, of course, asked if he were comfortable in working with me prior to our being assigned to one another.

Billy is nearly 2 years older than Jason, and he seemed at ease in talking about his life from the first session. Some rapport had already been established on that day when I spent several hours with him and his brother as we waited for a foster home placement. Billy never seemed to particularly mind talking about life with his parents, but as each week passed, it became more and more apparent that Billy was much more interested in talking about the current situation in his foster home. He would relate incidents of extremely harsh discipline by the foster mother, as well as a detached and demeaning attitude toward him as a person. Billy would talk at length about not feeling a part of the family, but would quickly add that he did not want to be. When I would return Billy to the foster home after our meetings, I observed the type of treatment that Billy was describing. It eventually became painfully obvious that Billy was suffering emotional abuse in this foster home, and his caseworker was contacted to facilitate a move to a more suitable environment. The Life Story Intervention, which was intended to assist Billy with his past experiences in living with his methamphetamine-involved parents, turned out to be a vehicle for him to share his feelings about his life in the present and discover that things could be different. Billy was moved to a foster home where love and acceptance abound, and he continues to live there today, 2 years later.

Billy is a personable young man, extremely bright and articulate, as well as polite in his interactions with adults. At the time of our work together, it would appear that he had been unscathed by his life with addicted parents and/or hostile foster parents. He would explain to me his philosophy on life regarding his concept of karma and his understanding that events in life happen for a reason. I recall asking him how he was feeling about the loss of his friends, family, and community following placement in foster care. Billy explained to me how he still sees his old friends on occasion when visiting his grandparents, and now he has friends in his new community and would not want to lose those relationships. Billy took great joy in teaching me about life and how to "roll with the punches." He would laughingly tell me how my emotional side just "gets in the way of your logical thinking." It was visibly apparent that, during these teaching moments, Billy's self-esteem, self-confidence, and self-efficacy were all on the rise.

When asked what advice he would give other foster children, Billy said, "When you're in foster care, everything changes. You have to adapt and adjust." Billy's first two foster homes were very rule-oriented, and he was confused by parents who took such an active role in a child's life. As previously stated, Billy was parentified and had basically been raising himself and his younger brother prior to the child welfare intervention. He had two grandmothers in close proximity whom he could count on in times of crisis, but had become quite adept in managing everyday matters. Billy knew how to get his brother ready for school, prepare meals, and do laundry, as well as other household chores. He knew the support systems in the community, such as church and school, and he was able to access services as needed.

I could relate to Billy's lifestyle, because I grew up with a single, alcoholic mother in the 1950s and have often told people that I was a social worker by age 10: able to network within my community and manage a household. In this respect, parental methamphetamine and alcohol misuse are not all that different. The effects of addiction, or any other debilitating mental illness, sometimes bring out the best in children. Not that any of us would advocate for children taking on parental responsibilities as a way of building character; however, the axiom of making lemonade when life gives you lemons is quite fitting. Unfortunately for Billy, his parenting skills and ability to make decisions for himself and his brother were a liability in his first foster home.

After Billy's relocation to a more appropriate foster home, our sessions focused on Billy's vision for the future. He talked a little about his life with his parents, but was much more focused on what he would do when he was on his own again. Due to Billy's age, his intellectual abilities, and his desire to plan for life after foster care, it was beneficial that he use the intervention time to look forward.

Closing the intervention with Billy was natural and went very smoothly. He would not have had it any other way. During our final sessions, we discussed Billy's plans for the future and the fact that, since we live in the same small community, we would most likely see one another from time to time. This indeed has been the case. I often see Billy at sports activities. He always says "hi," and frequently comes to sit by me at a basketball game and catch me up on the newest video game he has conquered. I send him a card on his birthday; he just turned 16 this week. Billy's ability to adapt and adjust continues, but his strong will and pattern of challenging adult authority have caused him to encounter problems at school and in his new home. He is facing these challenges with the support of a loving extended family, which remains in close contact, and the nurturance and guidance of foster parents who have now entered into a subguardianship* role with Billy and his brother as their parents serve extended prison sentences for methamphetamine

---

* Subsidized guardianship is an alternative to adoption that allows foster parents or other substitute caregivers to provide a permanent placement for a foster child without the legal ramifications of an adoption. The caregivers continue to receive a monthly stipend, and the child maintains a medical card as well as access to mental health services. This option is sometimes chosen if the child prefers not to relinquish his/her birth name, when the child is in mid to late adolescence, and sometimes because a caregiver needs to ensure that their biological children are the only ones entitled to their inheritance.

production. I fully expect that Billy will use his intelligence and life experiences as a springboard to a happy and healthy adulthood! I count it a privilege that I am able to continue to watch him grow.

Personal Reflection

As a professional social worker with over 20 years of experience, and as a participant observer of human behavior for a lifetime, the time I spent in Life Story Intervention was educational and certainly a time of personal growth. There were challenges as well as rewards. My experience with children in foster care, for the most part, has been that these kids open up easily and allow us to share in their lives. I believe they are looking for something permanent, someone who will be around in the long term. Too many changes in caseworkers and foster homes have left foster children to struggle with attachment issues. Yet, most of the time, when presented with another opportunity for positive attention and affection, they open up. Supervision was a place where this was discussed numerous times during my work with the intervention. Ultimately, the choice to maintain the connection between clinician and child after the intervention is completed is a personal one. As is true in most social work practice, there is no "one size fits all." The intervention needs to be flexible, meeting the differing needs of individual children.

It is sometimes difficult to articulate what happens in human relationships, both personal and therapeutic. It is even more challenging to assess the outcome of those relationships. Who can determine whether words spoken, time spent, and compassion felt is "life changing" for a child? I am able to recall teachers and community members who reached out to me as I was growing up with an alcoholic mother. Miss Ralston kept me after school to help her clean her classroom and wash blackboards. Miss Mercer tutored me in spelling and took me all the way to our state spelling bee, where I participated in a televised competition (a very big deal for a girl from a small town). Mrs. Knowles consistently provided praise for my high school English papers, implanting in me a desire to teach someday. Will Jason or Billy recall the days spent "riding in cars with Linda" as a time when they learned life lessons and came to a clearer understanding of their purpose in life? Only time will tell.

Part Four

Conclusion

Chapter Fourteen

The Value of the Case in Evidence-Based Social Work

*We first became involved with Keith shortly after his placement in
foster care. Keith and his mother had shared a trailer in a run-down
neighborhood in a small town. When Keith's mother began using
methamphetamine with her paramour, she rapidly became incapacitated.
Keith, who had been used to feeding and caring for himself while his
mother worked long hours or drank, found himself in a home without
food, electricity, or heat. Upon entrance into care, he was underweight,
dirty, ill, and had missed weeks of school. Keith began participating in
Life Story Intervention after his placement in a stable foster home. His
foster parents were kind and supportive, but Keith continued to mourn
the loss of his mother. He readily opened up to the community clinician, a
local social worker, with narrative accounts of happy as well as troubling
times with his mother, including violence between her and her paramour.
Two months into the intervention, Keith excitedly informed the community
clinician that his mother was better and that he would be returning home.
The community clinician and Keith's mother met and agreed that Keith
would continue in the intervention. Keith's mother clearly loved him and
was working hard to put their lives back together. Unfortunately, 1 month
of inpatient substance abuse intervention with outpatient follow-up was
inadequate, and she began to relapse. During one of the community clinician's
visits for Life Story Intervention, Keith's mother was sleeping deeply on the
couch and could not be roused. Keith began missing appointments for Life
Story Intervention as well as school. Unable to reach him at home, the
community clinician visited Keith at school where, dressed in an old t-shirt
with "Loser" written in permanent marker across the back, he refused
even to make eye-contact. Following his reinvolvement with child welfare
services, Keith again enrolled in Life Story Intervention, a sadder, more
guarded child. (Compiled from field notes and case notes, 2004–2005.)*

Grandparents can be important sources of support for children of methamphetamine-involved families. Photo by Linda Kingery.

As illustrated throughout this book, case-based research provides the thick description necessary to understand complex social phenomenon as they occur in everyday life and grounding for the design, implementation, and assessment of relevant, effective interventions. The case presented in this book is that of rural, East Central Illinois at the turn of the twenty-first century. It focuses on children who, like Keith, were in foster care because of parental methamphetamine misuse. Phase 1 of our research program was the creation of a case-based description of parental methamphetamine misuse in rural Illinois through ethnographic fieldwork, participant observation, interviews, and standardized psychological assessments of children. An overriding goal was to present the perspectives and voices of individuals who encounter methamphetamine misuse on a regular basis—parents who misuse methamphetamine, their children, foster parents, and professionals—and to understand this social problem from the perspectives of those involved, and in the complexities of their everyday lives

We set the stage for an understanding of children's lives with the narratives of four mothers who were recovering from methamphetamine addiction. They foreshadowed themes elaborated by other knowledgeable adults in the community, including the neglect of children and the exposure to adult criminality and substance misuse, and by the children themselves in their descriptions of profound loss. An important contribution of these mothers was to provide an understanding of the experience of methamphetamine addiction. They described being "in a fog," unable to think clearly, with an obsession to use methamphetamine that overshadowed even the children whom they loved. They also described the lasting impact of methamphetamine addiction on their physical health and relationships.

We then presented the experience and perspectives of children and knowledgeable professionals. These perspectives converged on a number of themes, with participant observation and reviews of child welfare case records. Consistent with recent research indicating high levels of violence among individuals who misuse methamphetamine (Cohen et al., 2003), both adults and children reported that children are exposed to adult violence within their homes. Violence occurred between parents, other adults, and sometimes involved children; for example, when a child intervened to protect a mother or younger sibling. Both adults and children also reported that children are exposed to adult substance misuse, often polysubstance misuse; for example, many parents who misused methamphetamine also misused marijuana and alcohol. Informants described violence and substance misuse as intertwined; for example, an adult using methamphetamine assaults his wife in front of their children.

Consistent with recent research indicating that methamphetamine misuse is associated with other illegal behavior such as stealing (Grella, Hser & Huang, 2006), adults and children also reported that children are exposed to criminal behavior. In addition to misusing illegal substances, parental drug-seeking behavior often involved crimes such as stealing ingredients to manufacture methamphetamine. Some participants reported that children were involved in these activities by their parents; for example, some parents taught children to steal the precursors they needed to manufacture the drug or to use guns to protect clandestine methamphetamine laboratories. More commonly, children were socialized to be very guarded in their communications and interactions with outsiders, even to lie to teachers, police officers, and child welfare workers to cover up their parents' illegal activities. In addition, some parents reportedly introduced their children to gateway drugs, as well as methamphetamine, at an early age. More indirectly, many children observed parents' antisocial behavior and arrests during police raids.

Adult and child perspectives did not always converge concerning salient features of the family contexts in which children were reared. Consistent with other research (see Holman et al., 2004), adult professionals emphasized environmental danger, chaos, neglect, and abuse. They reported that children may experience physical danger due to exposure to methamphetamine and its production. Users may leave drug paraphernalia within the reach of small children, and "Mom and Pop" cooks manufacture methamphetamine at home, exposing children to toxic chemicals, explosions, and fire. In addition, adults reported that children may experience extreme neglect as basic needs for food, sanitation, and medical and dental care are unmet. Children may live in chaotic, filthy homes with no electricity, running water, or phone service. More subtly, adults noted that children whose parents misuse methamphetamine may be deprived of the typical, joyful activities of childhood, such as play and recreation. Children may become caregivers not only for themselves and their young siblings, but for their incapacitated parents as well.

Consistent with a growing body of literature that indicates that children whose parents misuse drugs are much more likely to be maltreated than children whose parents do not misuse drugs (e.g., National Center on Addiction and Substance Abuse [CASA], 1999), adults also described high levels of physical and sexual abuse of children. For example, children may be sexually abused by adults who come by their homes to purchase and use methamphetamine, or physically abused by parents experiencing extreme irritability or paranoia.

In contrast to adults, many children emphasized the experience of separation and loss of their parents and families. Despite their experiences of neglect and abuse, when asked about a "sad or scary" time in their families, many children reported the loss of a parent. This loss typically was associated with being taken into protective custody. For example, 11-year-old Joseph described the "saddest, scariest" time in his life not as the periods of extreme neglect he and his siblings had experienced, but as, "The night we got taken away. . . ."

In addition to presenting children's perspectives based on interviews, we described their psychological functioning. Consistent with clinical discussions of children from substance-involved families (e.g., Black, 2001), the knowledge base of most children in our study with regards to methamphetamine was sketchy, with inaccuracies that may leave them vulnerable to psychological disturbances. Many children knew that methamphetamine was a "bad drug" that made adults "weird" or "wacko." Some children also viewed themselves as at fault for the problems in their families, their families as the only ones experiencing such problems, or adult substance misuse as "just normal." They described few social resources for understanding and coping with their family experiences. Indeed, many perceived that talking about their parents' methamphetamine misuse was taboo. To deal with family problems, most children described passive or avoidant responses, such as staying away from home or daydreaming. As reasons for their passive or avoidant responses, children noted a fear of adult users, not wanting to get their parents in trouble, fear of being taken away from their parents, other adults not wanting to get involved, and a lack of geographical or emotional closeness to relatives.

Children's psychological functioning also was examined through standardized assessments. Most children evidenced a pattern of trauma symptoms including anxiety, posttraumatic stress, depressed behavior, attention problems, and thought problems. Most children also had other significant emotional and behavioral problems, including rule breaking and aggressive behavior. Rates of problem behaviors were somewhat higher than that reported in other research with foster children (e.g., Clausen, Landsverks, Ganger, Chadwick & Litrownik, 1998).

Part 2 also underscores individual variation in family and child functioning. Recognizing diversity may suggest protective factors that may be enhanced through preventive and intervention services, counteract negative stereotyping, and emphasize the importance of tailoring interventions to meet individual needs. Consistent with reports of other parents who misuse methamphetamine (Brown & Hohman, 2006), some parents who misused methamphetamine reportedly were able, at least initially, to protect their children, for example, by sending them to stay with relatives while they used drugs. Some children rejected child welfare interventions, and others embraced the opportunity for a more normative lifestyle. Consistent with clinical discussions of children from substance-involved families (e.g., Black, 2001), some children vehemently denied their parents' methamphetamine misuse despite much evidence to the contrary. Others, however, provided straightforward, factual, and consistent reports. Some children had few relationships and failed in school, whereas others had positive relationships with peers and adult community members and performed well in school. Although most children evidenced trauma symptoms, a significant number had no trauma symptoms. Many children had other emotional and behavioral problems, but nearly half had no such problems.

These perspectives elaborated in Phase 1 of the research underscore a variety of themes for social work practice and policy. These include the importance of:

- Intensive, sustained, and accessible substance misuse intervention programs for rural parents involved with methamphetamine

- Informing foster parents of the contexts in which children have been reared, so that they may anticipate and appropriately respond to predictable challenges arising from inadequate socialization and trauma.
- Recognizing the complexity in assessing the psychological functioning of children from methamphetamine-involved families and responding with multiple assessments and informants
- Mental health interventions for rural children affected by parental methamphetamine misuse
- Substance misuse prevention programs designed for children whose lives have been disrupted by parental substance misuse
- Community-wide education to combat negative stereotyping and promote the wisest use of limited resources

We also discussed our attempts, in Phase 2 of our research program, to use this case-based description to design and implement a culturally sensitive mental health intervention for children like Keith who were in foster care because of parental methamphetamine misuse. Life Story Intervention was designed with an understanding of the cultural context of rural Illinois, issues facing many children from substance-involved families, and existing, evidence-based interventions for children suffering from trauma. We attempted in our narrative- and relationship-based intervention to capitalize on the strengths of rural Illinois. These include a tradition of oral narrative, and the flexible roles assumed by many professionals who work with children and families. We attempted to address limitations, such as access to specialized mental health services, by identifying rural professionals willing to provide Life Story Intervention to one or two children. We then provided these professionals with continuing education and weekly supervision with experienced, licensed clinicians located in an adjacent, urban area.

An account of Phase 3 of our research program, an empirical assessment of Life Story Intervention, will be forthcoming in future publications. Our goal in this book was to illustrate some of the complex responses of different children to the intervention over time, their struggles, and our attempts to support them. For many children, developing a supportive relationship with a community clinician through which they reflected on their lives appeared to correct misinformation, provide coherence, facilitate expression of emotion, and focus the child on a more positive developmental trajectory. For others like Keith, who experienced instability in placement or other ongoing trauma and disruptions, the process was much more complex. Clearly, mental health intervention, although necessary, is not sufficient. In the absence of safety and stability, children's energies are focused on adjusting and surviving, and their community clinicians are focused on case management. In the case of Keith, it was only through collaboration with educators to develop a plan to get him back in school, substance abuse professionals to re-engage Keith's mother in services, and child welfare professionals to find a safe and stable foster home that Keith could continue Life Story Intervention.

As we conclude our book, it is important to reflect on the value of this case-based research strategy for our broader understanding and practice. A colleague (Carl Johnson, personal communication, 2001) once remarked that the best case-based studies are those that find "the universal in the particular." Certain of our findings may reflect more general experiences, for example, of children in families involved with substance misuse, the child welfare system, or living in poverty. These experiences may include the role of secrecy and denial in substance-involved families, children's responses to parental criminality and traumatic events associated with parental substance misuse, the stress of foster care, and the importance of supportive adults in children's resiliency. Other of our findings may be more specific to rural families, for example, challenges in finding and accessing appropriate mental health services; or to rural families involved with methamphetamine, for example, hazards from clandestine methamphetamine laboratories and the rapid deterioration in parental functioning as the addiction progresses.

The extent to which the content of our specific findings are transferable to other contexts is an open empirical question. Our obligation was to provide adequate thick description to make assessment of such transferability possible. Indeed, as we write this book in September, 2007, even East Central Illinois has changed. For example, police are seizing fewer "Mom and Pop" home-based methamphetamine laboratories, probably due to legislation restricting the over-the-counter sale of cold medicines. The lasting contribution of this case-based research, however, may not be in the specific findings, but in finding the "universal in the particular," conceptually and methodologically:

Illustrating the Importance of Meaning for Child Welfare Practice and Research

The research program described in this book underscores the importance to child welfare practice and research of attending to the meanings clients and others ascribe to complex social events such as parental substance misuse, child maltreatment, or foster care. Our study was not an attempt to uncover one universal truth regarding the impact of parental methamphetamine misuse on children, which like a logical formula or mathematical proof is true from "no perspective," but rather to understand diverse perspectives of affected individuals acting in relation to a complex social problem embedded in a particular time and place (see Nagel, 1979; Shweder, 1996b). An adequate and complete understanding of parental substance misuse, child and community responses, or any complex human behavior, requires not only a description of external social patterns, but attention to their meaning—the beliefs, values, and interpretations of diverse participants.

Note that the beliefs about methamphetamine espoused by participants in our study were not necessarily accurate, nor did they necessarily map in a simple way onto their behavior. Beliefs about methamphetamine presumably did provide participants with a framework for responding. For example, the rationale for extended prison terms for individuals who misuse methamphetamine, and the stigmatization of these same individuals, is comprehensible in light of a common but inaccurate belief of many knowledgeable adults that methamphetamine addiction cannot be treated successfully. The private reluctance of some community members to act upon such a punitive public stance toward those addicted to methamphetamine is comprehensible in light of complex intergenerational relationships among families and neighbors. A thick description both of patterns of behavior and the meanings ascribed to them by clients provides professionals with a fuller understanding on which to base practice and policy decisions.

Illustrating the Importance of Context in Intervention, Practice, and Research

Our research program is undergirded by a sociocultural perspective. It highlights the necessity of examining substance misuse in context. Clearly, methamphetamine misuse does not occur in isolation. Attempts to isolate the "effects" of methamphetamine per se on children and families are largely academic. Within rural Illinois, we learned that many children, like Keith, were reared in a drug subculture permeated not only by the misuse of methamphetamine, but the misuse of other substances, violence, and criminality, often extending back for generations and, which, as a whole, affect their development. By the time children entered into foster care where their physical needs were met, many were suffering from unmet mental health needs. Effective and relevant interventions for children affected by parental methamphetamine misuse will address these mental health needs in the context of other socialization, educational, and community issues including education of foster parents regarding predictable challenges given children's contexts of rearing, adequate substance misuse intervention for parents, and preventative efforts to enhance educational and employment opportunities in impoverished rural areas.

Illustrating the Use of Evidence in Social Work Practice

The research program described in this book also illustrates the use of evidence, broadly construed, in social work practice and research. Although the philosophical origins of evidence-based practice in medicine actually date at least as far back as mid nineteenth-century Paris (Sackett, Richardson, Rosenberg & Haynes, 1997), the practice of applying evidence in practice and policy remains a hotly debated topic in contemporary social work. Applied to social work, evidence-based practice is the "conscientious, explicit, and judicious use of current best evidence in making decisions about the care of clients" (Gambrill, 2000). In medicine and in social work, "evidence" involves integrating individual practice or clinical experience with the best available external evidence from systematic research, as well as the values and expectations of the clients or patients. This integration of knowledge of research, context, and case is necessary. Without insider knowledge of the context and clinical knowledge of the individual case, practice risks "becoming tyrannized by external evidence, for even excellent external evidence may be inapplicable to or inappropriate for an individual patient. Without current best external evidence, practice risks becoming rapidly out of date, to the detriment of patients" (Sackett et al., 1997, p. 2).

Evidence-based practice in social work also poses formidable challenges to researchers. To develop the knowledge base for evidence-based practice, researchers must collect relevant types of external evidence. The type of data sought depends on the questions raised. Although some might narrowly construe certain types of quantitative or qualitative data derived from particular designs as the "gold standard" for external evidence, there are no such simple formulas. As with all good research, we start with the question and then seek appropriate methods and designs. If we are concerned with understanding the complexity of a certain kind of experience or social issue, then qualitative evidence may be most appropriate. In the absence of a complex understanding of the social phenomenon such as parental methamphetamine misuse, generalized descriptions run the risk of superficiality, and decontextualized interventions of ineffectiveness. If we are concerned about the effectiveness of an intervention designed with a complex understanding of the social phenomenon, then experimental studies are appropriate. In the absence of such approaches, clients and significant others can be harmed (see Gambrill, 2000).

Giving Voice to Hidden Children

In this book, we have attempted to give voice to highly vulnerable children, like Keith, from stigmatized families. The historic intersection of public concern with the impact of illicit methamphetamine laboratories on safety and water and food quality in rural communities and concern for the vulnerable, substance-involved families briefly focused public attention on children who otherwise would have remained hidden, as had generations of children preceding them. Many, but by no means all, of the children in our research came from families with generations of dysfunction, including alcohol and other substance misuse, violence, and poverty. For this subset of families, methamphetamine was only the latest reflection of generations of dysfunction. Some of these families may have desired to remain hidden, emphasizing secrecy with their children to prevent them from inadvertently disclosing illegal activities to outsiders such as teachers or child welfare workers. Others of us in the community also may have desired that these families whose lives cause us discomfort remain hidden. As several children speculated, other adults in their lives with whom they had positive relationships may not really have wanted to "see" or "know" about the problems in their families. Our research program provided one opportunity to see and know children affected by parental methamphetamine misuse and to help them to find some continuity, meaning, and hope in lives disrupted by parental substance misuse and foster care.

References

Achenbach, T., & Rescorla, L. (2001). *Manual for the ASEBA School-Age Forms & Profiles*. Burlington, VT: ASEBA.

Administration for Children and Families. (2003). *Child maltreatment: Reports from the states to the National Child Abuse and Neglect Data Systems National Statistics on Child Abuse and Neglect*. Washington, DC: U.S. Department of Health and Human Services. Administration for Children and Families, Administration on Children, Youth and Families, Children's Bureau.

Agathonos-Georgopoulou, H. (2003). Child maltreatment in sociocultural context: From a syndrome to the Convention on the Rights of the Child. *International Journal of Child and Family Welfare, 6*(1/2), 18–26.

Ainsworth, M. D. S., Blehar, M., Waters, E., & Wall, S. (1978). *Patterns of attachment*. Hillsdale, NJ: Erlbaum.

Altshuler, S. J. (2005). Drug-endangered children need a collaborative community response. *Child Welfare, 84*(2), 171–190.

American Academy of Child and Adolescent Psychiatry (AACAP). (1998). Practice parameters for the assessment and treatment of children and adolescents with posttraumatic stress disorder. *Journal of the American Academy of Child and Adolescent Psychiatry, 37*(10 Suppl.), 4S–26S.

American Psychiatric Association. (2000). *Diagnostic and Statistical Manual of Mental Disorder*, 4th Edition (DSM-IV-TR). Washington, DC: American Psychiatric Association.

Anglin, M. D., Burke, C., Perrochet, B., Stamper, E., & Dawad-Noursi, S. (2000). History of the methamphetamine problem. *Journal of Psychoactive Drugs, 32*(2), 137–141.

Arant, T., Henry, C., Clifford, W., Horton, D. K., & Rossiter, S. (2005). Anhydrous ammonia thefts and releases associated with illicit methamphetamine production-16 states, January 2000–June 2004. *CDC Mortality Morbidity Week in Review, 54*(14), 359–361.

Axline, V. (1989). *Play therapy*. New York: Church Livingston.

Baker, P. L., & Carson, A. (1999). "I take care of my kids": Mothering practices of substance-abusing women. *Gender & Society, 13*(3), 347–363.

Bamba, S., & Haight, W. (2007). Helping maltreated children to find their Ibasho: Japanese perspectives on supporting the well-being of children in state care. *Children and Youth Services Review, 29*(4), 405–427.

Bauer, R., & Olson, D. (2006). The evolution of methamphetamine in Illinois. *Research Bulletin, 4*(8), 1–4.

Beck, A. T. (1976). *Cognitive theory and emotional disorder.* New York: International Universities Press.

Becker, H. (1996). The epistemology of qualitative research. In. R. Jessor, A. Colby, & R. Shweder (Eds.), *Ethnography and human development: Context and meaning in social inquiry* (pp. 53–72). Chicago: University of Chicago Press.

Bender, L., & Cottington, F. (1942). The use of amphetamine sulfate (Benzedrine) in child psychiatry. *American Journal of Psychiatry, 99*,116–121.

Bion, W. R. (1962). *Learning from experience.* London: Heinemann.

Black, C. (1987) *Children of alcoholics: It will never happen to me!* New York, NY: Ballantine Books.

Black, C. (2001). *It will never happen to me: Growing up with addiction as youngsters, adolescents, adults.(Second edition).* Center City, Minnesota: Hazelton.

Black, C. (1989). *"My dad loves me, my dad has a disease."* Denver, Co: MAC.

Bowlby, J. (1982). Attachment and loss: Retrospect and prospect, *American Journal Orthopsychiatry,* (52), 664–678.

Bowlby, J. (1988). *A secure base: Clinical applications of attachment theory.* London: Routledge.

Bradshaw, J. (1995). *Family Secrets: What you don't know can hurt you.* New York: Bantam Books.

Brecht, M., O'Brien, A., von Mayrhauser, C., & Anglin, M. D. (2004). Methamphetamine use behaviors and gender differences. *Addictive Behaviors, 29,* 89–106.

Briere, J. (1996). *Professional manual for the Trauma Symptom Checklist for Children (TSCC).* Odessa, FL: Psychological Assessment Resources.

Bronfenbrenner, U. (1979). *The Ecology of Human Development: Experiments by nature and design.* Cambridge: Harvard University Press.

Bronfenbrenner, U., & Morris, P. (2006). The bioecological model of human development. In R. Lerner (Volume Editor), *Handbook of Child Psychology: Volume 1: Theoretical models of human development.* (6 ed.) Hoboken, New Jersey: John Wiley and Sons.

Brown, J. & Hohman, M. (2006). The impact of methamphetamine use on parenting. *Journal of Social Work Practice and Addictions, 6*(1–2), 63–88.

Bruner, J. (1986). *Actual minds, possible worlds.* Cambridge, MA: Harvard University Press.

Bruner, J. (1990). *Acts of meaning.* Cambridge, MA: Harvard University Press.

Burger, L. K., & Miller, P. J. (1999). Early talk about the past revisited: Affect in working-class and middle-class children's co-narrations. *Journal of Child Language, 26,* 133–162.

Carlson, E. (1998). A prospective longitudinal study of attachment disorganization/ disorganization: Lessons from research on maltreated infants' attachments to their caregivers. In D. Cicchetti & V. Carlson (Eds.), *Child maltreatment: Theory and research on the abuses and consequences of child abuse and neglect* (pp. 494–528). New York: Cambridge University Press.

Cernerud, L., Eriksson, M., Jonsson, B., Steneroth, G., & ZetterStorm, R. (1996). Amphetamine addiction during pregnancy: 14–year follow-up of growth and school performance. *Acta Paediatrica, 85*, 204–208.

Cho, G., & Miller, P. J. (2004). Personal storytelling: Working-class and middle-class mothers in comparative perspective. In M. Farr (Ed.), *Ethnolinguistic Chicago: Language and literacy in Chicago neighborhoods* (pp. 79–102). Mahwah, NJ: Erlbaum.

Cicchetti, D., Toth, S., & Maughan, A. (2000). An ecological-transactional model of child maltreatment. In A. Sameroff, M. Lewis & S. Miller (Eds.), *Handbook of developmental psychopathology* (2nd ed.) (pp. 689–722). New York: Kluwer Academic/Plenum.

Clausen, J., Landsverk, J., Ganger, W., Chadwick, D., & Litrownik, A. (1998). Mental health problems of children in foster care. *Journal of Child and Family Studies, 7*, 283–296.

Cohen J. A. (1998). Practice parameters for the assessment and treatment of children and adolescents with posttraumatic stress disorder. *Journal of the American Academy of Child and Adolescent Psychiatry, 36*(Suppl. 10), 4–26.

Cohen, J. A., Deblinger, E., Mannarino, A. P., & Steer, R. A. (2004). A multisite, randomized controlled trial for children with sexual abuse-related PTSD symptoms. *Journal of the American Academy of Child and Adolescent Psychiatry, 43*(4), 393–402.

Cohen, J. B., Dickow, A., Homer, K., Zweben, J. E., Balabis, J., Vanderstoot, D., et al. (2003). Abuse and violence history of men and women in treatment for methamphetamine dependence. *American Journal on Addictions 12*(5), 377–385.

Cohen, J., & Mannarino, A. (1996). Factors that mediate treatment outcome of sexually abused preschool children. *Journal of the American Academy of Child and Adolescent Psychiatry, 34*(10), 1402–1410.

Cohen, J. A., Mannarino, A. P., Berliner, L., & Deblinger, E. (2000). Trauma-focused cognitive behavioral therapy for children and adolescents: An empirical update. *Journal of Interpersonal Violence, 15*(11), 1202–1223.

Coles, R. (1989). *The Call of stories. Teaching and the Moral Imagination*. Boston, MA: Houghton Mifflin.

Copeland, A. L., & Sorensen, J. L. (2001). Differences between methamphetamine users and cocaine users in treatment. *Drug and Alcohol Dependence, 62*, 91–95.

Corder, B., & Haizlip, T. (1989). The role of mastery experiences in therapeutic interventions for children dealing with acute trauma: Some implications for treatment of sexual abuse. *Psychiatric Forum, 15*(1), 57–63.

Corsaro, W. (1996). Transitions in early childhood: The promise of comparative, longitudinal ethnography. In R. Jessor, A. Colby, & R. Shweder (Eds.), *Ethnography and human development: Context and meaning in social inquiry* (pp. 419–458). Chicago: University of Chicago Press.

Covington, S. (2002). Helping women recover: Creating gender-responsive treatment. In S. Straussner & S. Brown (Eds.), *The Handbook of Addiction Treatment for Women*. San Francisco: Jossey-Bass.

Cresswell, J. W., Fetters, M. D., & Ivankova, N. V. (2004). Designing a mixed methods study in primary care. *Annals of Family Medicine, 2,* 7–12.

Cretzmeyer, M., Sarrazin, M. V., Huber, D. L., Block, R. I., & Hall, J. A. (2003). Treatment of methamphetamine abuse: Research findings and clinical directions. *Journal of Substance Abuse Treatment, 24,* 267–277.

Deblinger, E., McLeer, S. V., & Henry, D. (1990). Cognitive behavioral treatment for sexually abused children suffering post-traumatic stress: Preliminary findings. *Journal of the American Academy of Child and Adolescent Psychiatry, 29,* 747–752.

Denzin, N. K., & Lincoln, Y. S. (2000). Introduction: The discipline and practice of qualitative research. In N. K. Denzin & Y. S. Lincoln (Eds.), *Handbook of Qualitative Research* (pp. 1–28). London: Sage.

Department of Justice (2008). National methamphetamine threat assessment. *National Drug Intelligence Center,* Johnstown, PA

Derauf, C., LaGasse, L., Smith, L., Grant, P., Shah, R., Arria, A., Huestis, M., Haning, W., Strauss, A., Grotta, S., Liu, J., & Lester, B. (2006). Demographic and psychosocial characteristics of mothers using methamphetamine during pregnancy: Preliminary results of the infant development, environment, and lifestyle study (IDEAL). *The American Journal of Drug and Alcohol Abuse, 33,* 281–289.

Dishion, T. J. (1996). Advances in family-based interventions to prevent adolescent drug abuse. National Conference on Drug Abuse Prevention Research: Presentations, Papers, and Recommendations. Plenary Session, September 19–20, Washington, DC.

Dishion, T. J., & McMahon, R. J. (1996). *Parental monitoring and the prevention of problem behavior: A conceptual and empirical* reformulation (*NIDA Research Monograph No. 177).* Rockville, MD: National Institute on Drug Abuse (NTIS No. PB 99–124315/LL).

Dunn, L. M., & Dunn, L. M. (1997). *Peabody Picture Vocabulary Test, Third Edition.* Circle Pines, MN: American Guidance Service.

Egeland, B. (1997). Mediators of the effects of child maltreatment on developmental adaptation in adolescence. In D. Cicchetti & S. Toth (Eds.), *Rochester Symposium on developmental psychopathology: Vol. 7. The effects of trauma on the developmental process* (pp. 403–434). Rochester, NY: University of Rochester Press.

e-PODUNK (2004). *The power of place.* Retrieved March 30, 2004 from http// www.epodunk.com.

Etz, K. E., Robertson, E. B., & Ashery, R. S. (1998). *Drug abuse prevention through family-based interventions: Future research* (NIDA Research Monograph No. 177). Rockville, MD: National Institute on Drug Abuse. (NTIS No. PB 99–124315/LL).

Fals-Stewart, W., Kelley, M. L., Fincham, F. D., Golden, J., & Logsdon, T. (2004). Emotional and behavioral problems of children living with drug-abusing fathers: Comparisons with children living with alcohol-abusing and non-substance-abusing fathers. *Journal of Family Psychology,* 18(2), 319–330.

Federal Bureau of Investigation. (2006). Semi-Annual Uniform Crime Report. http://www.fbi.gov/ucr/ucr.htm (accessed December 20, 2006).

Fivush, R. (1993). Emotional content of parent–child conversations about the past. In C. A. Nelson (Ed.), *Memory and affect in development* (pp. 39–78). Hillsdale, NJ: Lawrence Erlbaum Associates.

Fonagy, P. (2001). *Psychoanalysis and attachment theory.* London: Karnac.

Fraiberg, S. (1980). *Clinical studies in infant mental health.* New York: Basic Books.

Freedman, J., & Combs, G. (1996). *Narrative therapy: The social construction of preferred realities.* New York: W. W. Norton & Company.

Freeman, E. (1993). Substance abuse treatment: Continuum of care in services to families. In E. Freeman (Ed.), *Substance Abuse Treatment: A family systems perspective.* Newbury Park: Sage Publications.

Fullilove, M. (1996). Psychiatric implications of displacement: Contributions from the psychology of place. *American Journal of Psychiatry, 153,* 1516–1523.

Galante, R., & Foa, D. (1986). An epidemiological study of psychic trauma and treatment effectiveness for children after a natural disaster. *Journal of the American Academy of Child Psychiatry, 25,* 357–363.

Gambrill, E. (2000). The role of critical thinking in evidence-based social work. In P. Allen-Meares & C. D. Garvin (Eds.), *The handbook of social work direct practice* (pp. 43–63). Thousand Oaks, CA: Sage.

Gambrill, E. (2003). Evidence-based practice: Implications for knowledge development and use in social work. In A. Rosen & E. Proctor (Eds.), *Developing practice guidelines for social work intervention* (pp. 37–58). New York: Columbia University Press.

Gambrill, E. (2005). *Critical thinking in clinical practice: Improving the quality of judgment and decisions* (2nd ed.).New York: Wiley.

Garcia-Bournissen, F., Rokach, B., Karaskov, T., & Koren, G. (2007). Methamphetamine detection in maternal and neonatal hair; Implications for fetal safety. *Archives of Disease in Childhood—Fetal and Neonatal Edition, 92,* 351–355.

Gaskins, S., Miller, P., & Corsaro, W. (1992). Theoretical and methodological perspectives in the interpretive study of children. In W. Corsaro & P. Miller (Eds.), *Interpretive approaches to children's socialization: New directions for child development* (pp. 5–23). San Francisco: Jossey-Bass.

Glickman, E. (1957). *Child placement through clinically oriented casework.* New York: Columbia University Press.

Governor's Office News, (March 4, 2004). *Governor launches children's mental health partnership: Appoints 25 to create strategic plan.* Retrieved October 7, 2004, from http://www.illinois.gov/PressReleases/ShowPressRelease.cfm?SubjectID=3&RecNum=2828.

Grant, P. (2007). Evaluation of children removed from a clandestine methamphetamine laboratory. *Journal of Emergency Nursing, (33),* 31–41.

Grella, C., Hser, Y., & Huang, Y. (2006). Mothers in substance abuse treatment: Differences in characteristics based on involvement with child welfare services. *Child Abuse and Neglect, 30,* 55–73.

Gruber, K. & Taylor, M. (2006). A family perspective for substance abuse: Implications from the literature. In S. Straussner & C. Fewell (Eds.), *Impact of substance abuse on children and families: Research and practice implications.* Binghamton, NY: The Haworth Press, Inc.

Haight, W., Carter-Black, J. & Sheridan, K. (in press). Mothers' experiences of methamphetamine addiction: A case-based analysis of rural, midwestern women. *Children and Youth Services Review.*

Haight, W. L., Jacobsen, T., Black, J., Kingery, L., Sheridan, K., & Mulder, C. (2005). "In these bleak days": Parent methamphetamine abuse and child welfare in the rural Midwest. *Children and Youth Services Review, 27,* 949–971.

Haight, W., Ostler, T., Black, J., Sheridan, K. & Kingery, L. (2006). A child's eye view of parent methamphetamine abuse: Implications for helping foster families to succeed. *Children and Youth Services Review, 29*(1), 1–15.

Haight, W. L., & Taylor, E. H. (2007). *Human behavior for social work practice: A developmental-ecological framework.* Chicago: Lyceum Books.

Halfon, N. G., Mendonca, A., & Berkowitz, G. (1995). Health status of children in foster care: The experience of the Center for the Vulnerable Child. *Archives of Pediatrics & Adolescent Medicine, 149,* 386–392.

Hanney, L., & Kozlowska, K. (2002). Healing traumatized children: Creating illustrated storybooks in family therapy. *Family Process, 41*(1), 37–65.

Hans, S. L. (2004). When mothers abuse drugs. In M. Göpfert, J. Webster, & M. V. Seeman (Eds.), *Parental psychiatric disorder: Distressed parents and their families* (pp. 203–216). Cambridge, UK: Cambridge University Press.

Hans, S. L., Bernstein, V. J., & Henson, L. G. (1999). The role of psychopathology in the parenting of drug-dependent women. *Development and Psychopathology, 11*(4), 957–977.

Hartman, A. (1978). Diagrammatic assessment of family relationships. *Social Casework, 59,* 465–476.

Hawkins, J. D., Catalano, R. E., & Miller, J. Y. (1992). Risk and protective factors for alcohol and other drug problems in adolescence and early adulthood: Implications for substance abuse prevention. *Psychological Bulletin, 112*(1), 64–105.

Heath, S. B. (1996). Ruling place: Adaptation in development by inner-city youth. In R. Shweder, R. Jessor, & A. Colby (Eds.), *Ethnographic approaches to the study of human development* (pp. 225–251). Chicago: University of Chicago Press.

Herbert, M., & Harper-Dorton, K. V. (2003). *Working with children, adolescents and their families* (3rd ed.). Malden, MA: Blackwell.

Hodge, F. S., Pasqua, A., Marquez, C. A., & Geishirt-Cantrell, B. (2002). Utilizing traditional storytelling to promote wellness in American Indian communities. *Journal of Transcultural Nursing, 13,* 6–11.

Hohman, M., Oliver, R., & Wright W. (2004). Methamphetamine abuse and manufacture: The child welfare response. *Social Work, 49*(3), 373–381.

Holmes, J. (2001). *The search for the secure base: Attachment theory and psychotherapy.* Sussex: Brunner-Routledge.

Hser, Y., Evans, E. & Huang, Y. (2005). Treatment outcomes among women and men methamphetamine abusers in California. *Journal of Substance Abuse Treatment, 28*(1), 77–85.

Huber, A. Ling, W., Shoptaw, S. Gulati, V., Brethen, P., & Rawson, R. (1997). Integrating treatments for methamphetamine abuse: A psychosocial perspective. *Journal of Addictive Diseases, 16*(4), 41–50.

Humphries, D. (1999). Crack mothers: Pregnancy, drugs, and the media. Columbus, OH: Ohio State University Press.

Hymes, D. H. (1982). *Ethnolinguistic study of classroom discourse: Final report to the National Institute of Education*. University of Pennsylvania. Graduate School of Education.

Jacobsen, T., Levy-Chung, A, & Kim, J. (2002). Intervening with young children in foster care: Using countertransference reactions to facilitate the therapeutic process. *Zero to Three, 25,* 57–60.

Jessor, R., Colby, A., & Shweder, R. A. (Eds.). (1996). *Ethnography and human development: Context and meaning in social inquiry*. Chicago: University of Chicago Press.

Joe, K. A. (1996). The lives and times of Asian-Pacific American women drug users: An ethnographic study of their methamphetamine use. *Journal of Drug Issues, 26*(1), 199–218.

Johnson, B. D., Dunlap, E., & Maher, L. (1998). Nurturing for careers in drug use and crime: Conduct norms for children and juveniles in crack-using households. *Substance Use & Misuse, 33*(7), 1511–1546.

Johnson, J. L., & Leff, M. (1999). Children of substance abusers: Overview of research findings. *American Academy of Pediatrics, 103,* 1085–1099.

Jordan, C., & Franklin, C. (2003). *Clinical assessment for social workers: Quantitative and qualitative methods* (2nd edition). Chicago, IL: Lyceum Books.

Kalechstein, A., Newton, T., & Green, M. (2003). Methamphetamine dependence is associated with neurocognitive impairment in the initial phases of abstinence. *Journal of Neuropsychiatry & Clinical Neurosciences, 15*(2), 215–220.

Kandel, D. B. (1990). Parenting styles, drug use, and children's adjustment in families of young adults. *Journal of Marriage and the Family, 52*(1), 183–196.

Kearney, M. H., Murphy, S., & Rosenbaum, M. (1994). Mothering on crack cocaine: A grounded theory analysis. *Social Science and Medicine, 38*(2), 351–361.

Kiley, S. (Sept. 23, 2007). Rare shellfish bartered for drugs. Guardian Newspaper (UK). Retrieved October 4, 2007 from http://observer.guardian.co.uk/world/story/0,,2175010,00.html.

Klee, H. (1998). Drug-using parents: Analysis and stereotypes. *International Journal of Drug Policy, 9,* 437–448.

Klee, H. (2002a). Women, family and drugs. In H. Klee, M. Jackson, & S. Lewis (Eds.), *Drug misuse and motherhood* (pp. 3–14). New York: Routledge.

Klee, H. (2002b). Drugs and parenting. In H. Klee, M. Jackson, & S. Lewis (Eds.), *Drug misuse and motherhood* (pp. 145–164). New York: Routledge.

Klee, H. (2002c). Overcoming the barriers. In H. Klee, M. Jackson, & S. Lewis (Eds.), *Drug misuse and motherhood* (pp. 263–275). New York: Routledge.

Klee, H. (2002d). Drug policy and practice development in the United Kingdom. In H. Klee, M. Jackson, & S. Lewis (Eds.), *Drug misuse and motherhood* (pp. 285–297). New York: Routledge.

Kroll, B. (2004). Living with an elephant: Growing up with parental substance abuse. *Child and Family Social Work, 9*, 129–140.

Kumpfer, K., Olds, D., Alexander, J., Zucker, R. & Gary, L. (1996). *Family etiology of youth problems (NIDA Research Monograph No. 177)*. Rockville, MD: National Institute on Drug Abuse (NTIS No. PB 99–124315/LL).

Kyle, A. D., & Hansell, B. (2005). Two surveys of U.S. counties: The criminal effect of meth on communities. The impact of meth on children. Washington, DC: National Association of Counties.

Laidler K. A. J and Morgan P. (1997).Kinship and community: The "ice" crisis in Hawaii. In H Klee (Ed), Amphetamine Misuse: International Perspectives on Current Trends CRC Press, Boca Raton, FL

Lave, J., & Wenger, E. (1991). *Situated learning: Legitimate peripheral participation.* Cambridge, UK: Cambridge University Press.

Lieberman, A. F., Padrón, E., Van Horn, P., & Harris, W. W. (2005). Angels in the nursery: The intergenerational transmission of benevolent parental influences. *Infant Mental Health Journal, 26*(6), 504–520.

Lieberman, A. F., & Van Horn, P. (1998). Attachment, trauma, and domestic violence. Implications for child custody. *Child and Adolescent Psychiatric Clinics of North America, 7*(2), 423–443.

Lieberman, A. F., & Van Horn, P. (2005). *Don't hit my mommy! A manual for child-parent psychotherapy with young witnesses of family violence.* Washington, D.C.: Zero to Three Press.

Lieberman, A. F., Compton, N. C., Van Horn P., & Ghosh-Ippen, C. (2003). *Losing a parent to death in the early years: Guidelines for the treatment of traumatic bereavement in infancy and early childhood.* Washington, DC: Zero to Three Press.

Lincoln, Y., & Guba, E. (1985). *Naturalistic inquiry.* London: Sage.

Lineberry, T. W., & Bostwick, J. M. (2006). Methamphetamine abuse: A perfect storm of complications. *Mayo Clinic Proceedings, 81*(1), 77–84.

Luthar, S. S., Cushing, G., Merikangas, K. R., & Rounsaville, B. J. (1998). Multiple jeopardy: Risk and protective factors among addicted mothers' offspring. *Development and Psychopathology, 10*, 117–136.

Malinosky-Rummell, R. R., & Hoier, T. S. (1991). Validating measures of dissociation in sexually abused and nonabused children. *Behavioral Assessment, 13*, 341–357.

Mandell, A.J. (1976) The nightmare season. New York, NY: Random House.

Manning, T. (1999). Drug labs and endangered children. *FBI Law Enforcement Bulletin, 68*(7), 10–15.

Maxwell, J. (2005). Emerging research on methamphetamine. *Current Opinion in Psychiatry, 18*, 235–242.

Mayes, L. (1995) Substance abuse and parenting. In M. Bornstein (Ed.), *Handbook of parenting (Vol. 4): Applied and practical parenting.* Mahwah, NJ: Lawrence Erlbaum Associates.

Mayes, L., & Truman, S. (2002). Substance abuse and parenting. In M. Bornstein (Ed.), *Handbook of parenting, Vol.4: Social conditions and applied parenting* (2nd ed., pp. 329–359). Mahwah, NJ: Lawrence Erlbaum Associates.

McGoldrick, M., Gerson, R., & Shellenberger, S. (1999). *Genograms: Assessment and intervention.* New York: W. W. Norton & Company.

McIntyre, A., & Keesler, T. Y. (1986). Psychological disorders among foster children. *Journal of Clinical Child Psychology, 15,* 297–303.

McRoy, R., Aguilar, M. & Shorkey, C. (1993). A cross-cultural treatment approach for families with young children. In E. Freeman (Ed.), *Substance abuse treatment: A family systems perspective.* Newbury Park: Sage Publications.

Mecham, N., & Melini, J. (2002). Unintended victims: Development of a protocol for the care of children exposed to chemicals at methamphetamine laboratories. *Pediatric Emergency Care, 18*(4), 327–332.

Meisels, S. J. (2001). Fusing assessment and intervention: Changing parents' and providers' views of young children. *Zero to Three, 21*(4), 4–10.

Meredith, C. W., Jaffe, C., Ang-Lee, K., & Saxon, A. J. (2005). Implications of chronic methamphetamine use: A literature review. *Harvard Review of Psychiatry, 13*(3), 141–154.

Merikangas, K. R., Dierker, L., & Fenton, B. (1996). *Familial factors and substance abuse: Implications for prevention (NIDA Research Monograph No. 177).* Rockville, MD: National Institute on Drug Abuse (NTIS No. PB 99–124315/LL).

Miles, M. B., & Huberman, A. M. (1994). *Qualitative data analysis* (2nd ed.). Thousand Oaks, CA: Sage.

Millar, G. M., & Stermac, L. (2000). Substance abuse and childhood maltreatment: Conceptualizing the recovery process. *Journal of Substance Abuse Treatment, 19,* 175–182.

Miller, B., A., Smyth, N. J., & Mudar, P. J. (1999). Mothers' alcohol and other drug problems and their punitiveness toward their children. *Journal of Studies on Alcohol, 60,* 632–642.

Miller, M. A. (1997) History and epidemiology of amphetamine abuse in the United States. In H Klee (Ed), Amphetamine Misuse: International Perspectives on Current Trends CRC Press, Boca Raton, FL

Miller, M. A. (1991). Trends and patterns of methamphetamine smoking in Hawaii. *NIDA Research Monographs, 115,* 72–83.

Miller, P. (1982). *Amy, Wendy, and Beth: Language learning in South Baltimore.* Austin: University of Texas Press.

Miller, P. J., & Moore, B. B. (1989). Narrative conjunctions of caregiver and child: A comparative perspective on socialization through stories. *Ethos, 17*(4), 428–449.

Miller, P., Wiley, A., Fung, H., & Liang, C. (1997). Personal storytelling as a medium of socialization in Chinese and American families. *Child Development, 68,* 557–568.

Moore, T. (1991). The African-American Church: A source of empowerment, mutual help, and social change. *Religion and Prevention in Mental Health, 10,* 147–167.

Morgan P and Beck JE (1997). The legacy and the paradox: Hidden contexts of meth-amphetamine use in the United States. In H. Klee (Ed), *Amphetamine Misuse: International Perspectives on Current Trends.* CRC Press, Boca Raton, FL

Morgan, P., & Joe, K. A. (1996). Citizens and outlaws: The private lives and public lifestyles of women in the illicit drug economy. *Journal of Drug Issues, 26*(1), 125–142.

Morris, K., & Parry, C. (2006). South African methamphetamine boom could fuel further HIV. *The Lancet Infectious Diseases, 6,* 471–471.

Nagel, T. (1979). Subjective and objective. In. T. Nagel (Ed.), *Moral questions* (pp. 196–213). New York: Cambridge University Press.

National Center on Addiction and Substance Abuse at Columbia University (CASA). (1999). *No safe haven: Children of substance abusing parents.* New York: The National Center of Addiction and Substance Abuse.

National Institute of Drug Abuse (2006) Research report #8: Methamphetamine abuse and addiction. Bethesda, MD

Nelson, K. (1988). The ontogeny of memory for real events. In U. Neisser & E. Winograd (Eds.), *Remembering reconsidered: Ecological and traditional approaches to the study of memory* (pp. 244–276). New York: Cambridge University Press.

Newton, T., Cook, I., Kalechstein, A., Duran, S., Monroy, F., Ling, W., & Leuchter, A. F. (2003). Quantitative EEG abnormalities in recently abstinent methamphetamine dependent individuals. *Clinical Neurophysiology, 114*(3), 410–415.

Norton, D. (n.d.). *Ecology and plurality: An ecological systems framework for a pluralistic curriculum: Beyond the dual perspective.* Unpublished manuscript.

Nurco, D. N., Blatchley, R. J., Hanlon, T. E., O'Grady, K. E., & McCarren, M. (1998). The family experiences of narcotic addicts and their subsequent parenting practices. *American Journal of Drug and Alcohol Abuse, 24*(1), 37–59.

Oetting, E. R., Edwards, R. W., & Beauvais, F. (1985). Reliability and discriminant validity of the children's drug-use survey. *Psychological Reports, 56,* 751–756.

Oetting, E. R., Edwards, R. W., Kelly, K., & Beauvais, F. (1997). Risk and protective factors for drug use among rural American youth. In E. Robertson, Z. Sloboda, G. Boyd, L. Beatty, & N. Kozel (Eds.), *Rural substance abuse: State of knowledge and issues (NIDA Research Monograph No. 168).* Rockville, MD: National Institute on Drug Abuse.

Ogawa, J. R., Sroufe, L. A., Weinfield, N. S., Carlson, E. A., & Egeland, B. (1997). Development and the fragmented self: Longitudinal study of dissociative symptomatology in a nonclinical sample. *Developmental Psychopathology, 9,* 855–879.

Office of National Drug Control Policy (2006). *Pushing back against meth: A progress report on the fight against methamphetamine in the United States.* Washington, DC: Government Publishing Office.

Ogbu, J. U. (1974). The next generation: An ethnography of education in an urban neighborhood. New York: Academic Press.

Ostler, T., Haight, W., Black, J., Choi, G., Kingery, L., & Sheridan, K. (2007). Case series: Mental health needs and perspectives of rural children reared by parents who abuse methamphetamine. *Journal of the American Academy of Child and Adolescent Psychiatry, 46*(4), 500–507.

Otero, C., Boles, S., Young, N. K., & Dennis, K. (2006). Methamphetamine addiction, treatment, and outcomes: Implications for child welfare workers. Report to Substance Abuse and Mental Health Services Administration, Center for Substance Abuse Treatment.

Pach, A., III., & Gorman, E. M. (2002). An ethno-epidemiological approach for the multi-site study of emerging drug abuse trends: The spread of methamphetamine in the United States of America. *Bulletin on Narcotics, LIV*(1& 2), 87–102.

Peleg-Oren, N. & Teichman, M. (2006). Young children of parents with substance use disorders (SUD): A review of the literature and implications for social work practice. In S. Straussner & C. Fewell (Eds.), *Impact of substance abuse on children and families: Research and practice implications*. Binghamton, NY: The Haworth Press, Inc.

Phillips, S. (1983). *The invisible culture: Communication in classroom and community school and community*. Chicago: University of Chicago Press.

Pine, D.S., & Cohen, J. A. (2002). Trauma in children and adolescents: Risk and treatment of psychiatric sequelae. *Biological Psychiatry, 51*(7), 519–531.

Poertner, J. (2002). *Children and Family Research Center report on child safety and permanency in Illinois for fiscal year 2001*. Urbana, IL: The Children and Family Research Center.

Potter, M.J., and Kolbye, K.F.(1996). Effects of D-Methamphetamine. National Drug Intelligence Center, U.S. Department of Justice.

Preskorn, S. (1996). *Clinical pharmacology of SSRIs*. Caddo, OK: Professional Communications.

Putnam, F. W. Helmers, K., & Trickett, P. K. (1993). Development, reliability, and validity of a child dissociation scale. *Child Abuse and Neglect, 17*(6), 731–741.

Ray O.S. and Ksir C.J. (2004). Drugs, Society, and Human Behavior, 10/e. New York: Mcgraw Hill.

Rawson, R. A., Anglin, M. D., & Ling, W. (2002). Will the methamphetamine problem go away? *Journal of Addictive Diseases, 21*(1), 5–19.

Rawson, R. A., Gonzales, R. & Brethen, P. (2002). Treatment of methamphetamine use disorders: An update. *Journal of Substance Abuse Treatment, 23,* 145–150.

Rhodes, J. E. (2002). *Stand by me: The risks and rewards of mentoring today's youth*. Cambridge, MA: Harvard University Press.

Robertson, E. B., David, S. L., & Rao, S. A. (2003). *Preventing drug use among children and adolescents: A research-based guide for parents, educators, and community leaders*. NIH publication, no. 04–4212(A). Bethesda, MD: National Institute on Drug Abuse, National Institutes of Health.

Rogoff, B. (1990). *Apprenticeship in thinking: Cognitive development in social context*. New York: Oxford University Press.

Roll, J. M., Petry, N. M., Stitzer, M. L., Brecht, M. L., Peirce, J. M., McCann, M. J., et al. (2006). Contingency management for the treatment of methamphetamine use disorders. *The American Journal of Psychiatry, 163,* 1993–1999.

Ryan, J. (2006). *Illinois Alcohol and Other Drug (AODA) waiver demonstration: Final evaluation report.* Champaign-Urbana, IL: Children and Family Research Center, University of Illinois at Urbana-Champaign.

Sackett, D. L., Richardson, W. S., Rosenberg, W. & Haynes, R. B. (1997). *Evidence-based medicine: How to practice and teach EBM.* New York: Churchill Livingstone.

Schlaepfer, T. E., Pearlson, G. D., Wong, D. F., Marenco, S. & Dannals, R. F. (1997). PET study of competition between intravenous cocaine and [11C]raclopride at dopamine receptors in human subjects. *American Journal of Psychiatry, 154,* 1209–1213.

Schwandt, T. A. (2001). *Dictionary of qualitative inquiry.* Thousand Oaks, CA: Sage.

Shahmoon-Shanok, R., Gilkerson, L., Eggbeer, L., & Fenichel, E. (1995). *Reflective supervision: A relationship for learning.* Washington, DC: Zero to Three Press.

Shelby, J. S. (2000). Brief therapy with traumatized children: A developmental perspective. In H. G. Kaduson & C. E. Schaefer (Eds.), *Short-term play therapy for children.* New York: Guilford Press.

Shinn, J. (2000). *Shabu in America.* Retrieved October 4, 2007 from www.lazamboangatimes.com/shabu.html.

Shoptaw, S., Klausner, J. D., Reback, C J., Tierney, S., Stansell, J., Hare, B., et al. (2006). A public health response to the methamphetamine epidemic: The implementation of contingency management to treat methamphetamine dependence. *BMC Public Health, 6,* 214–218.

Shweder, R. A. (1996a). True Ethnography: The lore, the law, and the lure. In R. Jessor, A. Colby, & R. A. Shweder (Eds.), *Ethnography and human development: Context and meaning in social inquiry* (pp. 15–52). Chicago: University of Chicago Press.

Shweder, R. A. (1996b). Quanta and qualia: What is the "object" of ethnographic method? In R. Jessor, A. Colby, & R. A. Shweder (Eds.), *Ethnography and human development: Context and meaning in social inquiry* (pp. 175–182). Chicago, IL: The University of Chicago Press.

Shweder, R. A., Goodnow, J. J., Hitano, G., LeVine, R. A., Markus, H. R., & Miller, P. J. (2006). The cultural psychology of development: One mind, many mentalities. In W. Damon & Lerner R. M. (Eds.), *Handbook of child psychology, Vol. 1: Theoretical models of human development* (6th ed.) (pp. 716–792). Hoboken, NJ: Wiley.

Smith, L. M., Chang, L., Yonekura, M. D., Grob, C., Osborn, D., & Ernst, T. (2001). Brain proton magnetic resonance spectroscopy in children exposed to methamphetamine in utero. *Neurology, 57,* 255–260.

Smith, L. M., LaGasse, L. L., Derauf, C., Grant, P., Shah, R., Arria, A., et al. (2006). The infant development, environment, and lifestyle study: Effects of prenatal methamphetamine exposure, polydrug exposure, and poverty on intrauterine growth. *Pediatrics, 118*(3), 1149–1156.

Sperry, L. L., & Sperry, D. E. (1995). Young children's presentations of self in conversational narration. In. L. L. Sperry and P.A. Smiley (Eds.), *Exploring young children's concepts of self and other through conversation. New Directions for Child Development, No. 60* (pp. 47–60). San Francisco, CA: Jossey-Bass.

Sperry, L., L. & Sperry, D. E. (1996). Early development of narrative skills. *Cognitive Development, 11,* 443–465.

Spoth, R. L., Kavanagh, K. A., & Dishion, T. J. (2002). Family-centered prevention intervention science: Toward benefits to larger populations of children, youth, and families. *Prevention Science, 3*(3), 145–152.

Sroufe, L. A., Dougal, S., Weinfeld, N., & Carlson, E. (2000). Relationships, development and psychopathology. In A. Sameroff, M. Lewis & S. Miller (Eds.), *Handbook of developmental psychopathology* (2nd ed.) (pp. 75–92). New York: Kluwer Academic/Plenum.

State of Illinois, Department of Children and Family Services. (2004). *Final report: Illinois child and family services review.* U.S. Department of Health and Human Services.

Steinberg, J. (2005). *The illicit abalone trade in South Africa* (Paper 105). Pretoria, SA: Institute for Security Studies.

Stewart, J. L., & Meeker, J. E. (1997). Fetal and infant deaths associated with maternal methamphetamine abuse. *Journal of Analytical Toxicology, 21,* 515–517.

Substance Abuse and Mental Health Services Administration (SAMSHA), Center for Substance Abuse Treatment. (1999). *Treatment for Stimulant Use Disorders* (Treatment Improvement Protocol Series #33), (DHHS Publication No. 02–3745). Rockville, MD: U.S. Department of Health and Human Services.

Suchman, N., Pajulo, M., DeCoste, C., & Mayes, L. (2006). Parenting interventions for drug-dependent mothers and their young children: The case for an attachment-based approach. *Family Relations, 55*(2), 211–226.

Suwaki H, Fukui S, and Konuma K (1997). Amphetamine abuse in Japan: Its 45 year history and the current situation. In H. Klee (Ed), *Amphetamine Misuse: International Perspectives on Current Trends.* Boca Raton, FL: CRC Press.

Symington, J., & Symington, N. (1999). *The clinical thinking of Wilfred Bion.* London: Routledge.

Szymaszek, J. (Oct. 3, 2007). Drug trade, once passing by, takes root in Mexico. *New York Times.* Retrieved October 4, 2007 from http://www.nytimes.com/2007/10/03/world/americas/03addicts.html.

Tamura, M. (1989). Japan: Stimulant epidemics past and present. *United Nations Office on Drugs & Crime Bulletin,* 83–93.

Tashakkori, A., & Teddlie C. (Eds.). (2003). *Handbook of mixed methods in social and behavioral research.* London: Sage Publications.

Thompson, P. M., Hayashi, K. M., Simon, S. L., Geaga, J. A., Hong, M. S., Sui, Y., et al. (2004). Structural abnormalities in the brains of human subjects who use methamphetamine. *The Journal of Neuroscience, 24*(26), 6028–6036.

Tobar, H., & Martinez, C. (March 17, 2007). Mexico meth raid yields $205 million in U.S. cash. *Los Angeles Times.* Retrieved October 4, 2007 from http://www.latimes.com/news/la-fg-meth17mar17,0,3877797.story?.

U.S. Drug Enforcement Agency. (n.d.). *State fact sheet*. Retrieved September 9, 2006 from http://www.usdoj.gov/dea/statistics.html.

U.S. Drug Enforcement Agency. (2006). *National drug threat assessment 2007*. Washington, DC: Government Publishing Office.

Utah Division of Substance Abuse and Mental Health (2005). *Drug court & methamphetamine fact sheet*. Retrieved October 3, 2007, from http://www.dsamh.utah.gov/docs/fact_drugcourtmeth_2005.pdf.

Van de Kolk, B., & Fisler, R. (1996). Dissociation and the fragmentary nature of traumatic memories: Overview. *British Journal of Psychotherapy, 12*, 352–361.

Volkow, N. D., Chang, L., Wang, G. J., Fowler, J. S., Leonido-Yee, M., Franceschi, D., et al. (2001). Association of dopamine transporter reduction with psychomotor impairment in methamphetamine abusers. *The American Journal of Psychiatry, 158*, 377–382.

Walsh, C., MacMillian, H., & Jamieson, E. (2003). The relationship between parental substance abuse and child maltreatment: Findings from the Ontario Health Supplement. *Child Abuse and Neglect, 27*(12), 1409–1425.

WANDTV & Lin Broadcasting. [Executive Producers]. (2004, October 6). *WAND Six O'clock Evening News* [Television Broadcast]. Champaign-Urbana, IL. Lin Broadcasting.

Wenger, C. (1982). The suitcase story: A therapeutic technique for children in out-of-home placement. *American Journal of Orthopsychiatry, 52*(2), 353–355.

Wermuth, L. (2000). Methamphetamine use: Hazards and social influences. *Journal of Drug Education, 30*, 423–433.

West, K., McKenna, J. J., Stuntz, S., & Webber-Brown, S. (2000). Drug endangered children & clandestine methamphetamine labs. In K. West & S. Stuntz (Eds.), *The drug endangered children response team: Training for trainers curriculum (Unit 2)*. Los Angeles: The Drug Endangered Children Resource Center.

West, K., & Stuntz, S. (Eds.). (2000). *The drug endangered children response team: Training for trainer's curriculum (Unit 2)*. Los Angeles: The Drug Endangered Children Resource Center.

Wilens, T. E., Faraone, S. V., Biederman, J., & Gunawardene, S. (2003). Does stimulant therapy of attention-deficit/hyperactivity disorder beget later substance abuse? A meta-analytic review of the literature. *Pediatrics, 111*, 179–185.

Wiley, A. R., Rose, A. J., Burger, L. K., & Miller, P. J. (1998). Constructing autonomous selves through narrative practices: A comparative study of working-class and middle-class families. *Child Development, 69*(3), 833–847.

Winnicott, D. (1965). *The maturational processes and the facilitating environment*. London: Hogarth Press.

Woodhouse, L. D. (1992). Women with jagged edges: Voices from a culture of substance abuse. *Qualitative Health Research, 2*(3), 262–281.

Woodson, J. (2002). *Our Gracie Aunt*. New York, New York: Hyperion Books for Children.

World Health Organization (1997). Amphetamine-Type stimulants. World Health Organization, Geneva.

Wouldes, T., LaGasse, L., Sheridan, J., & Lester, B. (2004). Maternal methamphetamine use during pregnancy and child outcome: What do we know? *Journal of the New Zealand Medical Association, 117*(1206), 1–10.

Yampolskaya, S., & Banks, S. (2006). An assessment of the extent of child maltreatment using administrative databases. *Assessment, 13*(3), 342–355.

Zernicke, K. (July 11, 2005). *New York Times.* A drug scourge creates its own form of orphan.

Zule, W. A., & Desmond, D. P. (1999). An ethnographic comparison of HIV risk behaviors among heroin and methamphetamine injectors. *American Journal of Drug and Alcohol Abuse, 25,* 1–23.

Index

Note: Figures (or photographs), tables, and footnotes are indicated by *f, t,* and n after the page number, respectively.

Addiction
  addictive power of crystal methamphetamine, 19–20
  addictive power of methamphetamine, 64, 66–67, 76, 123
  biology of, 17–20
  crack cocaine, addictiveness and "rush," 19
Amphetamines
  government regulation, 20
  medical uses, 19, 20, 23
  misuse, 16, 20, 23–24, 25
  See also Methamphetamine

Benzedrine (bennies), 20, 23–24
Black, James, 120
  See also Narrative of a Midwestern psychiatrist
Blood–brain barrier, 18

California, history of methamphetamine misuse, 24–25
Case histories and examples involving adults
  Amy, a recovering mother, 66–67, 68–71
  case of parental methamphetamine misuse (Billy and Justin), 54–58
  Joshua, pastor of a Baptist church, 79–80
  Margaret, a community clinician, 147
  Margie, a recovering mother, 61–62
  Mary, a recovering mother, 66–67, 71–72
  Meryl, a recovering mother, 66–67, 72–74
  Nora, a recovering mother, 66–67, 74–76
  See also Experiences and perspectives of knowledgeable adults; Experiences and perspectives of recovering mothers; Narrative of a Midwest psychiatrist
Case histories and examples involving children
  Alex (15-year-old boy), 147
  Alice (10-year-old girl), 178, 186–94, 202–3
  Amy (9-year-old girl), 98

Andy (14-year-old boy), 98, 99, 101, 103, 104
Billy (13-year-old boy), 54–58, 205–7, 210–13
Brad (13-year-old boy), 104
Bradley (7-year-old boy), 105–6
case of parental methamphetamine misuse (Billy and Justin), 54–58
Jake (10-year-old boy), 178–86, 202–3
Jason (11-year-old boy), 205, 206–10
Jay (9-year-old boy), 106, 108
Jerry (11-year-old boy), 98, 102
Jess (12-year-old girl), 95–96, 97
John (10-year-old boy), 165
Karen (13-year-old girl), 98–99, 100–101
Keith, 217, 222–23
Kim (11-year-old girl), 102
Mark (10-year-old boy), 178, 194–203
Mary (10-year-old girl), 99–100
Mary (11-year-old girl), 102
Sally (13-year-old girl), 110
Sam (13-year-old boy), 102
Steve (8-year-old boy), 106
Steve (9-year-old boy), 102
Terry (7-year-old boy), 106, 108
Tim (13-year-old boy), 106–7
Tim (14-year-old boy), 99, 101–2
Tom (13-year-old boy), 105
Tony (14-year-old boy), 99
See also Experiences and perspectives of children
Child abuse/neglect investigation process
  case of parental methamphetamine misuse (Billy and Justin), 54–58
  collaboration and interdependence with law enforcement personnel, 48, 80*f,* 81
  indicated *vs.* unfounded reports, 53
  information gathering process, 51–52

Child abuse/neglect investigation
  process (*Continued*)
  initiation of child abuse/neglect investigation,
    47–51, 47*f*
  making a finding, 52–53
  potential for violence, 47–51
  protective custody, 53–58
  reporting process, 46–47
Children's experiences and perspectives. *See*
  Experiences and perspectives of children
Children's Mental Health Partnership, 94
Child welfare workers
  apprehension about personal safety,
    47–51, 82
  dual roles of community clinicians, 151–52
  interdependency of educators and child
    welfare professionals, 81
  interdependency of law enforcement
    professionals and child welfare
    professionals, 48, 80*f*, 81
  recruitment into research study, 34, 131,
    150–52
  windshield time, 129
  See also Community clinicians; Experiences
    and perspectives of knowledgeable
    adults; Narrative of rural child welfare
    professional
Cocaine, 17–19, 25
Cohort effects, 20
Community clinicians
  dual roles, 151–52
  eligibility in Life Story Intervention, 150–52
  Jane, a community clinician, 195–201
  Mae, a community clinician, 180–85, 203
  Margaret, a community clinician, 147
  Marie, a teacher and community clinician,
    188–92
  recruitment for research study, 34, 131,
    150–52
  supervision of clinicians, general, 150, 173–75
  supervision of Linda Kingery, 205, 208,
    209–10, 213
  See also Narrative of a community clinician
Crank, 3, 24
Crystal methamphetamine
  addictiveness, 19–20
  availability of instructions for producing, 9
  foil "boats" used to heat product for
    inhalation, 107n
  in Hawaii, 26
  ice, 26
  marketing and distribution, similarity to
    crack cocaine, 25
  tik in South Africa, 22–23

Danville, Illinois, 120
Death of family members related to
  methamphetamine, 125, 148*f*, 183,
  208–9
Depression and sexual abuse, 6
Drug Abuse Resistance Education (DARE),
  103, 114

Effects of methamphetamine misuse
  biology of addiction, 17–20
  cognitive effects, 124
  dopamine depletion syndrome, 5
  initial effects of use, 4
  lasting problems due to methamphetamine
    addiction, 67, 75–76, 76–78
  methamphetamine-induced psychosis, 21,
    23, 81, 104, 124
  neurological effects, overview, 5, 18
  pharmacology, 17–20
  physical effects of regular use, 5
  psychological effects, overview, 5
  tweaking, 4–5, 122–23
  See also Experiences and perspectives
    of children; Experiences and
    perspectives of knowledgeable adults;
    Experiences and perspectives of
    recovering mothers
Epidemiology and demographics of
  methamphetamine misuse, 16–17
  See also History of methamphetamine
    misuse
Exculpatory evidence, 53
Experiences and perspectives of children
  active role in socialization, 102–3
  Alex (15-year-old boy), 147
  Amy (9-year-old girl), 98
  Andy (14-year-old boy), 98, 99, 101,
    103, 104
  basic needs for food and shelter, 96*f*
  belief in parents' love, 96
  Brad (13-year-old boy), 104
  Bradley (7-year-old boy), 105–6
  death of family members related to
    methamphetamine, 125, 148*f*, 183,
    208–9
  divergence from adult perspectives, 96,
    101–2, 109, 220
  exposure to adult criminality and antisocial
    activities, 98–99, 102–3, 108, 219–20
  exposure to adults' substance misuse, 98,
    219–20
  exposure to adult violence, 99–100,
    108, 219
  exposure to rural drug subculture, 97, 108

implications for helping children to succeed,
108–9
interviews with children, overview, 10, 37,
96–97, 112, 155–56
Jay (9-year-old boy), 106, 108
Jerry (11-year-old boy), 98, 102
Jess (12-year-old girl), 95–96, 97
John (10-year-old boy), 165
Karen (13-year-old girl), 98–99, 100–101
Keith, 217, 222–23
Kim (11-year-old girl), 102
loss and separation from parents, 84, 102,
109, 220
maltreatment and neglect deemphasized by
children, 96, 101, 109
Mary (10-year-old girl), 99–100
Mary (11-year-old girl), 102
overview, 96–97, 107–9
parenting and caregiving roles of children,
91, 96, 100f, 113, 206–8
participation in antisocial activities,
100–101, 219
perception of parents' methamphetamine
use, 97
physical and sexual abuse, 101, 110, 179,
186–87, 194
protective custody and child welfare
interventions as cause of distress, 102,
109, 219
relationships with parents, 113, 117
relationships with siblings, 113, 117
religion as a support system, 103, 111f,
114, 207
Sam (13-year-old boy), 102
social and emotional experiences in families,
112–15, 117
socialization against discussing substance
misuse, 39, 51–52, 84, 114,
117–18
Steve (8-year-old boy), 106
Steve (9-year-old boy), 102
Terry (7-year-old boy), 106, 108
Tim (13-year-old boy), 106–7
Tim (14-year-old boy), 99, 101–2
Tom (13-year-old boy), 105
Tony (14-year-old boy), 99
understanding of methamphetamine, 103–7,
109, 220
variation in knowledge and responses to
probes about methamphetamine,
104–7, 220–21
See also Case histories and examples involving
children; Psychological functioning of
children

Experiences and perspectives of knowledgeable
adults
advice and suggestions for supporting
children, 89–91, 92–94
apprehension about personal safety, 47–51, 82
chaos, neglect, and isolation of children, 83–84
children as caregivers, 84, 91
educational disturbances of children, 86, 91
effect of length of exposure to parental
methamphetamine misuse, 87
exposure of children to antisocial behavior,
84–85, 91, 219–20
fear of contamination and accidents from
meth labs, 82, 220
importance of foster parent information
about children's background, 108, 117,
118, 138
individual variation among children, 87, 91, 93
interdependency of educators and child
welfare professionals, 81
interdependency of law enforcement
professionals and child welfare
professionals, 48, 80f, 81
interviews with adults, 10, 37
Joshua, pastor of a Baptist church, 79–80
losses experienced by children, 84, 102,
109, 220
need for basic physical requirements for
children, 89
need for developmental experiences for
children, 89
need for quality mental health services for
children, 86, 89–90, 92–94
need for substance abuse education, 90, 92,
108–9
need for timely child welfare
involvement, 92
perception of abuse of children, 84, 91
perception of danger for children, 83, 91
perceptions of effects of parental
methamphetamine misuse on children,
85–91
protective effect of child's extended family,
88, 218f
protective effect of child's interpersonal
context, 87–88
protective effect of child's school, 88–89
protective effect of temperaments of
children, 87
psychological disturbances due to parental
substance abuse, 85
rural drug subculture effect on children,
83, 84–85, 91
social development of children, 85–86

Experiences and perspectives of
    knowledgeable adults (*Continued*)
    See also Narrative of a Midwest psychiatrist;
        Narrative of rural child welfare
        professional
Experiences and perspectives of recovering
        mothers
    addictive power of methamphetamine, 64,
        66–67, 76, 123
    adult perceptions of methamphetamine
        abuse, 81–82
    Amy, a recovering mother, 66–67, 68–71
    attempts to protect children, 64–65,
        77, 221
    children as primary motivation for recovery,
        62f, 67, 74–75, 77, 126
    fear of prison as primary motivation for
        recovery, 67, 74, 77
    functional use of methamphetamine, 63, 77
    interviews, 10, 37, 66–67, 219
    lasting problems due to methamphetamine
        addiction, 67, 75–76, 76–78
    Margie, a recovering mother, 61–62
    Mary, a recovering mother, 66–67, 71–72
    Meryl, a recovering mother, 66–67, 72–74
    mixed attitudes, 81–82
    mothers in research program, overview, 10,
        34–35, 66–67
    Nora, a recovering mother, 66–67, 74–76
    previous research on mothers, 62–66
    recognition of risks to children from
        substance misuse, 64–65, 67, 77
    risk factors associated with drug misuse,
        63–64, 76–77
    stigmatization of substance misuse, 63

Families involved with methamphetamine,
        overview, 12–13
Foster parents
    Mrs. Bernard (Jake's foster mother), 179–80,
        181–82, 185–86
    Childhood Behavior Checklist (CBCL), 10,
        39, 115–18, 154
    importance of information about children's
        background, 108, 117, 118, 138
    Mrs. Karny (Mark's foster mother), 195, 202
    need for continuing education, 90
    roles in Life Story Intervention, 144, 149,
        154, 170–72, 177
    Mrs. Weaver (Alice's foster mother), 187,
        191, 194

Hawaii, history of methamphetamine misuse,
        25, 26

History of methamphetamine misuse
    in California, 24–25
    epidemiology and demographics of
        methamphetamine misuse,
        16–17
    in Hawaii, 25, 26
    in Illinois, 120–21
    increased production and misuse in east
        central Illinois, 4f, 9
    in Japan, 8–9, 20, 21–22
    overview, 8–9, 16–17, 20, 27–29
    prescription drug abuse and "script doctors,"
        23–24
    recipes available from the Internet, 3, 9
    rural Midwest, 3, 9, 27, 121, 129
    in Texas, 25–26
    in United States, 23–27
    in Utah, 120–21
    in Wyoming, 26–27

Ice, 3, 26
    See also Crystal methamphetamine
Illinois
    Danville, Illinois, 120
    history of methamphetamine misuse in
        Illinois, 120–21
    increased production and misuse in east
        central Illinois, 4f, 9
    laboratory seizures in Illinois, 9, 17,
        18f, 33
    methamphetamine seizures in Illinois, 9, 17,
        18f, 33
    rural east central Illinois countryside, 4f, 17f,
        121f, 130f
Inculpatory evidence, 53
Integrated Assessment Program (State of
        Illinois), 93
Interventions. *See* Life Story Intervention

Japan, history of methamphetamine misuse,
        8–9, 20, 21–22

Kingery, Linda
    background and experience, 11–12, 36,
        46, 212
    on effects of parental methamphetamine
        misuse, 11–12
    See also Narrative of a community clinician;
        Narrative of rural child welfare
        professional
Knowledgeable adults' experiences and
        perspectives. *See* Experiences and
        perspectives of knowledgeable
        adults

Legislation
  Comprehensive Methamphetamine Control
      Act, 27
  Controlled Substances Act, 27
  Health Insurance and Portability
      Accountability Act (HIPAA), 152
  Mental Hygiene Law (Japan), 21
  Stimulant Control Law (Japan), 21–22
Life books, 135
Life Story Intervention, children's responses
  Alice (10-year-old girl), 178, 186–94, 202–3
  Jake (10-year-old boy), 178–86, 202–3
  Keith, 217, 222–23
  Mark (10-year-old boy), 178, 194–203
  overview, 178–79, 202–4
Life Story Intervention, conceptual and
      empirical bases
  attachment theory, 140–42
  attention to children's medical needs, 136–37
  bringing treatment to the child in the
      community, 133
  children's understanding of events, 138–39
  cognitive distortions of children, 139
  cognitive therapies, 138–39
  collaboration with local professionals, 42,
      131, 132–33, 177
  community clinician recruitment, 34, 131,
      150–52
  containment of children's intense emotion,
      142–43, 164–65
  cultural adaptations and cultural
      appropriateness, 132–33
  exosystems, 144
  focal system, 131, 135
  goals, 130, 137, 139–40, 142, 173
  helping children create new life experiences,
      143–44
  helping children interpret trauma, 143,
      164, 175
  importance of in-depth examination of
      complex cases, 206f, 218
  life books, 135
  macrosystem, 132
  mesosystem formation, 144–45
  microsystem development, 135–36
  overview, 13–15, 40–41, 129–32, 145–46,
      222–23
  personal narratives in sociocultural context,
      134–35, 222
  personal narratives in therapies, 135
  psychotherapeutic intervention for trauma,
      overview, 138
  relationships of children with professionals,
      130–31, 139–44, 159–62, 175–76, 179f

  sociocultural framework, 131, 132–36,
      145–46, 174–75
  storytelling, 130, 134–35, 163, 192
  substance misuse education, 137, 166–67
  suitcase stories, 135
  See also Research program, overview
Life Story Intervention, implementation
  assessing children, 153–58, 180,
      187–88, 195
  assessment of perspectives and experiences,
      155–56
  caregiver component, 170–72
  child eligibility, 148–49
  child-paced intervention, 177
  child welfare professionals' component,
      172–73, 177
  community clinician eligibility, 150–52
  confronting and correcting erroneous
      beliefs, 167
  containment of children's intense emotion,
      142–43, 164–65
  creating memento of the intervention, 169
  debriefing, 156
  discussing separation from clinician, 168–69,
      184
  dual roles of community clinicians, 151–52
  foster parents' role, 144, 149, 154, 170–72, 177
  guidelines for developing relationships, 160–62
  helping children create new life experiences,
      143–44
  helping children interpret trauma, 143,
      164, 175
  helping children learn to regulate emotions,
      165–66
  identifying and meeting mentors, 144, 169,
      171, 176, 202
  individualized intervention, 176
  intervention setting, 152–53
  language assessment, 154–55
  overview, 147–48
  phase 1, orientation and relationship-
      building, 159–63, 171, 180–82,
      188–90, 195–97
  phase 2, co-constructing the child's life story,
      163–68, 171, 182–84, 190–92, 197–99
  phase 3, endings, 168–70, 171, 184–85,
      192–94, 199–201
  post-test and follow-up assessments, 170,
      185–86, 194, 201–2
  psychotherapeutic intervention for trauma,
      138–44, 175
  rapport building and informed consent, 154
  relationship of assessment to intervention,
      158–59

Life Story Intervention, implementation
    (*Continued*)
    review of children's records, 154
    six months later, 186, 194, 202, 203–4
    strengths-based intervention, 176
    substance misuse education, 137, 166–67
    supervision of clinicians, 150, 173–75
    sustained period of intervention, 43–44, 176
    trauma assessment, 155
    See also Psychotherapeutic intervention for
        trauma
Losses experienced by children, 84, 102, 109, 220

Macrosystem of social ecology, 132
Mandell, Arnold, 24
Mental health needs of rural children in foster
        care, overview, 13–15, 110–12, 117–19
    See also Psychological functioning of children
Mental Hygiene Law (Japan), 21
Mentors
    identifying and meeting mentors, 144, 169,
        171, 176, 202
    Mr. Jasper (Mark's football coach and
        mentor), 202
    Mrs. Albert (Jake's counselor and mentor), 185
    Mrs. Johnson (Alice's teacher and mentor), 193
Methamphetamine, general information
    initial effects of use, 4
    medical uses, 18, 19, 20
    other names for methamphetamine, 3
    pharmacology, 17–20
Methamphetamine laboratories
    early labs in San Francisco, 24
    explosion and fire hazards for children, 7, 111
    fear of contamination and accidents, 82
    laboratory seizures, 9, 17, 27, 28t, 33
    "Mom and Pop" laboratories, 7, 27, 83,
        220, 223
    toxic hazards for children, 7, 111,
        136, 220
    See also Methamphetamine production
Methamphetamine misuse. *See* Effects of
    methamphetamine misuse;
    Epidemiology and demographics of
    methamphetamine misuse; History of
    methamphetamine misuse; Parental
    misuse of methamphetamine;
    Sociocultural context of
    methamphetamine misuse
Methamphetamine production
    history of synthesis methods, 8, 20, 24
    hydrochloric acid generators used in Birch
        methamphetamine process, 110n
    pseudoephedrine use, 3, 22, 27
    recipes available from the Internet, 3, 9

    See also Methamphetamine laboratories
Methamphetamine seizures in Illinois, 9, 17, 18f
Mothers' experiences and perceptions. *See*
    Experiences and perspectives of
    recovering mothers; Parental misuse of
    methamphetamine
Motorcycle gangs and biker groups, 24–25, 120

Narrative of a community clinician
    Billy (13-year-old boy), 54–58, 205–7, 210–13
    Jason (11-year-old boy), 205, 206–10
    personal reflection, 213
    supervision, 205, 208, 209–10, 213
    See also Community clinicians; Kingery,
        Linda; Life Story Intervention,
        implementation
Narrative of a Midwestern psychiatrist
    addictive power of methamphetamine, 123
    death of child's family members related to
        methamphetamine, 125
    effects of exposure to violence, 125
    effects of methamphetamine on families, 125
    functional use of methamphetamine, 122
    patients with history of substance misuse and
        untreated mental illnesses, 122–23
    possibility of recovery, 125–26
    psychiatric symptoms associated with
        methamphetamine misuse, 124–25
    social use of methamphetamine, 123
    See also Black, James; Experiences and
        perspectives of knowledgeable adults
Narrative of rural child welfare professional
    case of parental methamphetamine misuse
        (Billy and Justin), 54–58
    cognitive effects of methamphetamine, 124
    family reluctance to share information
        ("conspiracy of silence"), 51–52
    initiation of child abuse/neglect investigation,
        47–51
    potential for violence, 47–51
    protective custody, 53–58
    reporting process, 46–47
    uninsured addicted patients, 123–24
    See also Experiences and perspectives of
        knowledgeable adults; Kingery, Linda

Organized criminal groups, 8, 22, 25, 26, 29

Parental misuse of methamphetamine
    case of parental methamphetamine misuse
        (Billy and Justin), 54–58
    effects of prenatal exposure, 5–6
    effects on children, 6–7, 85–91
    Linda Kingery on effects of misuse, 11–12
    maltreatment of children, 6

overview of effects on children, 6–7
parental deterioration from misuse, 7
strain placed on child welfare systems, 7
See also Experiences and perspectives of
    recovering mothers
Phases of Life Story Intervention
  caregiver component, 170–72
  overview, 159
  phase 1, orientation and relationship-
      building, 159–63, 171, 180–82,
      188–90, 195–97
  phase 2, co-constructing the child's life
      story, 163–68, 171, 182–84, 190–92,
      197–99
  phase 3, endings, 168–70, 171, 184–85,
      192–94, 199–201
  post-test and follow-up assessments, 170,
      185–86, 194, 201–2
Philopon, 21
Post traumatic stress disorder (PTSD)
  in children, 116*t*, 138–39, 165, 221
  as effect of methamphetamine use, 5
  and sexual abuse, 6
Prenatal exposure to methamphetamine, 5–6
Protective custody
  child abuse/neglect investigation process, 53–58
  fear and distress experienced by children,
      102, 109, 219
  and parental methamphetamine involvement,
      33, 34
Pseudoephedrine use in methamphetamine
    production, 3, 22, 27
Psychological functioning of children
  avoidance or passive coping strategies, 113,
      117, 119, 221
  isolation of children, 83–84, 113
  mental health according to the CBCL,
      115–17, 115*t*, 118
  mental health according to the TSCC,
      116–18, 116*t*
  psychological disturbances due to parental
      substance abuse, 85, 110–12, 221
  reactive attachment disorder, 186–87
  relationships with parents, 113, 117
  relationships with siblings, 113, 117
  social and emotional experiences in families,
      112–15, 117
  socialization against discussing substance
      misuse, 39, 51–52, 84, 114, 117–18
  social resources used for coping, 113–14, 117
  See also Experiences and perspectives of
      children; Mental health needs of rural
      children in foster care
Psychosis induced by methamphetamine use,
    21, 23, 81, 104, 124

Psychotherapeutic intervention for trauma
  attachment theory, 140–42
  aversive stimuli, 139
  children's understanding of events, 138 39
  cognitive distortions of children, 139
  cognitive therapies, 138–39
  containment of children's intense emotion,
      142–43, 164–65
  desensitization techniques, 139
  flooding, 139
  helping children create new life experiences,
      143–44
  helping children interpret trauma, 143,
      164, 175
  helping children learn to regulate emotions,
      165–66
  overview, 138
  See also Life Story Intervention, implementation

Recovering mothers' experiences and
    perspectives. *See* Experiences and
    perspectives of recovering mothers
Research program, overview
  case-based research strategy, 41, 218–26
  clinically sophisticated researchers, 44
  clinical methods, 30, 32
  credible analyses, 44
  data set characteristics, 11
  developmental methods, 30, 31–32
  ethnographic methods, 30–31
  evidence-based social work practice and
      research, 40, 225
  giving voice to hidden children, 225–26
  importance of context in intervention,
      practice, and research, 224
  importance of meaning for child welfare
      practice and research, 223–24
  interviews, 10, 37–39
  key characteristics of research program,
      41–44
  lack of contact with children before foster
      care, 45
  limited parental participation, 44
  limited systemic information on children's
      development, 44
  mixed-method approach, 30–31, 42, 45
  multiplism, 42–43
  participant observation, 9, 31*f*, 36
  rapport building, 43
  research site, 9, 33
  standardized assessment methods, 10,
      37–39
  strong practitioner–researcher collaboration,
      42, 131, 132–33, 177
  sustained involvement, 43–44, 176

Research program, overview (*Continued*)
　themes for social work practice and policy,
　　221–22
　transdisciplinary research team, 42
　visits with children, 10
　See also Life Story Intervention
Research program, phase 1 (ethnographic–
　developmental overview)
　children in program, 10, 35–36
　children's exposure to parental substance
　　abuse and criminality, 35, 35*t*, 219–20
　entering the community, 36
　foster parent childhood behavior checklist
　　(CBCL), 39
　interviews with adults, 10, 37
　interviews with children, 10, 37, 96–97, 112,
　　155–56
　knowledgeable adults in program, 10, 34,
　　80–81, 219
　mothers in program, 10, 34–35, 66–67, 219
　participant observation, 9, 31*f*, 36, 80–81
　participants, 10, 34–36
　procedures, 36–39, 218
　research site, 9, 33
　standardized assessment methods, 10, 37–39
　transcription and analysis of interviews, 37,
　　39–40
　See also Experiences and perspectives of
　　children; Experiences and perspectives
　　of knowledgeable adults; Experiences
　　and perspectives of recovering mothers
Research program, phase 2 (intervention
　design). *See* Life Story Intervention,
　implementation
Research program, phase 3 (evaluation of
　intervention), overview, 41
Rural drug subculture effect on children, 83,
　84–85, 91, 97
Rural Midwest and methamphetamine
　barriers to providing support services, 7, 14
　Danville, Illinois, 120
　history of methamphetamine misuse, 3, 9,
　　27, 121, 129
　history of methamphetamine misuse in
　　Illinois, 120–21
　increased production and misuse in east
　　central Illinois, 4*f*, 9
　laboratory seizures in Illinois, 9, 17, 18*f*, 33
　methamphetamine seizures in Illinois, 9, 17,
　　18*f*, 33
　numbers of substance-exposed infants
　　reported, 9
　rural east central Illinois countryside, 4*f*, 17*f*,
　　121*f*, 130*f*

Sociocultural context of methamphetamine
　misuse
　Life Story Intervention, sociocultural
　　framework, 131, 132–36, 145–46,
　　174–75
　overview, 3, 7–12, 224
　personal narratives in sociocultural context,
　　134–35, 222
Speed (speedball), 24
Standardized assessment methods
　American Drug and Alcohol
　　Survey–Children's Form (ADAS),
　　18–19
　Childhood Behavior Checklist (CBCL), 10,
　　39, 115–18
　Peabody Picture Vocabulary Test (PPVT,
　　PPVT-3), 10, 37–38, 105
　Trauma Symptom Checklist for
　　Children (TSCC), 10, 38,
　　115–18
Stimulant Control Law (Japan), 21–22
Storytelling
　life books, 135
　in Life Story Intervention, 130, 134–35,
　　163, 192
　personal narratives in sociocultural context,
　　134–35, 222
　personal narratives in therapies, 135
　suitcase stories, 135
　See also Life Story Intervention; Narrative of
　　a community clinician; Narrative of a
　　Midwest psychiatrist; Narrative of rural
　　child welfare professional
Subsidized guardianship, 212n
Substance abuse education
　Drug Abuse Resistance Education (DARE),
　　103, 114
　importance of, 90, 92, 108–9
　substance misuse education in Life Story
　　Intervention, 137, 166–67
Suitcase stories, 135

Texas, history of methamphetamine misuse,
　25–26
Tik, 22–23
　See also Crystal methamphetamine
Tweaking, 4–5, 122–23

Utah, history of methamphetamine misuse,
　120–21

Windshield time, 129
Wyoming, history of methamphetamine misuse,
　26–27